ज्ञान गरिमा के
68 वर्ष

भारतीय
ज्ञानपीठ

Structure and Functions of Soul in Jainism

by

Dr. S.C. Jain

BHARATIYA JNANPITH

ISBN 978-81-263-4036-1

Moortidevi Granthamala No. : English 7

Structure and Functions of Soul in Jainism
by Dr. S.C. Jain

Printed at : Vikas Computer & Printers, Delhi-110032

Published by
Bharatiya Jnanpith
18, Institutional Area, Lodi Road,
New Delhi-110 003
e-mail : jnanpith@satyam.net.in, sales@jnanpith.net
website : www.jnanpith.net

Fourth Edition : 2012
Price : Rs. 150

General Editorial

Philosophy is an enquiry into the nature of life and of existence; and this way of dealing with reality depends on the exercise of thought and reason. Since the dawn of human civilization, numerous thinkers, in different times and climes, have applied themselves to solving the riddle of the universe, to unravelling the mystery of existence and to explaining what life really is. Consequently, we have quite a good number of schools of philosophical thought, often contradictory or widely divergent, such as Nihilism, Materialism, Spiritualism, Idealism, Realism. Neutralism, Sensationalism, Associationism, Structurism, Monism, Dualism, Pluralism, Absolutism, Non-absolutism, and so on.

In the midst of this conglomeration of philosophies, stands out the Jaina system which starts with the scientific postulate *ex nihilo nihil fit,* and is thus grounded in reality. It may look strange, that although it is a very ancient Indian system, it is highly and peculiarly consistent with modern realism and modern science. Since it establishes the existence of soul and matter as the two separate, distinct, independent and immutable entities, it is often described as a dualism or dualist realism. Again, since each of the two categories comprises infinite individual entities, the system may also be called a realistic pluralism. The fact that every real is dynamic owing to the co-presence in it of change and permanence, gives it the character of a realistic dynamism. Moreover, since an absolute unqualified affirmation of existence is not in conformity with the nature of reality, the Jaina philosophy affirms the possibility of diverse attributes in a unitary entity, which fact characterises the system as a non-absolutist one. Position and negation are obtained simultaneously in a real, wherefore unqualified existence or non-existence is meaningless, unless qualified by proper context, not only for the sake of predication but also for the sake of existence. The Syādvāda logic helps a clear grasp of the truth which is Anekāntic (non-absolutist) in its essence, and, with its powerful organ, the seven-combinational mode of predication, it enabled the Jaina philosopher to avoid adopting philosophical extremes like the nihilism of the Buddhists and the absolute monism of the Vedāntists, and to steer clear of the shallow realism of the Chārvākas and the ludicrous idealism of the Nyāyavādins.

The soul being the *terminus a quo* as well as the *terminus ad quem* of his pursuit, the Jaina philosopher goes on to explore at length its structure and its varied functions, hence incidentally its relationships with matter, wherein lie the roots of the Jaina doctrine of Karma, the soul's efforts to shake off the Karmic shackles and attain liberation, the state in which the pure and perfect soul lives in omniscience and unalloyed everlasting bliss.

In the present thesis, Dr. S.C. Jain, its learned author, has presented a detailed, critical and comparative study of the Jaina conception of soul, its structure and its functions, against the background of the Anekāntic philosophy and Syādvādist dialectics, in a lucid manner. Connected topics like Jaina epistemology, eschatology, liberation and omniscience have been paid due attention.

The chief merit of this work lies in the fact that it examines almost every aspects of the Jaina conception of soul in context with other systems of philosophy, particularly the western thinkers of the modern age, and has also not left out Indian writers on the subject. For the Jaina view, he has generally gone direct to the original texts.

This book should be a welcome addition to modern philosophical literature and would certainly help in understanding and rightly assessing the Jaina conceptions.

We congratulate Dr. S.C. Jain for producing this valuable work and are thankful to him for giving it to the Bharatiya Jnanpith for publication.

We are also grateful to the President, Managing Trustee, Secretary and staff of the Bharatiya Jnanpith, who have been instrumental in bringing out this book.

Kailash Chandra Shastri

2nd September, 1978 **Jyoti Prasad Jain**

Preface

Structures may be spatial or non-spatial. A material structure is always spatial, whereas a mental one is held to be non-spatial. For the Jaina extension means the quality of space-occupation and it is a necessary implication of the existence of a substance. Hence the soul as a substance must have an extended structure. The Jaina conception of the structure of the soul differs from that of 'mind' in modern psychology in being substantial and spatial. At the same time a structure implies the possibility of its analysis into its components. The plurality of components in the soul's structure may be conceived in terms of its attributes and modes. Moreover the Jaina conception of the soul-units (*ātmapradeśas*) in the soul along with its substantial oneness (*dravyaikatva*) suggests that every soul has a structure.[1] Thus in Jainism the soul has a distinct structure and functions. Hence it is felt necessary that while expounding the Jaina theory of the soul equal emphasis should be laid on both the facts of structure and function of the soul.

Besides, epistemology has been a great source of attraction for the present age; but the importance of epistemology is not to be recognized at the expense of ontology. The soul is an equally important subject both for epistemology and ontology. Moreover the structure of the soul demands an ontological treatment of the problem. It is for this reason that the ontology of the soul finds its due place in the present dissertation.

The soul constitutes the most important theme of the Jaina philosophy. Different parts of the system appear to be

1. Cf. Umāsvāti: *Tattvārthasūtra, 5.6 and 8.*

woven round this central theme. The aim of this dissertation is not an analytic description of all the aspects of the Jaina philosophy of the soul. Nor does this thesis mark an entirely new approach to the principle of consciousness, for, as A.C. Mukerjee thinks, no one "can expound an entirely original doctrine without being indebted to his predecessors."[1] I, therefore, have sought to make my humble contribution to the Jaina theory of the soul in respect of some of its aspects to be specified in this preface while giving an analysis of the contents of the thesis.

Though the writer has taken due care to present the Jaina tenets in a faithful way, yet, at places, he has found himself in disagreement with the Jaina orthodoxy; because loyalty to reason imposed on him by the Muse of Philosophy has left him no choice in the matter. Regarding such deviations from the traditional positions in Jainism Rājamalla states: "I speak mainly on the ground of the Jaina scriptures, but something (I say) from my own experience."[2] This may be taken to mean that the contributions based on one's experience but made in strict obedience of reason may also form an essential part of the system.

As regards the use of the technical terms in philosophy, specially those of the Jaina system, the Sanskrit ones have been given along with suitable English equivalents so as to minimize the danger of a loss of meaning, which is likely to be caused in the absence of the original terms.

The thesis is divided into nine chapters. The first two chapters deal with the two foundational concepts of the Jaina philosophy. The first chapter deals with the Anekānta theory of existence. My contribution to this theory lies in the research of the region of traits or *dharmas* so as to give a consistent interpretation of the concepts of negation, attributes and modes. The opposition which the Anekānta theory implies and which has rather been supposed to exist in the realm of traits. The second chapter contains a

---

1. A.C. Mukerjee: *Nature of Self*, p. 253
2. Rājamalla, *Pañcādhyāyī*. II, verse 960

discussion of the Jaina dialectic and aims to establish the validity of partial comprehensions. A new meaning is given to the *pramāṇa*-knowledge by introducing the conception of system. Then follow the five chapters dealing with the substance of the soul and its various functions. In the third chapter the dualism of soul and matter is sought to be established. The Jaina dualism of the soul *(jīva)* and the non-soul *(ajīva)* is not based on absolute opposition. Hence the theory of relation between them is shown to transcend both interactionism and parallelism. The fourth chapter deals with the Jaina theory of knowledge. Consciousness, the identity of which has so far been a riddle, has been found to be no distinct attribute of the soul. In accordance with the Jaina theory of substance the soul is shown to possess a multiplicity of attributes. In respect of some of their attributes both the soul and the non-soul agree with each other. The special attributes of the soul like conation *(darśana)*, knowledge *(jñāna)*, bliss *(sukha)*, etc., distinguish it from the non-soul;[1] and the general implication of such attributes is termed as consciousness. Thus not only conation *(darśana)* and knowledge *(jñāna)* are found to be conscious, but many other attributes of the soul are also conscious. The old controversies regarding conation and knowledge, the sensuous (*mati*) and perceptual (*śruta*) types of knowledge, the non-difference of clairvoyance (*avadhi*) and telepathy *(manaḥparyaya)* and the non-distinction of bliss *(sukha)* and knowledge *(jñāna)* have received varied interpretations at the hands of the Jaina writers themselves. They have failed to pacify our curiosity in one or the other way. These problems are so represented in the present treatise as to yield a fresh solution in the light of the Jaina theory of attributes. The fifth chapter deals with extension as an implicate of the soul's existence. It leads to the conclusion that the soul as a substance has an extended structure. Bliss, the topic of the next chapter, has been variously conceived by the Jaina writers. It has been sought

1. Devasena: *Ālāpapaddhati*, p. 33

to be shown that bliss stands for the feeling capacity of the soul, and is responsible for the generation of pleasure and pain. Many critics of the Jaina philosophy are of the opinion that the Jaina has not been able to establish the plurality of the souls. This topic has been discussed in the seventh chapter wherein the writer has sought to maintain that the very theory of the soul as propounded by the Jaina leads to the truth of the plurality of souls. The eighth chapter divided into four sections deals with different aspects of Jaina eschatology. The materiality of Karmas, which is a unique contribution of the Jaina to the theory of Karma, has been established by means of a number of arguments. Another ingredient of the Jaina theory of Karma is the conception of the negativity of the soul, which, in the light of the theory of *dharmas* or traits, finds a fresh interpretation in this thesis. A new classification of the Karma-forces is made to bring the Jaina doctrine of Karma into close agreement with modern psychology. The problem of determinism and indeterminism seems to have been better solved if considered in the light of the non-absolutism of the Jaina. The ninth chapter is divided into two sections. The first section is devoted to the Jaina theory of liberation—its possibility and the manifestation of the soul's powers in the state of liberation. The second section begins with Kundakunda's theory of the pure soul which directly leads to the theories of the absolute. The conceptions of the absolute as given by Śaṅkara, the Mādhyamika (as interpreted by T.R.V. Murti, Hegel and Bradley) have been considered. It is concluded that reality does not imply an absolutism, but is of the nature of the non-absolute.

I feel highly grateful to Dr. B.G. Tiwari, M.A., Ph.D., D. Litt. under whose scholarly and encouraging guidance I had the fortune to conduct my work. I must here express my hearty thanks to all the thinkers whose works and views I have used and quoted in the present dissertation.

My most sincere thanks are due to Bharatiya Jnanpith for sponsoring the publication of this work in that prestigious Granthamala, under the patronage of Shri Sahu Shriyans

Prasad Jain, its President and Shri Ashok Kumar Jain, Managing Trustee. I am personally indebted to Shri L.C. Jain, Secretary of the Trust for his continuous guidance as the finalisation of the manuscript progressed from stage to stage. Dr. Gulab Chandra Jain of Jnanpith has been very painstaking in seeing the work through the Press.

Vidya Varidhi Dr. Jyoti Prasad Jain and Siddhantacharya Pandit Kailash Chandra Shastri, Editors of the series deserve my gratitude for favouring me with an editorial to the book.

New Delhi **S.C. Jain**
20th September, 1978

CONTENTS

Chapter 1

The Anekānta Theory of Existence

Two Basic Conceptions of Jaina Philosophy

Before embarking upon an exposition of the soul or the *jīva* or the principle of consciousness in Jaina philosophy it is desirable to have an idea of the basic concepts of the system, in the light of which the discussion on the soul will follow. The Anekānta theory of existence and the Syādvāda theory of judgement are two such concepts. The entire philosophy of the Jaina may be taken to be an illustration of his unique theory of existence and judgement. The principle of consciousness equally illustrates the two aforesaid conceptions. According to the Jaina Anekāntavāda, which is understood to include both the Jaina theories of existence and judgement, is a sovereign principle embracing the entire system of the cosmos. Amṛtacandra Sūri remarks that *Anekānta* is the very basis of the highest of the scriptures.[1] The position of the Jaina is marked from that of others mainly for his *anekānta* (non-absolute) outlook on reality in general and the principle of consciousness in particular.

Meaning of Anekānta

The term *anekānta* yields two meanings when interpreted etymologically. The popular meaning refers to the plurality of determinants in a real. But this position will be found common nearly to all the pluralistic systems of philosophy. The Jaina concept of *anekānta* implies something more than the mere plurality of components in a real. It is very often

1. Amṛtacandra Sūri: *Puruṣārtha-siddhyupāya*. verse 2

said that the distinctive feature of the *anekānta* theory lies in the affirmation of opposites in the same real. Reality does not merely admit of multiple forms of existence; but it is, at the same time, a substrate of opposite elements. The other meaning of the term *anekānta* may be taken as the antithesis of *ekānta*, i.e., an absolutism. An absolutism affirms one uniform character of reality, and the non-absolutism denies such an affirmation. Vidyānandin says, "*Anekānta* means the negation of the absolutism of existence, non-existence, permanence and momentariness."[1] If reality is held to be absolutely permanent as in Vedānta, the non-absolutism of the Jaina denies the very contention. If reality is held to be absolutely transitory as in Buddhism, the non-absolutism of the Jaina refutes this position also. The Jaina in the denial of the former affirms the latter and vice versa; and he is able to maintain such a position consistently only by resorting to the non-absolute way of thinking. The position held by the Jaina amounts to the contention that a real is a substrate of opposing elements. This brings us face to face with the problem of negation or *abhāva* which constitutes a vital part of the Anekānta theory of existence.

Śaṅkara criticizes the *anekānta* position of the Jaina as "On account of the impossibility (of contrary attributes) in one and the same thing (the Jaina doctrine) is not (true)."[2] It means what is a substrate of opposing elements cannot be one. The Jaina is said to admit the co-presence of opposite elements in a real not with reference to temporal or spatial differences but with reference to the same unitary entity. S. Mookerjee observes: "The central thesis of the Jaina is not only diversity of reals; but each real is equally diversified."[3] Diversity does not connote simple plurality but a plurality which involves opposition; it is a plurality and opposition in one. Samantabhadra remarks: "*astitva* (position) is concomitant with *nāstitva* (negation) in the same substrate.

1. Vidyānandin: *Aṣṭasahasrī*, p. 286
2. *Brahma-sūtra* 2.2. 34 (Translated by Swami Vireswaranand, 2nd ed. 1948) p. 229
3. S. Mookerjee: *The Jaina Philosophy of Non-absolutism.*

Nāstitva (negation) is concomitant with *astitva* (position) in the same substrate."[1] Position and negation are copresent in the same real and possess an equal status. This may appear to be a contradiction, but "the Jaina solves the difficulty by means of the law of *anekānta*, which affirms the possibility of diverse attributes in a unitary entity."[2] "Absolute unqualified affirmation of existence is not in conformity with the nature of reality. Absolute negation of existence is self-contradictory. Fidelity to experience and thought demands that existence and non-existence both are to be accepted as equally valid traits in the make-up of a real"[3]. S. Mookerjee herein means that the real is a substratum of opposing attributes. The Jaina writers have not taken due care to guard themselves against a lax use of the term 'attribute'.[4] Kānji Swāmi of Songarh has pointed out that in the Jaina works "sometimes a mode has been called an attribute..., and to call a mode an attribute is the main style of the commentator....Thus it has been the style of the commentator to call a made, whether pure or impure, an attribute".[5] S. Mookerjee, as quoted above, uses the terms 'attributes' and 'trait' to convey the same meaning. The position amounts to an admission of opposing attributes in the same substratum. If two mutually hostile attributes inhere in the same substratum, they will annul each other's function and hence destroy the identity of the substratum itself. "If the identity of the substances becomes contradictory to itself, then no substance will be able to exist in the world,

---

1. Samantabhadra: *Āptamīmāṅsā*, verses 15 and 16, p. 20
2. S. Mookerjee: *The Jaina Philosophy of Non-absolutism*, p. 29
3. It will be seen that in Jainism every peculiarity of a substance is not taken to be an attribute. Attributes are constitutive elements of a substance, their unity constitutes the substance. Hence they must be ever present with the substance. Substance and its attributes always go together. The generality of a few selected modes may be termed as a quality; it cannot be an attribute, because it is not always found with the substance.
4. *Ibid.*, p. 88
5. *Ātmadharma*, Bhādrapada, 2482, p. 193

because the identity of things by contradicting itself will destroy itself.[1] Moreover, if to negate a positive entity a negative entity is needed then to negate the latter one another entity will be required; and the series has to be continued infinitely. The position is made still worse by the fact that we are required to negate not only the infinite positive elements in a real by means of the negative ones, but each one of the negative elements stands in need of being negated by other elements. Such a process can never come to an end. From this it follows that in an identical substance no attributes or powers can oppose any of the other attributes or powers and the negative function must be due to the positive attributes themselves. Generally speaking no entity can include in its structure elements which oppose each other. P.T. Raju has correctly observed: "If negation is an existential category; it must be the function of something which exists. This something must be negative. This negative something performs its function by negating or repelling. But this function is also found in the positive. So there is no need of postulating a negative in order to assign the function of negating to it".[2] What the critic means is that the negative function is also due to the positive elements in reality. The positive and the negative functions are determined by the self-same entity. There is no distinct attribute of negation to which the function of repelling may be assigned. The self-same entity is capable to establish itself and, at the same time, to negate entities other than itself. This leads to the conclusion that the truth of negation cannot be accepted at the level of attributes or powers.

Negation as a Dharma or a Trait

The facts of positive and negative cannot be denied, they are facts of our experience and require proper explanation. "To call the differences of the phenomenal

---

1. M.C. Jain: *Tattvārtha Cintāmaṇi,* vol: II, p. 293
2. P.T. Raju: *Thought and Reality,* p. 98

world an illusion is to give them a new name and not to explain them. Even an illusion is a fact of experience and has got to be seriously treated".[1] The Jaina traces the origin of theory of the *saptabhaṅgī* or the seven fold predication in the momentary mode of an attribute. It is said that the *saptabhaṅgī* applies to every mode.[2] Akalaṅka also observes that the *saptabhaṅgī* proceeds on account of affirmation and negation dependent upon the divisions (of reality) into substance, mode, universal and particular.[3] It means that the seven predicates are related to a singly momentary mode of an attribute or a unitary entity. The unitary mode of an attribute implies the seven traits technically known as the *dharmas* in Jaina philosophy. A mode in an expression of an attribute and implies the seven traits. It is with reference to these traits or implicates that the distinction between position and negation must be maintained by the Jaina. Vimaladāsa says: "The seven forms of prediction are dependent upon the seven varieties of questions....These arise on account of the seven forms of inquisitiveness which, in turn, arise from the seven forms of doubt. The doubts are seven on account of the seven traits which are the subject-matter of the seven *bhaṅgas*.[4] These seven traits may be taken to be the implicates of a real or an entity and it is through them that the real or the entity is able to establish itself or differentiate itself from other reals and entities. The number of the *bhaṅgas* does not matter very much in the present context. The first two *bhaṅgas* connected with the positive and the negative *dharmas* of a real are sufficient for the purpose under consideration. Thus in Jainism an ontological basis for negation, like that of position, is admitted; but for such a distinction we shall have to go deep into the region of traits or *dharmas* or implicates where they may be seen to coexist peacefully. Aurobindo also

---

1. H.L. Haldar: *New Hegelianism,* p. 256
2. "Pratiparyāyaṁ saptabhaṅgī vastunī", Vidyanadion's *Tattvārtha ślokavārtik a,* p. 130
3. Akalaṅka: *Nyāyaviniścaya, II.* verse 66
4. Vimaladāsa: *Saptabhaṅgī-taraṅgiṇī,* p. 5

remarks: "*sat* and *asat,* if they have both to be affirmed, must be conceived as if they obtained simultaneously. They permit each other though they refuse to mingle".[1] We can stop at the level of substance where it will be found to be establishing itself with the help of position (*sat*) and differentiating itself with the help of negation (*asat*). A similar situation will be found at the level of attributes, modes and powers and also at the level of the universals. In this way the Jaina allows full scope to a substance, an attribute, a mode or in general to every entity to oppose everything other than itself along with its own establishment. The Jaina also does not resort to any substantial, spatial, temporal or modal distinctions to establish the reality of negation. It must mean that the self-same real or entity is responsible for self-establishment and its differentiation from what is other than itself. It is an unintelligible piece of logic to say that an entity establishes itself but fails to negate what is other than its own identity. If there is no such negation concomitant with position, then position itself becomes meaningless. Significant negation as T.R.V. Murti thinks, must have an affirmative side;[2] and the Jaina holds a necessary concomitance between position and negation. In the same way Collingwood holds "a peculiar intimacy in the relation between the two kinds of elements. The negative elements give point to our affirmation by indicating what exactly they are intended to deny."[3] Both the positive and the negative functions are determined by the positive and the negative traits or *dharmas* of a real. The Jaina must locate this simultaneous existence of position and negation in the realm of traits or implicates. Behind these traits there is the unity of the entity which includes substance, attribute, power and mode. Samantabhadra aims at establishing concomitance between position and negation in this realm of traits, a fact suggested by the use of the term *eka-dharmin*

---

1. Aurobindo: *Life Divine,* p. 43
2. T.R.V. Murti: *Central Philosophy of Buddhism,* p. 154
3. Collingwood: *Philosophical Methods,* p. 106

in the verses already quoted (*Āptamīmāṁsā*, verses 15 and 16). So the *anekānta* philosophy does not advocate the opposition of attributes or powers in a substance independently of their implicates and the implicates may be taken to constitute a unity in spite of the fact that they are different from each other on account of their differing functions. The secret of the Jaina theory of negation is that for the reality of negation one has to enter the region of traits or implicates, and this type of opposition is implied by the term, *anekānta*.

Hegel and the Jaina on Negation

Commenting upon the Hegelian form of dynamism Collingwood observes: "Nature is permeated for Hegel as for Aristotle, by nisus; everything in nature is trying to become something definite; but the convergence of the process upon its own proper goal is always asymtotic and never reaches the point of coincidence".[1] If a philosophy of dynamic reality is advocated the implied dynamism must be due to something inherent in the constitution of reality itself. This element must be forcing reality to oppose the form which it has already attained by a tendency to take one different from the present one. Thus reality will have to perform a double function of sustaining the present form and forsaking the same for the sake of a future one. Hence reality is position and negation in one. Hegel must point to this very element, when he emphasises the concept of negation. Position is there at the root in Hegel's negation. In the absence of the positive aspect reality could not have begun its negative function. Position and negation are so finely interwoven in reality that neither of them can be eliminated. Creation and limitation are the two traits evinced by reality at every moment of its existence. Negation or contradiction alone cannot be held to be the backbone or

1. Collingwood: *The Idea of Nature*, p. 24

reality, position is equally important in its constitution. Andrew Seth says: "The position which Hegel makes his fulcrum is contrary or real opposition; the second is not simply the negation of the first, but both are real determinations of things."[1]

Something in the thesis itself is responsible for the production of the antithesis. Hegelian negation thus will mean the potentiality behind an actuality, and the situation is saved from self-contradiction by accepting one element as potential and the other as actual. Actuality and potentiality both belong to the same real; and the latter opposes the former. Similarly the Jaina makes his conception of negation non-absolute by introducing the necessity of a proper context for its predication. For him position and negation are mutually concomitant but with a limitation imposed by the introduction of reference systems. From the analytical view-point dynamism must be applied to every element that may be called an attribute. So the Hegelian negation must be admitted in case of every existential category in the constitution of reality; and no such element can be held to be self-contradictory or as contradicted by any other category belonging to the same real, F.S.C. Northrop justly contends: "It is the character of any positive form or quality, which we immediately sense, that it is logically related to its opposite. It is because the immediately sensed qualities of positive forms are not bare data but are logically connected to their opposites by the relation of opposition, that in sensing the windowpane to be cold we are also able to assert that it is not hot. To be sure in another experience we may sense the hot directly as positive form, but in this case we are then able to assert that the object is not cold.[2] The Jaina is of opinion that every attribute in its momentary states evinces symptoms of position and negation both, position and negation both are incumbent upon the momentary mode of an attribute. Because positivity

1. Andrew Seth: *Hegelianism and Personality,* p. 97
2. F.S.C. Northrop: *The Meeting of East and West,* p. 269

and negativity are distinctly perceived, the Jaina conceives the two diverse traits or implicates in the same momentary mode. What has been called the logical connection between opposites must be founded on something ontologically true, or it would be merely a mental construction. This very element is the trait of negation *(nāsti dharma)* in the constitution of reality as conceived by the Jaina.

An Objection Answered

Now we are in a position to consider the objections raised by Susil Kumar Maitra who says: "When existence and non-existence are both predicated of the same real, they are not predicated in respect of its different parts and there is thus no possible escape from the contradiction involved. If it be urged that existence belongs in form and non-existence in another form and thus there is no contradiction, the answer is that the contradiction could have been avoided if we have predicated existence and non-existence at different times."[1] According to the above critic, contradiction would have been avoided, if existence and non-existence were affirmed in respect of different parts of a real or in the same part with a temporal distinction. It clearly shows that position and negation are being taken as attributes. Their simultaneous manifestation is held impossible on account of the hostility between the two attributes. On the contrary, the Jaina is of opinion that position and negation are obtained in a real with no distinction of parts and temporal differences. Such a distinction to account for the co-existence of position and negation in a real will destroy the very unity of the real. It also leads to the conclusion that a real, while establishing itself, is not differentiating itself from others; and while differentiating itself from others, is not establishing itself. This position thus involves alternate suspension of the

1. S.K. Maitra: *Fundamental Questions of Indian Metaphysics and Logic*, p. 98

function of the two attributes. If position and negation are taken to be *dharmas* or traits, or implicates of a real as the Jaina does, the aforesaid inconsistency must not come in. All the traits connected with a unitary mode are implied simultaneously, but for their prediction they require different contexts. Samantabhadra rightly remarks: "Who does not desire all to be existent with respect to its own identity and non-existent with respect to the identity of the others"[1] Hemacandra remarks: "From the view-point of its own identity everything exists, and from the view point of other's identity it does not exist. If it is not so everything will be found to exist simultaneously or it will lose even its own identity.[2] Position and negation must be obtained simultaneously in a real, they do not repel each other. Unqualified existence or non-existence have no meaning, they must be qualified by proper contexts not only for the sake of predication but also for the sake of existence. Besides the traits, that effect self-establishment of a real and its differentiation from what is other than itself, must be held as valid constituents. Joachim has correctly observed: "And all movement, and process, and life certainly involve a negative element. They exhibit a being which emerges in contrast with not-being. They manifest an identity which perhaps overcomes otherness and difference, but assuredly does not extinguish them."[3] "Such negations would not barely exclude or vaguely imply a positive to be revealed by the advance of knowledge. They would, in and by their denials, throw into relief the positive aspect of the otherness which they emphasize, just as the affirmations within the system would also negate, in-as-much, as, to reveal the distinctions of that which they affirm from its others."[4] To conclude negation cannot be dismissed as a non-entity or a mental construct. It obtains along with position in a real.

1. Samantabhadra's *Ātptamīmāṁsā*, verse. 15
2. Hemacandra: *Pramāṇamimāṁsā*, p. 12
3. Joachim : *Nature of Truth*, p. 122
4. *Ibid*., p. 138

But its identity cannot be established at the level of attributes, or the criticism as given by P.T. Raju will apply to the conception of negation. We must differentiate between levels of attributes modes, traits or implicates. Negation exists at the level of traits or implicates.

Reality as a Featureless Entity

Every existent can be conceived in terms of substance, attributes, modes and traits. Umāsvāti holds a substance to be that which has attributes and modes.[1] Modes and attributes are not numerically distinct members in the constitution of a substance, a substance cannot stand independently of its attributes and modes. Price has correctly said: "A characteristic is pretty obviously a characteristic of something or other, and cannot easily be supposed to be an independent entity like the weevil".[2] This something living behind characteristics must not be absolutely distinct from its characteristics, for, in that case, that something will be left without features and hence without a form of existence. The Nyāya theory of substance is ultimately based on the concept of a featureless reality. According to it substance and attributes are distinct categories brought into relationship by a third category of *samavāya* or inherence. In spite of effecting a relationship the category of *samavāya* just becomes a member standing in need of a relationship with the members which it aims to relate. Thus the conception of *samavāya* fails to solve the problem and leads to an infinite regress. The idea of a featureless reality reduces reality to a non-entity. It is meaningless to hold reality to have no features. Features are actually the forms of existence of a real; and, if it is deprived of all such forms, it must lose its existence.

Kant's conception of the thing-in-itself seems to be based on an admission of numerical difference between the features

1. Umaāsvāti: *Tattvārtha-sūtra,* v. 29
2. H.H. Price: *Thinking and Experience,* p. 12

and their substrates. It is why Kant thinks of the thing-in-itself as independent of all the appearances. He abstracts reality from all its forms of existence and then denies the possibility of its knowledge. Actually speaking the remainder in the Kantian process of abstraction is not something unknowable but nothing which must be unknowable. Kant does not seem to be consistent in upholding the existence of the thing-in-itself, for existence itself should have been eliminated along with other features, thus leaving nothing behind to be designated as the unknowable. The conception of the thing-in-itself has no logical ground to stand upon. A.C. Ewing states that "in Kantianism thing-in-itself is only dogmatically asserted."[1] We can give no meaning to such a conception, because our knowledge of it cannot be mere nescience. Collingwood rightly holds: "The thing-in-itself is a non-sense phrase and it makes every argument, where it enters, non-sense".[2] This leads to the conclusion that nothing is absolutely unknowable and hence absolutely featureless. If a featureless entity which amounts to nothing can also become the subject-matter of philosophy, we fail to appreciate the form of knowledge which such a philosophy will yield. This nothing, if taken as a negation of everything positive, comes out to a non-entity; hence in the absence of the subject matter the concerned branch of knowledge must also vanish. Philosophy will have some meaning only when its 'nothing' is interpreted as something positive. C.R. Jain observes: "The idea of nothing involves a contradiction. In the popular sense nothing is an empty concept, and, as such, is inconceivable by the mind. We might describe the state of nothingness as a condition of existence, when this thing, that thing, the other thing, that is, when each and every and all things were not, but when we have merely a notion of the sense objects; and when we endeavour to think away substance itself, the mind refuses to obey the impulse and the lips to formulate speech".[1] Thus the conception of

1. A.C. Ewing: *Idealism—A Critical Survey,* p. 102
2. Collingwood: *Nature of Reality,* p. 117

a featureless reality does not come out to be tenable.

Reality as Pure Being

The continuum theory of reality will reduce itself to the view of pure neutral being, if it allows scope for undifferentiated continuum. Such a theory of reality, as Collingwood holds, is untenable, because such a being will have nothing to be investigated and the concerned science having no problems to solve will also disappear.[2] When differentiation is the very nature of the continuum, it is inconceivable how we ever get undifferentiated continuum. In the flow of reality one state will be superseded by another, and by going forward we can never reach a stage where the flow ceases so as to make room for undifferentiated continuum. By calling reality a continuum or a process stress is laid on its flowing or dynamic aspect; but at the same time the unity of the continuum is also maintained. The Sanskrit equivalent of the term substance is *dravya* which has been explained by Devanandin as "that which, by nature, flows towards its modes".[3] Thus the Jaina also aims at emphasising the fluidity of reality but not to the negation of its unity which has been affirmed as one of the two traits, i.e., permanence and impermanence. As already pointed out the Jaina position does not mean that permanence and impermanence are the numerically different elements in the structure of reality. This will lead to the self-contradictory constitution of reality. The English term 'substance' is suggestive of something unchanging behind the changes, and thus implies a division of reality into two numerically different fragments. The Jaina sees permanence in the impermanent, and impermanence in the permanent. By effecting a change of context the aforesaid two aspects of reality can be comprehended. Neither permanence nor

1. C.R. Jain: *Key of Knowledge*, p. 19
1. R.G. Collingwood: *An Essay on Metaphysics*, pp. 14, 15
2. Devanadin: *Sarvārthasiddhi*, p. 153

impermanence taken singly sums up the nature of reality. They are abstractions from one unity and their togetherness in the sense of an aggregate will not yield a consistent solution. If these abstracted elements are predicated of reality without defining the necessary context, contradiction is the natural result.

The Jaina will not agree with the Mādhyamika view, as interpreted by T.R.V. Murti, that "all viewing. *dṛṣṭi* as such, is *avidyā; dṛṣṭi* is *kalpanā, kalpanā* is ascription of features which are non-existent in reality".[1] The difference between the Mādhyamika and the Jaina is that for the former all *dṛṣṭis* are false, while for the latter they are false if taken in an absolute sense. A *dṛṣṭi* for its sublation by another must establish itself, then alone it can be sublated. Hence the establishment and the sublation of a *dṛṣṭi* both are facts of our experience. The Jaina accepts both of them as true but solves the contradiction by referring to different contexts. The *pāramārthika* entity cannot be absolutely unknowable and featureless, because, as T.R.V. Murti himself thinks, the Mādhyamika denies metaphysics not because there is no real for him, but because it is inaccessible to reason".[2] Thus for the Mādhyamika reality is almost like the thing-in-itself of Kant with the exception that for the former it is knowable by intuition or *prajñā.* The right conclusion from the views of Kant and the Mādhyamika is the denial of the absolutism of the partial views or *dṛṣṭis;* and failing to solve the apparent contradiction involved therein, they resort to the conceptions of the thing-in-itself and the *śūnyatā.* Whatever partial views we get about reality are not merely subjective aberrations but are caused by the objects themselves as Kant held. The flaw in calling such views false lies in the fact that the object is conceived in its synthetical aspect and its correspondence is considered with a knowledge obtained analytically. In Jaina philosophy the truth of the partial

---

1. T.R.V. Murti: *The Central Philosophy of Buddhism,* p. 240
2. *Ibid.* p. 126

views is based on something ontologically true; and reality must yield such views, if an analytical approach to it is made.

Substance as Unity-cum-Diversity

Parker states: "To make identity real there must be some substantial core which persists, despite of continual change".[1] In a dynamic system of philosophy reality cannot be split up into two parts, one of which shows dynamism while the other determines persistence, for in that case the principle of dynamism will not be applicable to a part of reality. The flow of reality is ever continuous, it is a process wherein momentary modes can be recognized as point-events. Still it implies the identity of the flow. A number of variations are attributed to the same entity, still there is a factor which is responsible for the perception of identity. Permanence and impermanence are the mutually concomitant traits of reality. So both of them are supposed to coexist in the same real. This permanent element is the substantial core behind the variations....If change implies substance, substance equally implies change. As the conception of change depends upon the reference of them to an identical substance, so we can think of the latter only as the connecting principle of changes. Substance is not an unknown and unknowable substratum in which determinations inhere, but it is the principle which finds expression in its successive states and, as such is the link that connects them with each other".[2] To conceive the universe as a process or a function just raises the question 'whose process, whose function can it possibly be?' Bahm rightly holds; "substance as that which stands under or remains through change. Whenever there is a functioning there is a substance,...Each entity has its substantial and

1. Parker: *The Self and Nature.* p. 32
2. H.L. Haldar: *Neo Hegelianism,* p. 35

functional poles".[1] We cannot do merely with a process, a function, or a differentiation; something which is implied by it must be included in the system. In a way this something can be distinguished from the process, the function or the differentiation. The same entity has to be doubly designated as permanent and impermanent, the substance and the modes. Bradley found this situation difficult to comprehend. Explaining his views Dr. Haldar says: "How to bring together permanence and change consistently we do not know. Our usual procedure is to evade the difficulty by shutting our eyes now to the aspect of unity, now to the aspect of diversity, as suits our purpose. This is a make-shift practically convenient, but theoretically the problem remains unsolved".[2] So long as we are seeking for distinct constitutive elements or attributes to determine identity and diversity simultaneously, the problem must remain unsolved. The Jaina solves it by going deep into the region of traits where, actually speaking, the opposition between position and negation does not exist, for what may be held to be opposites require different contexts for their predication. In this respect the Jaina will agree with Bradley in holding that "...what is rejected as appearance is not mere non-entity. It forms a constituent element of the real. The character of the real is to possess everything phenomenal in a harmonious form. It is a self-consistent whole and excludes contradiction. What is self-contradictory cannot be real."[3] The *anekānta* philosophy holds the so-called absolute views true with reference to a proper context. Absolute views stand as organs of the *anekānta* philosophy. There is no inadequacy in accepting an absolutism, if it is governed by a proper view-point. When such specifications of the governing conditions are not made, the *anekānta* or the non-absolute position is the most consistent one to which one would like to adhere.

---

1. *Philosophy: Eastern and Western,* pp. 270, 271
2. H.L. Haldar: *New Hegelianism,* p. 220
3. *Ibid.,* p. 226

Substance, Attributes, Modes and Traits

Substance has been variously described with a view to emphasise one or the other of its aspects. Rājamalla says: "A substance has attributes and modes. A substance is a collection of attributes."[1] Umāsvāti also thinks: "A substance has attributes and modes."[2] Such descriptions may be taken to suggest a distinction between the substance and its attributes and modes, but the Jaina holds this distinction in a non-absolute way. A substance is a unity of attributes and modes, it is a unity which is constituted of a diversity. Modes and attributes are not numerically different elements in a substance, nor in substance numerically different from attributes and modes. A substance is identified with its attributes which appear when its unity is analysed. Pandit Sukh Lal in his commentary on the *Tattvārthasūtra* says: "The cause of the individual flows of the infinite modes in all the three times is the individual power called an attribute, and a group of such infinite powers is the substance. It is said from the differential point of view. From the non-distinctive point of view a mode is identical with the substance, which, for this reason, is called identical with attributes and modes".[3] Prof. A.N. Whitehead sums up the nature of dynamic reality as "Actuality with permanence requires fluency as its component and actuality with fluency requires permanence as its component".[4] Permanence or fluency alone cannot give a true picture of reality. Permanence and fluency, when considered with respect to reality, must imply each other. A. C. Ewing has justly observed: "It is clear that there is no sense in talking about what a substance is apart from its qualities and relations, it is also clear that qualities and relations, if they are to have

1. *Pannādhyāyī*, verses 72, 73
2. Umāsvāti: *Tattvārthasūtra*, 5.38
3. *Tattvārthasūtra* (commentary by Pt. Shukhlal), Saṁvat 1996) p. 231
4. A.N. Whitehead: *Process and Reality*, P. 491

a place in the existent world, must be qualities and relations of something".[1]

An attribute is something which invariably accompanies a substance. The very unity of a substance implies that it can never be found without the diversity of attributes. Hence an attribute is something in the structure of a substance, which never leaves the substrate. Devanandi states: "What are found inhering in the permanent substance are the attributes".[2] An attribute may undergo changes in degrees of manifestation from a minimum to a maximum, but it can never disappear totally from its substratum. Attributes are the principles of division of a substance. Umāsvāti again contends that the attributes inhere in a substance, but, in themselves, cannot be supposed to have attributes".[3] He emphasises two facts. Firstly, the attributes presuppose a substance for their inherence, and secondly in themselves they are not substrate for other attributes. The unity of the attributes gives birth to what is called the substance. By following a process of abstraction we may talk of attributes distinctively of the substance; but, if all the attributes are shaken off, the unity of attributes, and hence the substance, vanishes. Thus a talk of substance independently of the attributes becomes impossible. The second fact implied means the limit of the process of analysis of a substance into its attributes. We can analyse the unity of a substance to a stage where we come across elements which are termed as attributes. The process of analysis may be carried on further, but we shall not get attributes therefrom. By this Umāsvāti also means that the attributes are not mental constructions but have ontological validity. This limit of the process of analysis is such as would allow no overlapping of the elements so obtained. Rājamalla emphasises the same fact when he says: "No

1. S.K. Maitra: *Fundamental Problems of Philosophy,* P. 96
2. Devanandin: *Sarvārthasiddhi*, p. 95
3. Umasvātī: *Tattvārthasūtra,* 5. 41

attributes can be covered under other attributes".[1] Still no part of a substance is without all the attributes into which it can be analysed. Parker remarks: "The qualities of an individual are all involved in one another, and it is impossible for any one of them to exist separately from the rest, that is, separate from a thing of which we say it is a quality".[2] So the attributes are mutually distinct, but each one of them inheres the whole of the substance. It is only at a particular depth of the analysis of a substance that we can get its attributes.

When reality is held to be dynamic, dynamism must apply to everyone of its attributes. The flow of a substance means the totality of the constituent flows determined by its various attributes. The cross sections of these flows as related to a particular moment of time are the modes. The modes may be said to be the forms of existence of a substance with respect to its various attributes. The flow of a substance is ever continuous and this continuity is conceived as analysed into elements like the point-events which are called the modes. Devasena remarks: "The variations of an attribute are the modes".[3] The modes are, thus, the principles of division of an attribute. Modes depend upon attributes, being the forms of existence of a substance with respect to its attributes. A mode may be said to be the expression of a substance with respect to an attribute. It attains its true meaning in the ultimate division of an attribute with respect to an ultimate division of time; but the term has also been used to represent the states of a substance with respect to a number of attributes and also as extended over a number of moments.

Jaina Dynamism of Substance

The Jaina mentions *sat* or existence as the differentia of a substance, but for him *sat* does not mean the absolute

1. Rājamalla: *Pañcādhyāyī, verse, 1013*
2. Parker: *The Self and Nature, p. 267*
3. Guṇa-vikārāḥ paryāyāḥ (Devasena): *Ālāpapaddhati,* p. 37

permanence of Vedānta. A substance by its very nature, undergoes variations, still it is able to maintain its identity. Hence *sat* has been defined as the copresence of origination, decay and permanence."[1] The secret of the Jaina dynamism of substance lies in the fact that the substance undergoes variations by negating old forms of existence and assuming new ones and thereby safeguarding its persistence. Mc Taggart has very correctly remarked: "Thus the continuity of the attributes is always sufficient to preserve personal identity, not because it would be sufficient if the substance changed, but because it proves that the substance remains unchanged."[2] Continuity and change are coexistent in a real. There is no temporal distinction among the states of origination, decay and permanence. It is one existence which implies origination, decay and permanence simultaneously. Hence a substance would mean origination, decay and permanence in one. Amṛtacandra Sūri remarks: "There is no creation without destruction, no destruction without creation, no creation and destruction without persistence, and no persistence without creation and destruction."[3] Bergson also observes: "At the very instant that my consciousness is extinguished, another consciousness lights up or rather, it was already alight: it has arisen the instance before, in order to witness the extinction of the first, for the first could disappear only for another and in the presence of another"[4]. Appearance and disappearance or origination and decay must be taken to be copresent; and it is possible only when the same entity is able to imply them simultaneously. The aforesaid trio cannot be given the status of an attribute or a mode in a substance for fear of self-contradiction. Still the Jaina stresses its ontological validity; and by that be means that it is not a mental construction but has objective reality as a trait or a *dharma*. Samantabhadra

1. *Ibid.*, 5.30
2. Mc Taggart: *Studies in Hegelian Cosmology*, p. 50
3. Amṛtacandra: *Pravacansāra (Tattvārtha-dīpikā-vṛtti)*, p. 136
4. Henri Bergson: *Creative Evolution* (Translated by Arthur Mitchell), 1944, p. 303

advances an argument in support of its ontological validity. "Persons desirous of a pot, a crown and gold become sad, happy and indifferent at the destruction (of the pot), origination (of the crown) and persistence (of gold) on account of their causes."[1] The psychological states of sadness, happiness and indifference, though generated in the self, have their causes in the external world. As these states are caused by the self-same mode, origination, decay and permanence must be affirmed of the same momentary mode; and a mode can accommodate them all simultaneously only as its traits. Thus to get at their ontology we shall again have to go deep into the region of traits. Parker has very justly said: "Existence and non-existence can no more cohere than any two contradictories can; yet in the same thing, in the same least moment of reality creation and decay are present to gether with the permanent, just as colour and extension and hardness coexist in the same object. Becoming and passing out must be recognized as ultimate categories, subforms of existent on an equal footing with the permanent."[2] A dynamism attains its true meaning only when it implies a peaceful unity of change and permanence. If change and permanence are affirmed of a substance at the level of attributes, they, being contradictory, will make the existence of the substance impossible. If they are held to be two distinct modes of a substance, they will be distinct on account of the attributes whose modes they are; or on account of a temporal distinction, if they are modes of the same attribute. In the first case we come to a position where contradiction is found at the level of attributes. In the second case we come to the opposition between modes and the underlying attribute—which is impossible, for the modes are the expressions of the attribute itself. For this reason origination, decay and permanence cannot be held to be the modes of the same attribute. This position creates another difficulty. Origination, decay and

---

1. Samantabhadra: *Āptamīmāṁsā*, verse. 59
2. Parker: *Self and Nature*, p. 99

permanence as modes of the same attribute most follow in succession. This would mean that for a moment the real is only origination or decay or permanence; and the next moment one of these three modes is transformed into another. Permanence which changes into decay or origination, and decay and origination which change into permanence are meaningless, Hence in the Anekānta philosophy change and permanence are consistently united in the region of traits or *dharmas.* The copresence of change and permanence is the very soul of the Jaina dynamism.

Absolutism of Dynamism of Reality Considered

There are thinkers who uphold the absolutism of the modal side of substance. "Reality", according to Prof. James, "appears to be one stream of immediate experience, and nothing beyond this real".[1] The Buddhistic philosophy of momentariness also propounds a similar view. "Buddha finds no centre of reality or the principle of permanence in the flux of life and the whirl of the world."[2] This philosophy is not nihilsm, but it objects to the existence of the principle of continuity. The discreteness of existence is real, while the perception of continuity is a delusion. The two perceptions of discreteness and continuity are simultaneously had, but the former is considered faithful to reality while the latter is not held to be so. The difference between the associationists and the Buddhists is that for the former the perception of continuity is a creation of the percepient's mind, but for the latter there is a sort of modalization of latter events by the former ones. So according to the Baudha there is a sort of objectivity in the form of a series of events, which determines the perception of continuity. The Jaina agrees with the associationists in holding that the perception of continuity is a psychic manifestation but is not purely determined by the mind. He also agrees with the Baudha in

1. Bradley: *Essays on Truth and Reality,* p. 99
2. Radhakrishnan: *Indian Philosophy,* vol. l, p. 375

holding that the perception of continuity is caused by the series of modes of the objects, When the two perceptions are experienced every moment, the Jaina finds it fallacious to prefer one to the other. He holds that the modes are mutually distinct on account of the traits of change and difference *(anitya-dharma)* which they imply. At the same time the trait of persistence (*nitya-dharma*) determines the perception of continuity. It so, neither the perception of discreteness nor that of continuity can be said to be untrue to reality. Neither permanence nor impermanence, taken singly, can give us the full view of reality. The real is such as absorbs both permanence and impermanence into its identity.

No doubt reality is a stream, but it must be a stream of something. Flow is only an aspect of reality and it cannot be taken to represent the whole of reality. The stream without the support of a continuous factor will not be a stream at all. The ideas of unity and diversity are simultaneously implied by a real. How can they be seen united, if not by going deep into the region of traits? The continuum theory of reality explicitly recognizes the unity of the continuum behind the differentiations, hence the continuum must be sucl as would include integration and differentiation in one. Regarding simultaneous existence of unity and diversity Mc Taggart says: "Reality is a differentiated unity, in which the unity has no meaning but the differentiations, and the differentiations have no meaning but the unity. The differentiations are individuals for each of whom the unity exists and the whole nature consists in the fact that it is for the individuals. And, finally, in this harmony between unity and the individuals neither side is subordinated to the other, but the harmony is an immediate and ultimate fact."[1] So a substance must mean a copresence of position and negation, permanence and impermanence and diversity and unity without involving any contradiction therein. If these

1. Mc Taggart: *Studies in Hegelian Cosmology,* p. 19

elements are affirmed of a substance in the same context, contradiction is inevitable. The Jaina establishes his position consistently by assigning different contexts for their predication. Like position and negation unity and diversity are the two implicates or traits of a real, the same real is perceived as a unity and also as a diversity. As already quoted S. Mookerjee thinks: "The central thesis of the Jaina is that there is not only diversity of reals, but each real is equally diversified."[1] To complete the exposition it may be supplemented by the proposition that there is not only unity of a real but all reals are equally united. "All substances are diversified with respect; to their origination, decay, persistence, attributes, modes, names, differentia and purpose, still from the view-point of existence they are not so distinguished. Reality assumes such a form by nature."[2] Thus a true theory of reality must include all the elements enumerated above and their ontological validity is to be sought in the region of traits.

Jaina Theory of Reality as Illustrated by a Propositional or a Mathematical Function

As regards the nature of existence of the aforesaid elements H.H. Price has given a very suitable suggestion. He states: "In the technical symbolism of Formal Logic the most appropriate expression for referring to one of these features of the world is not a single letter such as P or R which might possibly be mistaken for the name of an entity, but a propositional function such as Px or x R y or R (x, y, z). Here, x, y, and z are variables so that the propositional function is an overtly incomplete expression, To complete it one must replace the variables by a constant, denoting some object, which satisfies the function; if there are several variables, each of these must be replaced by a constant."[3] A

1. S. Mookerjee: *The Jaina Philosophy of Non-absolutism,* p. 68
2. Jayasena: *Pravacana-sāra.* (Commentary by Jayasena), p. 125
3. H.H. Price: *Thinking and Experience,* p. 12

proposition depends upon the terms used in it but is not identical with their aggregate. The propositional function is a synthetic unity of the terms which stand as elements in its structure. The proposition requires no other elements except the terms, but still marks a transcendence over them. The attributes and modes, according to the Jaina theory of reality, occupy the same position in a substance as the terms, in a proposition.

The unity of the substance, attributes and modes and their diversity may be equally illustrated by a mathematical function involving a plurality of variabilities. With the variation of the variables the function itself undergoes variations, but still it cannot be conceived as distinct from the variables. The function results from the unity of the variables, and in the unity the diversity of the variables is not sublated. So the mathematical function is a unity and a diversity at the same time. The Jaina theory of reality affirms unity and diversity of a real after the manner of a mathematical function. The attributes are the variables, and modes are like the constant values given to the variables. The process of reality is ever continuous, and by stopping at the intermediate stages of the process we get the modes of a substance with respect to the various attributes, The values of the function can be obtained for the constant values of one or more variables, so also in case of a substance the modes can be determined with respect to one or more attributes. Thus we come to the attributive modes *(guṇa-paryāyas)* and the substantial modes *(dravya paryāyas).* To illustrate the Jaina theory of reality by a mathematical function the function must be taken as F (x, y, z....) where the variables involved are infinite.

Chapter 2

The Doctrine of Syādvāda or The Jaina Dialectic

Introduction

We have seen that the structure of reality consists of both unity and diversity at the same time. It can be further analysed into attributes, modes and traits. The relational nature of reality makes its structure all the more complicated. On the other hand human capacity for comprehension is so limited that it cannot know a thing in its totality. Thus the Anekānta theory of existence and the discursive nature of human thinking necessitate the formulation of the doctrine of Syādvāda or the Jaina dialectic, which is mainly concerned, as W.T. Stace thinks, with "the correct joining and disjoining of ideas"[1]. It aims at finding a suitable explanation for the fragmentary advance of our thought and comprehension. It also aims at seeking the type of consistence which such an advance of knowledge will evince.

Main Spirit of the Jaina Dialectic

Another spirit which the doctrine of *Syādvāda* shows is that nothing can be affirmed of a real in an absolute way. Samantabhadra remarks that *Syādvāda* is a way of comprehension of an entity be renouncing the absolute views about it. *Syādvāda* emphasizes the fact that no predicate affirmed of a real is able to yield the whole truth

1. W.T. Stace: *A Critical History of Greek Philosophy*, p. 190.

about it. It gives us only a partial view of the real and such a view is effected by isolating some of the elements from the totality of the real. It means that the *Syādvāda* doctrine is based on an analysis of reality into its constituent elements. "*Syādvāda* effects a division or analysis of reality and the *naya* enlightens the particularity of the divided elements."[1] *Syādvāda* is the theory of fragmentary or partial *comprehension* and the *nayas* embody the principles by which the process of such a comprehension is governed. The possibility of an analysis of reality just shows that the process of comprehension based on such an analysis cannot be merely a subjective imposition. There must be something in the structure of the real itself to effect a partial comprehension about it. If it is said that the universe is permanent or transitory, the universe must contain something to correspond to such comprehensions. We have seen how the traits like position and negation, unity and difference, and permanence and impermanence are united in a real. Thus the subject-matter of *naya*-knowledge has an ontological validity. At the same time such characteristics cannot be affirmed of a real in the same context; this will involve contradiction. The world cannot be permanent in the same context in which it is held to be impermanent. Hence the application of contexts or reference systems is also an ingredient of the theory of *Syādvāda*. The main function of the Jaina dialectic comes out to be the selection of a proper context and the discernment of the truth implied in it. Devanandi says: "A consistent comprehension of a particular element in realty having many determinants by assigning a proper reason (i.e., context) is the *naya*."[2] Again "that particular view-point of the knower, which comprehends a part of the real (by throwing the rest into relief) and which has become the subject-matter of the *śruta pramāṇa*, is the *naya*."[3] Dr. Radhakrishnan also observes: "A *naya* is the

1. Samantabhadra: *Āptmīmāṁsā*, verse 104.
2. Devanandin: *Sarvārthasiddhi*, p. 78
3. Vādideva: *Pramāṇanaya tattvāloka*, p. 316

stand-point from which we make a statement about a thing."[1] The idea underlying these expositions is that the *naya* knowledge depends upon an analysis of a real effected from a particular view-point of the knower.

Some Illustrations of Partial Comprehensions

In our actual experience knowledge always advances in fragments, i.e., not by grasping a real in its entirety. Here are a few illustrations of the fragmentary process of comprehension. The different sciences take for their subject-matter the different aspects of reality, and there is no science which could boast of making the whole of reality its subject-matter. The various departments of philosophy take for their study the various aspects of reality, and the partial comprehensions so effected go to constitute the body of knowledge. Thinkers have often resorted to this way of partial comprehension in the course of their discussions.

(i) Kant on Partial Comprehension

Kant draws a distinction between the two worlds of the noumenon and the phenomenon; and holds that some truths find validity in the noumenal world while others, in the phenomenal world. This is the way by which he tries to solve his antinomies. For this he mentions the transcendental and the empirical points of view. What is transcendentally wrong may be empirically true and vice-versa. The idea that our empirical perceptions are not purely subjective but have a cause in the noumenal world just connects our perceptions to the thing-in-itself. The appearances are related to something beyond themselves; they refer to the thing whose appearances they are. Kant fails to do due justice to the appearances, when he propounds the theory of unkowability of the noumenon. H.M. Bhattacharya rightly remarks: "But the net result of Kant's epistemology has been that he has left a great gulf yawning between knowledge

---

1. S. Radhakrishnan: *Indian Philosophy,* vol. I, p. 298

and existence, between what our understanding constructs as the world of objects and the real world of things-in-themselves to which understanding has no access."[1] This very fact has led Hegel and Bradley to establish a closer relation between the phenomenal and the noumenal worlds. It is true that in the fragmentary process of knowledge our cognition must suffer a distortion as compared with the cognition of the noumenon itself; but, in spite of it, it must remain an appearance of the same noumenon. In this sense the phenomenal knowledge may be said to connect itself with the noumenon. The two view-points, that is, the transcendental and the empirical, form an important part of Kantian epistemology.

(ii) Hegel on Partial Comprehensions

Hegel makes the principle of contradiction the very back bone of his philosophy. The union of the thesis and the antithesis is effected only by rising to higher systems. The thesis and the antithesis never lose their opposition in the same system. So the truth of opposition and unity is based on the distinction of systems. In other words Hegel makes one of the synthetic view point in one system, and of the analytic viewpoint in the other. He has not been able to establish absolute unity, as Dr. Haldar complains that "Hegel goes from the lower to the higher without solving the contradiction of the lower and wants to include them under the latter."[2] The conclusion from Hegel's position is that the truths he establishes are valid only in their proper systems, and he cannot belittle them for the sake of something whose absolute truth he tries to maintain. About Bradley's position it is said that "no appearance is lost in the Absolute. Each one is indispensable and constitutes the whole. Take away from the Absolute anyone of its elements and it is at once reduced to nothing. None of the fundamental aspects of the world can be resolved into others and none is useless and

1. H.M. Bhattācharya: *The Principles of Philosophy,* p. 105
2. P.T. Raju: *Thought and Reality,* p. 78

insignificant."[1] This amounts to the position that reality admits of analytic and synthetic judgments, and the validity of such partial comprehensions is not totally rejected by Hegel or Bradley.

(iii) Śaṅkara on Partial Comprehensions

As regards Śaṅkara's position it is very often said that he has not explained the world but has explained it away. To meet the criticisms of the opponents he distinguishes among the three levels of existence. Thus a sort of reality is assigned to all the *prātibhāsika* (ephemeral), the *vyāvahārika* (empirical) and the *pārmārthika* (absolute) worlds. Then in the same breath the principle of *māyā* along with its products in the form of ephemeral and empirical worlds is admitted to be absolutely unreal. It is on this ground that Śaṅkara's explanation of the world is held to be insufficient. Max Müller points to the same difficulty as "To steer between all these rocks is no easy matter. Brahman, though called the material cause *(upādāna)* of the world, is himself immaterial, nay the world of which he is the cause, is considered as unreal, while at the same time cause and effect are held to be identical in substance".[2] The absolute truth of the Brahman must mean the absolute untruth of the world. So the absolute defence of the one must lead to the absolute unreality of the other. Thus the conceptions of the ephemeral and empirical worlds are unable to explain the reality of the world. Still the empirical truths are valid though only in a particular world. Hence this much can be admitted about Śaṅkara that for the validity of empirical truths the proper worlds must be taken into consideration. Whatever may be the status of these empirical truths this much can be accepted that Śaṅkara has not totally discarded them.

(iv) Mādhyamika on Partial Comprehensions

The Mādhyamika school of Buddhism, like Śaṅkara's

---

1. H.L. Haldar: *Neo Hegelianism,* p. 242
2. Max Müller: *Indian Philosophy,* vol. II, p. 45

absolute truth of Brahman, upholds the truth of *śūnyatā*, and tries to undermine the validity of the partial comprehensions. T.R.V. Murti observes: "For the Mādhyamika all viewing, *dṛṣṭi* as such, is *avidyā; dṛṣṭi* is *kalpanā* and *kalpanā* is ascription of features which are non-existent in reality".[1] It is again said: "The Mādhyamika dialectic remove the conflict inherent in reason by rejecting both the opposites taken singly or in combination. The Mādhyamika is convinced that the conjunctive or disjunctive synthesis of the opposites is but another view."[2] The conception of *saṁvṛti satya* (empirical truth) in Buddhist philosophy just points to the admission of partial comprehensions, and such truths are needed to explain the visible world. Now the only problem is whether the Buddhist can uphold the validity of empirical truths (because *saṁvṛti* is also *satya* or true) and designate them as absolutely false. Waiving aside the problem of the validity of empirical truths this much can be admitted of this school of philosophy that partial comprehensions as truths find a place in it. Then absolute falsehood of the *dṛṣṭis* cannot be consistently maintained. The falsehood of *dṛṣṭis* consists of the fact that they fail to comprehend reality in its entirety but for this reason they cannot be ascriptions absolutely unconnected with reality.

Almost all the thinkers have to believe in the efficacy of the partial way of thinking and comprehension. All the systems of philosophy make a start from what is comprehensible to the thinking mind and such comprehensions are partial by their very nature. The only difference among them is that they assign varying import to them. We shall see that the partial comprehensions are not absolutely false or subjective; but at the same time they cannot be perfectly faithful to things perceived, as they are born of a analytical view-point. Such comprehensions will be found to be valid only in the systems which form a suitable context for them. For the Jaina the partial

---

1. T.R.V. Murti: *The Central Philosophy of Buddhism,* p. 240
2. *Ibid.,* p. 128

comprehensions are true conditionally i.e. in a particular context. If a context is defined, the Jaina will find no fault with the resulting partial comprehension. He holds it true to reality because reality must yield such a partial view if an abstraction from reality in accordance with the view point of the knower is effected.

Import of Contexts or Reference-Systems in the Jaina Dialectic

Reality shows signs of difference and unity sumultaneously and the Jaina holds that both of them belong to it as its traits. Hence our perceptions of the one or the other aspect must be equally true. According to the Jaina the partial comprehensions always need a context. The same real, when placed in different contexts yields different views; and our experience will also show that the partial views are not merely mental constructions. There is something ontologically valid in the things themselves, which makes its isolation and partial comprehension possible. Prof. Einstein illustrates the relativity of perception as "If a stone is dropped from a running train it will appear to describe a parabola to man on the embankment and a perpendicular downward line to man in the train."[1] It must be held that the *path* of the stone is such that it can be seen as a perpendicular from one angle of vision and as a parabola from another. Both the perceptions cannot be said to be absolutely independent of the object perceived. The same fact is seen in different ways, when the contexts governing them are changed. The Jaina dialectic just supplies the necessary reference-systems with reference to which a real must be comprehended. There is a way by following which reality can be perceived as a multiplicity or a unity; and when contexts are further multiplied the partial comprehensions become all the more varied. The author of the *Sanmati-tarka* says, "There are as many *nayavādas* (partial comprehensions)

1. Albert Einstein: *Theory of Relativity,* p. 3

as there are ways of verbal expression."[1] By this it is emphasized that the Jaina dialectic has manifold ways for its movement. The Cartesian system of coordinates includes only the three dimensions, while some other systems may be conceived to include more dimensions. There must be something in the point itself which enables it to admit of an application of different systems of coordinates. Thus the Jaina dialectic makes varied comprehensions of the same real possible by effecting a change of the reference systems or contexts. No one can afford to ignore the importance of the universe of discourse in his discussion without landing himself in a net-work of fallacies. The conception of contexts or reference-systems occupies the same position in Jaina philosophy as the universe of discourse in logic and the systems of coordinates in analytic geometry. The conception of the thing-in-itself will mean the comprehension of a real, when it is governed by no contexts. It is almost like reading the coordinates of a point, when no system of reference is given. A point is a centre of a circle, a point of intersection of two curves and the foot of a perpendicular by its own virtue and by virtue of the setting in which it is placed. From this follows the conclusion that the partial comprehensions must presuppose the application of one or the other contexts; and the varying descriptions of the same real in different contexts are valid but only in proper contexts.

W. James rightly holds: "Every single event is ultimately related to every other and is determined by the whole to which it belongs."[2] Andrew Seth has also said: "Everything is connected with everything else, its existence involves a multitudinous reference beyond itself."[3] Prof. A.N. Whitehead points out: "An actual entity has a definite bond with each item in the universe. This determinate bond is its prehension of that item."[4] Lord Haldane contends: "Relativity is every

1. Siddhasena: *Sanmatitarka. 3.47.*
2. W. James: *A Pluralistic Universe,* p. 76
3. Andrew Seth: *Hegelianism and Personality, p. 8*
4. *History of Philosophy—Eastern and Western,* p. 261

where obvious. It is inherent in the order or nature as much as it is inherent in the order of knowledge."[1] This relational side of reality is responsible for bringing a real in different settings, but according to the Jaina there in no absolutism of the relational side which at the same time implies the non-relational one. Before having a connection, a relation, a bond with other entities, an entity must establish its own identity. Self-establishment and relationship with other entities must be held simultaneously. Samantabhadra argues: "If things have nothing by their own right, no relations can contribute anything to them, or the relations must be held to be creating something real out of a void. If we hold that things are established absolutely independently of all relations then we fail to understand how and why they should at all enter into a relationship with each other, and in this way the possibility of the universal and hence also of the particular is destroyed."[2] Hence our conclusion is that the partial comprehensions are also based on something ontologically valid and are true in their proper contexts.

Validity of Partial Comprehensions

A.C. Ewing does not simply question the validity of partial comprehensions but denies even their possibility. He says: "I see a black patch, Socrates is man, all men are mortal, Socrates is mortal, are not only partially true but completely true. It is nonsense to say that 2 + 2 = 4 is partly false and 2 + 2 = 5 is partly true."[3] Joachim also holds a similar view. According to him "Relative truth is a contradiction in terms, what is true is *eo ipso* absolutely true. There may be truths about the relative, but the truth about the relative is itself absolute, i.e., true neither more nor less... the indeterminate judgement affirms only a part of truth. But the part affirmed is true absolutely and

---

1. Haldane: *Reign of Relativity*, p. 214
2. Samantabhadra: *Āptamīmāṁsā, verse* 73
3. A.C. Ewing: *Idealism: A Critical Survey*, p. 210.

completely, and remains true to all eternity, it is the whole truth about a part of the matter."[1] It means that objects admit of relativity but their knowledge cannot be said to be relative. Such knowledge must comprehend only a part or an aspect of the objects governed by a particular system of reference. So its validity must hold good in that particular system. When the validity of a comprehension depends upon some conditions, we cannot say that it is absolutely true, unless the limited context it taken to be absolute. When we think that 2 + 2 = 4, we unwittingly take the necessary context for granted i.e. the first 2, the second 2 and the 4 are taken in the same context. If the first 2 stands for days, the second 2 for weeks and the 4 for months, the given equation will come out to be false. If the equation is held to be absolutely true, the aforesaid specification of the terms in the equation must not have any bearing on it.

Bradley on Partial Truths

Supporting the truth of partial comprehension Bradley has rightly observed: "To gain truth the conditions of the predicate must be stated ideally and must be included within the subject. This is the goal of ideal truth, a goal at which truth never arrives completely; and hence every truth, so long as this end is not attained, remains more or less untrue... Every partial judgement therefore is partly true and opposite also has truth. This of course does not mean that any given truth is merely false, and, of course, also, it does not mean that the opposite of any given truth is more true than itself."[2] If propositions are made without specifying the necessary contexts, they admit of their own truth as well as the truth of their opposites. As we cannot hold that such prepositions are absolutely true or absolutely false, they must be held to be only partially true. When the

---

1. Joachim: *Nature of Truth*, p. 87
2. Bradley: *Essays on Truth and Reality*, p.232

necessary reference system is given, the logical conclusion is that the proposition is true only in the given system.

The Jaina View

Dr. Tatia observes: "Certainly the knowledge of a slice of reality cannot be false unless the fanaticism of the observer makes it the sole and sufficient character of it."[1] A real represents a multitudinous structure; and a truth, which comprehends only an aspect of it, cannot be absolutely faithful to it. If by such absolutism is meant only an absolutism within a particular system the Jaina will see no inconsistency in it. But such comprehensions must allow scope for other comprehensions. Samantabhadra has said: '*Nayas*, when taken in indifference to other view-points, are false; and when taken with due allowance for other views, establish truth about reality."[2] The Jaina dialectic establishes the truth of the partial comprehensions about reality not by negating other similar truths about it but 'by bringing one of the many traits of the real to the focus of our attention and by assigning a secondary place to others."[3] "The latter *naya*, when it apprehends an aspect of the real, does not obstruct the application of the other *nayas*."[4] "If an alternative is selected for exposition, the connected *naya* invariably emerges; and if the alternative is not so meant, the *naya* invariably recedes."[5]

Dr. Radhakrishnan's View of Partial Comprehensions

Dr. Radhakrishnan criticizes the Jaina theory of partial comprehensions on the ground that it implies the truth of an absolute principle which the Jaina does not like to advocate.

---

1. N.M. Tatia: *Nayas—Way of Approach and Observation*, p.4
2. Samantabhadra: *āptamīmāṁsā*, verse 108
3. Devanandiṇ: *Sarvārthasiddhi*, p. 175
4. *Nayavivaraṇa*, verse 114
5. Rājamalla: *Pañcādhyāyī*, verse 508

He says: "If Jainism stops short with plurality which is at best a relative and partial truth, and does not ask whether there is any higher truth pointing to a one which particularizes itself in the objects of the world, connected with one another vitally, essentially and immanently, it throws overboard its own logic and exalts a relative truth into an absolute one."[1] As has been pointed out in the previous chapter, plurality and unity upon which the critic centres his attention, are the traits of reality concomitantly connected with each other. If so, the aspect of unity can never be neglected but it again constitutes only an aspect of reality, and hence gives rise to another partial comprehension. What the critic expected to be the most exalted truth of the absolute comes out, on the ground of Jaina logic, to be another partial comprehension which was never dismissed by the Jaina.

The Jaina Dialectic and the So-called Absolute Views

The *anekānta* philosophy adheres to no form of *ekānta* or absolutism. For the Jaina *ekānta* finds a meaning only within a reference-system, and there is nothing like an absolute view in Jaina philosophy. Dr. S. Mookerjee remarks: "The non-absolute is constituted of absolutes as its elements, and as such would not be possible if there were no absolutes. As the tree disappears if the branches and members are taken out, the non-absolute would similarly vanish if the absolute elements are not there."[2] The distinction of unity and difference, one and many, existence and non-existence are all relative, while reality includes them all as merely part characteristics. Discussing Lenin's view of absolute and relative truths it is said: "He recognizes the presence of relative elements in the process of knowledge and explains that the distinction between relative and absolute truths is itself a relative one...absolute truth results from the sum

1. Radhakrishhan: *Indian Philosophy,* vol. 1, p. 305
2. S. Mookerjee: *The Jaina Philosophy of Non-absolutism,* p. 171

total of relative truths in the course of their development, the relative truths represent relatively faithful reflections of an object existing independently of man, that those reflections become more and more faithful, that very scientific truth, notwithstanding its relative nature, contains an element of absolute truth."[1] The Jaina touches what Lenin calls an element of the absolute truth by mentioning the non-relational side of reality. To be relational and to be non-relational are the two concomitant traits of a real, and they require different contexts for their predication. We cannot maintain one or the other of them without specifying the necessary context. It is why the Jaina accepts the relational-cum-non-relational nature of reality. The question whether he upholds a relative absolutism or an absolute relativism, will find meaning only in the non-absolute philosophy of the Jaina. Outside the span of Anekānta philosophy a combination of relativism and absolutism will not be possible. The Jaina philosophy of non-absolutism can be interpreted as relative absolutism or absolute relativism by supplying the necessary context; and in that the admission of the one will never be antagonistic to the admission of the other but there must be a difference of contexts applied. Samantabhadra remarks: "Non-absolutism, which is established by the *pramāṇa* and *nayas,* is non-absolute. It is non-absolute as comprehended with the help of a *pramāṇa,* and becomes absolute when a *naya* is applied to it."[2]

The Prāmaṇa Type of Knowledge and its Essential Nature

The *naya* is not the only form of knowledge. "Knowledge is accomplished", saya Umāsvāti, "by means of *pramāṇas* and *nayas.*"[2] Generally we come across two types of knowledge. Firstly, there is a type which follows the

1. B.G. Tiwari: *Lenin's Doctrine of Absolute and Relative Truth, pp. 59 and 61*
2. Samantabhadra: *Bṛhat-svayambhū-stotra*, verse 103
3. Umāsvāti: *Tattvārtha-sūtra*, 1.6

fragmentary process of comprehension and touches only a slice of reality. The other type of knowledge aims at giving a comprehensive view of a real. The *pramāṇa* and the *naya* types of knowledge are mutually distinguished for their total and partial approaches to a real. Devanandi says: "A *pramāṇa* takes the whole of a real as its subject-matter."[1] Vimaladāsa also mentions: "A total comprehension of reality is the knowledge of the *pramāṇa* type."[2] This may appear to lead to the impossibility of the *pramāṇa* type of knowledge. Our experience testifies to the fact that we are never able to comprehend the totality of reality. Samantabhadra, therefore, has well said: "The knowledge of reality which enlightens the whole of it simultaneously is the *pramāṇa*."[3] Thus perfect knowledge or the *kevalajāṇna* alone can be designated as the *pramāṇa* type of knowledge; and in the lower stages of existence a *pramāṇa* cannot be experienced. But in the Jaina works along with the Kevalajñāna sensuous knowledge, scriptural knowledge, clairvoyance and telepathy have also been enumerated as yielding *pramāṇa* type of knowledge, though they never apprehend reality as a whole. The totality common to all the aforesaid types of knowledge must not be taken to mean the all inclusive totality of reality whose comprehension is held to be possible only in the perfect stage. So all the *pramāṇa* types of knowledge except the perfect knowledge as enumerated by the Jaina comprehend reality only partially; and the total comprehension of reality does not form the criterion for the *pramaṇa* type of knowledge, Hence in the *pramāṇa* type of knowledge the meant totality is not vitiated by the fact that it does not comprehend reality as a whole. It also leads to the conclusion that the *pramāṇa* knowledge is possible in spite of the fragmentation it may involve. The Jaina will have to give a similar meaning to the term *sakalādeśa* which is taken to be the differentia of the *pramāṇa* knowledge. *Pramāṇa* knowledge must not

1. Devanadin: *Sarvārthasiddhi*, p. 8
2. Vimaladāsa: *Saptabhaṅgītaraṅgiṇī*, p. 19
3. Samantabhadra: *Āptamīmāṁsā*, verse 101

presuppose a totality in the sense of all-inclusiveness, as the term *sakalādeśa* may suggest, but it must be the totality of a system. When we aim at an isolation of one or the other aspects from a system presented as an object, we get *naya*-knowledge; and when such isolation is not aimed at we get *pramāṇa* knowledge. Kevljñāna comprehends the entire system of the universe, and the lower and smaller systems are comprehended by other *pramāṇas.* The totality of a system should not be taken to mean the aggregate of its constituents. So also an aggregate of partial comprehensions cannot yield a *pramāṇa*. Rajamalla opposes the view that a *pramāṇa* is an aggregate of the *nayas.* "A *pramāṇa* has a different taste (essence) from the aggregate of *nayas.*"[1] "Negation in preceded by affirmation, and affirmation by negation. The knowledge which comprehends the union of the two is the *pramāṇa*"[2] Joachim also maintains a similar view. He observes: "To treat science as a sum, aggregate, collection or class of single truths, each of which is what it is in its singleness and remains unchanged in the collection is utterly inadequate as a theory of knowledge".[3] A *pramāṇas* may include the *nayas* but is not identified with them, it always transcends the aggregate of the *nayas.* The totality of the *nayas* gains in essence which is lost when a surgical analysis of a *pramāṇa* is effected. This special essence is suggested by assigning a different taste (*rasa)* to the *pramāṇa.* In the bits of sensuous knowledge the entity presented to the senses is comprehended as a whole and no isolation is meant therein, so this type of knowledge is classed with the *pramāṇas.*

Relation Between the Naya and the Pramāna Types of Knowledge

If reality is not completely comprehended by the *naya* and also by some of the *pramāṇas* the question of their

1. Rājamalla: *Pañcādhyāyī*, verse 675
2. *Ibid*, verse 665
3. Joachim: *Nature of Truth*, p. 100

validity needs consideration. The problem is what kind of validity the Jaina would like to assign to the partial comprehensions. We have seen that the determination of the partial comprehensions is also based on something ontologically true in the structure of the objects, so also the *pramāṇas* that fail to comprehend reality as a whole must proceed on a similar ground. The *nayas* as well as the *pramāṇas* yield a valid type of knowledge. "A *naya* comprehension is also valid as it yields a right cognition of its subject-matter."[1] A *naya* is not admitted as an antithesis of a *pramāṇa* because it embodies a type of knowledge. It is a part of the *pramāṇas.* A *naya* is neither a *pramāṇa* nor an antithesis is of *pramāṇa*, being free from contradiction."[2] Vidyānanda also establishes a relation between the *nayas* and the *pramāṇas* by saying that the former are the parts of the latter."[3] At the same time the Jaina would like to emphasize the fact that a *pramāṇa* transcends the totality of the *nayas* by gaining a different essence. The *pramāṇa* does not oppose the possibility of the constituent *nayas* but oppose the possibility of the constituent *nayas* but accepts them as elements in its own structure. When the *nayas* go to constitute a *pramāṇa*, their individuality though not totally wiped out, does not remain the same as it was in isolation. In this sense alone we can say that *nayas* lose their existence when they enter into a system to yield a *pramāṇa*. A *pramāṇa* is an integrated system of the *nayas;* and it is a system in which as Blenshard holds. "integration would be so complete that no part could be seen for what it was without seeing its relation with the whole, and the whole itself could be understood only through the contribution of every part."[4]

1. Vidyānandin: *Ślokavārtika*, 1.65
2. *Nayavivaraṇa*, verse 10
3. Cf. Vidyānandin: *Ślokavārtika*, 1.6.5
4. Blenshard: *Nature of Thought*, Vol. II, p. 267

Hegelian and the Jaina Dialectics

Distinguishing between the Hegelian and the Jaina dialectics T.R.V. Murti observes: "The Hegelian dialectic is a conjunctive or integrating synthesis; at every stage the alternatives are unified and transcended, and this leads to a higher or lower view. The Jaina dialectic is a disjunctive synthesis or alternatives, as we have seen it is more a syncretism than a synthesis."[1] It is true that Jaina writers have failed to emphasize the concept of a system as explicitly as Hegel has done; but it can never mean the concept is totally absent in Jaina Philosophy. The special essence assigned to the *pramāṇa* type of knowledge just points to the unity of the system involved therein. The Jaina, by emphasizing both the aspects of unity and multiplicity, saves himself from falling into the absolutism of either. Disjunction and conjunction are the two aspects of the Jaina dialectic, and the one is affirmed not by vanquishing the other but by assigning a secondary position to it as the nature of the dialectic demands. Hegel's philosophy does not reduce multiplicity to insignificance, and he has to accept the copresence of unity and multiplicity in reality. Such a view can be maintained only in the non-absolute way of the Jaina. If the Jaina dialectic is interpreted as disjunctive, it can also be interpreted as conjunctive by effecting a change of context. To call the Hegelian dialectic purely conjunctive is to introduce an inconsistency in the Hegelian philosophy itself. It will amount to absolute negation of difference and opposition—a position which Hegel does not seem to advocate. On the other hand regarding the element of conjunction in Hegelian system P.T. Raju and H.L. Haldar complain that Hegel has not been able to solve the contradiction of the lower. P.T. Raju observes: "In the dialectic so long as the opposites are there, the contradiction is not solved. But when the synthesis is attained the lower ones are merged in it and therefore

---

1. T.R.V. Murti: *Central Philosophy of Buddhism*, p. 128

lost."[1] Starting from opposites Hegel attains unity by rising to higher system where the opposites are supposed to exist but they do not oppose each other. If opposition is absolutely abandoned by the opposites, they must lose their existence, as the aforesaid critic mentions. Such a position becomes inevitable, if absolute unity is meant. Hence to obtain unity and difference simultaneously the position must be interpreted in the non-absolute way of the Jaina, or the charge against Hegel must stand.

Merit of the Jaina Dialectic

The great merit of the Jaina philosophy of non-absolutism lies in the fact that it is able to maintain the truth of the opposite elements like unity and multiplicity in a consistent manner. It establishes its truth not by rejecting the partial views about reality but by taking all of them into consideration. The partial comprehensions, so far as they approach reality, are held to be true, but they are unable to give us a full picture of reality. "The only thing the Jaina dislikes in other thinkers is the dogmatic claim of each that he alone is in the right. The claim amounts to a fallacy of exclusive predication *(ekāntavāda)*."[2] The Jaina does not simply uphold a spirit of easy and illogical compromise among the different views, but fully agrees with what has been said of K.C. Bhattācarya. D.M. Datta recognizes the merit of Bhattacarya's philosophy as "his superiority lies not in demolishing the views of others, but in being able to work out their unknown and unthought of implications, showing them at their best, and assigning them a place among the many possible alternate views which would make partisans voluntarily give up all airs of self-sufficiency."[3] And to achieve this aim the Jaina effects a

1. P.T. Raju: *Thought and Reality*, p. 80
2. Chatterjee and Datta: *An Introduction to Indian Philosophy*, p. 93
3. D.M. Datta: *Contemporary Philosophy*, p. 124

very deep analysis of the structure of reality which he finds to possess no absolute character. Thus equipped with the knowledge of the *Anekānta* theory of existence and the Jaina dialectic we shall be better able to do justice to the various aspects of the Jaina theory of the soul.

Chapter 3

The Soul

Introduction

The fact of conciousness is a necessary presupposition for every system of philosophy with the exception of the behaviourist school of psychology which does not distinguish between behaviour and consciousness. Philosophy, or rather every branch of knowledge, being through and through a conscious function, must base itself on the truth of the fact of consciousness. An attempt to deny the truth of consciousness is again based on consciousness. Without presuming consciousness no exposition, no discussion can be advanced. Consciousness is an undeniable fact of our experience. Waiving aside the problem how and whence consciousness is caused it must be the common assumption of all the systems. Opinions may differ as regards the origin and nature of consciousness, but no one can deny it without the risk of self contradiction. It is established by the very first attempt we make to investigate its identity and nature.

Classification of the Theories of the Soul

On the functional side consciousness is an undisputed fact of our experience; it is only the structural side of consciousness which has been variously conceived by the philosophers. Their views may be broadly classified as follows:

(a) Materialism holds that consciousness originates from matter. There is nothing like a spiritual reality or substance distinct from matter to determine the conscious function. For this school consciousness is a manifestation of matter.

(b) Idealism posits ultimate value in the conscious principle. Though idealism takes varied forms, the ultimate truth of the conscious principle is their common implication. The visible world of our experience is taken to be either a delusion or a manifestation of the conscious principle. Some idealists also go to the extent of denying delusion as a manifestation of the conscious principle which is held to be perfectly immutable.

(c) Between extremes of materialism and idealism stands the doctrine of neutralism. For it the ultimate source of the world is neither material nor spiritual, but it is something which gives rise to material as well as spiritual manifestations. The continuum theory of the world also holds that the material and the spiritual manifestations are derived from the same continuum, and, in this respect, it may be said to agree with neutralism.

(d) The Śaṁvedanātvaita of Buddhism, the associationism of Hume, and the structurism of modern psychology form another group. All of them start with the distinct atomic conscious functions and do not presuppose any substantial reality to determine such functions. They postulate a tying principle, named variously, to connect them.

(e) The last group consists of the dualists who believe in the distinct existence of soul and matter. They hold that soul and matter are two distinct substances, the one cannot be transformed into the other.

Materialism and the Soul

The basic conception underlying different forms of materialism is that matter alone is the ultimate reality in the world; and it is matter that takes the form of consciousness at one or the other stage of its existence. On the ground of sense perception the Cārvāka school of Indian materialism holds that "consciousness is generated from the four material entities when they get transformed into an organism, like the intoxicating power of wine."[1] Matter in its entirety is not the source of consciousness. It is in a particular form of material existence that consciousness appears. Consciousness is thus a novel quality of matter, much distinguished from the material qualities. Sometimes a fine type of matter is held responsible for the generation of consciousness. Joad observes: "Mind is a matter of a very refined and attenuated type, a glow surrounding the brain, a halo round the head."[2] Epicurus also establishes the material origin of the soul on the ground of sense perceptions which show us nothing but material bodies. For him the soul is material and is composed of extremely minute atoms of matter diffused all over the body.[3] Thus only a part of the substance of matter becomes the source of consciousness. With Aristotle we see that it is not necessary to isolate any part of matter for the generation of consciousness. For him "the human soul is nothing but the organization of the body. It stands to the body in the relation of form and matter."[4] Mc Dougall also observes: "Life is a continuous activity. It may be that it is manifested to us only when matter exists in a peculiar collocation we call protoplasm, just as magnetism is manifested only where certain unusual collocations of matter are formed:"[5] Herein we see that emphasis is laid not on a particular type of matter as was done before, but consciousness is held to be dependent upon a form of existence of matter. This view does not aim at drawing a distinction between the conscious and the unconscious types of matter. Matter is, throughout the same, the credit of originating consciousness goes mainly to material collocation and organization. According to this view we shall have to suppose that matter constituting a

---

1. Mādhavācārya: *Sarvadrasána-saṁgraha*, p. 2
2. Joad: *Workings of Mind*, p. 19
3. Cf. Frank Thilly: A *History of Philosophy*, pp. 90-91
4. W.T. Stace: *A Critical History of Philosophy*, p. 296
5. Mc Dougall: *Modern Materialism*, p. 95

collocation or an organism must gain in quality, though the gain may be held to be due to a particular setting of matter. To avoid the antagonism of spirit and matter it is also held that consciousness is always found with matter but in a rudimentary form. In an organism the manifestation of consciousness becomes explicit, and there is no emergence of a novel quality in matter. All forms of materialism agree in holding the ultimate reality of matter which can give rise to consciousness in one or the other stage of its existence.

Jaina Criticism of Materialīsm

The entire Jaina criticism of the theory of the soul as given by materialism is based on the contention that matter and consciousness are so different that one cannot be derived from the other. In the commentary of the Sūtrakṛtāṅga Śīlānka points out that "Consciousness cannot be found in a collocation of matter, because, though the senses are constituted of matter and apprehend thing severally, they cannot give rise to unity of consciousness."[1] The organism is a plurality of material atoms; and, if matter can give rise to consciousness, it must be a plurality of consciousness—a conclusion which is contradicted by our experience. "If consciousness is regarded as a secretion of matter, it must be a composite substance, every atom emanating a distinct consciousness."[2] Again it is explicitly said by Haribhadra that "the nature of material entities being different, consciousness cannot be found in their collocation."[3] The Jaina just opposes the basic thesis of the materialist that there is no opposition between matter and consciousness. According to him consciousness cannot be an attribute, an emergent quality or a manifestation of matter. He holds that an attribute is that which is always found with its substratum, though it may undergo variations of degrees.

---

1. Sūtrakṛtāṅga (Āgamodaya Samiti, Mahesana), p. 16
2. C.R. Jain: *Key of Knowledge*, p. 45
3. Haribhadra: *Śāstravārtā-samuccaya*, p. 22

Thus colour is an attribute of matter, but red colour is only a form of manifestation of colour. Red colour does not always accompany the substratum which can never be found to be colourless. So what is called an emergent quality is only a form of manifestation of an attribute. It cannot be absolutely novel and distinct from the attribute. With this definition of an attribute the Jaina does not accept consciousness as an attribute of matter. Matter is said to be unconscious and inert by nature hence it cannot gain something which is not found in it as an attribute. If materialism gives a true explanation of consciousness, then it cannot consistently isolate a particular type of matter as having the capacity for consciousness. This matter will ultimately lead to the reality of the spiritual substance, because its distinction from other matter will gradually lead to its immateriality. Vidyānandin has correctly remarked: "(if to explain consciousness) some fine matter, responsible for self experience and having no colour, etc., is supposed, then, for the Cārvāka the fifth element is proved."[1] This fifth element with its special characteristics may be held to be the substance of the soul. The conclusion is that all matter should be supposed to have the potentiality for producing consciousness. In other words consciousness must be there in matter in all forms of its existence, though at certain stages it may show only rudimentary consciousness. Then the question is 'if this basic substance has both the capacities for material and conscious manifestations, why it should be at all called a material substance' The moment the materialist supposes that consciousness can be produced from matter he commits himself to the position of the neutralist. The absolutism of matter or soul can be held only by drawing a distinction between the material and the spiritual. By deriving one position from the other we do not get the truth of the former but reduce it to a third position. Hence the conclusion from

1. Vidyānandin: *Tattvārtha-ślokavārtika* (Bombay; 1918), p. 29 (verses 115, 116)

the above discussion is that the conscious and the unconscious entities must be distinguished both in their structural and functional aspects. If so, materialism cannot be said to have established the truth of the soul.

Vidyānandin's Criticism of Materialism

Vidyānandin puts forth a number of arguments to show the existence of the self as distinct from matter. Firstly the existence of the soul is proved by the experience of 'I'. Secondly the distinctive characteristics of the soul and matter prove the soul to be a distinct substance. Thirdly the ways of their comprehension being different, the soul must be held to be a distinct substance from matter.[1] The feeling of selfhood has been taken to be a proof for the existence of the soul. Everyone feels himself as distinct from his organs, his nerves and his brain; and this distinct experience leads to the existence of the soul as a distinct entity from matter. "The Jīva exists because we perceive it directly, in the form of bliss, etc. The experience of 'I' is independent of the senses and is felt clearly and consistently."[2] This self experience is a presupposition of all conscious processes. In the Viśeṣāvaśyaka Bhāṣya it is said, "Oh Indrabhūti, the self is indeed directly cognisable to you also. Your knowledge about it which consists of doubt, etc., is itself the self. What is proved by your own experience should not be proved by other means of knowledge. No proof is required to prove the existence of happiness, misery, etc....If the object about which one has doubt is certainly non-existent, who has a doubt as to whether I do exist or I do not exist."[3] Descartes also proved the existence of 'I' on the possibility of thinking. To take a general view of his argument we can say that the self is established on the ground of its functions.

---

1. *Ibid.*, p. 27 (verses 102 & 103)
2. *Ibid.*, p. 26 (verses 96 & 97)
3. Jinabhadra: *Viśeṣāvaśyaka Bhāṣya*, verses 1554, 1555 (quoted by M.L. Mehta in *Jaina Psychology*, p. 37)

One can be conscious of his psychic functions directly; and therefrom the existence of the self is deduced. Max Müller remarks "There is in man something that can be called *Ātman* or self. It requires no proof, but if a proof were wanted it would be found in the fact that no one can say, 'I am not (I being the disguised *ātman*) for he who would say so, would himself be not, or would not be."[1] "Mind is the first and most direct thing in our experience, all else is remote inference."[2] It may be argued that it is always the experience of some psychic functions which we get in self-consciousness. We never come across, as Hume held, the substance of the soul. We shall consider Hume's position at a later stage. At present it will suffice to say that, if one accepts the substance of matter, the substance of the soul cannot be denied. We certainly draw a distinction between the functions of the soul and matter, and so they must have been determined by two different substances. The difficulty of assigning an object of self-experience arises out of the fact that we want to perceive the soul in the same manner as we would see a piece of matter. The substances of matter and soul are so different that the ways of their comprehension are not the same. Matter is comprehended in terms of its attributes and modes, so also a soul must be known in terms of its attributes and modes. The feelings of pleasure and pain, the cognition and other psychic phenomena are the terms by which the soul can be known. These are the forms of its existence, and we can know it only in terms of the forms of its existence. As these forms of the soul's existence are different from those which we find in matter, we come to the conclusion that the soul must be a different substance from matter. Even the protoplasm of the materialist has been shown to be insufficient to explain the phenomenon of consciousness. Bausfield rightly replaces protoplasm by psychoplasm which he holds to be

---

1. Max Mūlar: *Indian Philosophy*, vol. II, p. 50
2. Eddington: *Science and the Unseen World*, p. 24

the substance of the psychical structure. The introduction of psychoplasm brings us back to the position where a very fine type of matter was supposed to explain the origin of consciousness. Unless this substance is so different from matter that it may be called immaterial, it cannot prove a suitable substratum for consciousness. The very idea that we need something different from matter to explain consciousness goes to prove that the soul is a different substance from matter the soul has distinct forms of existence and comprehension and for this reason it is a distinct substance from matter, as Vidyānandin observed.

Idealistic Theories of the Soul

Just as materialism tries to derive consciousness from matter, so also idealism tries to derive matter from the principle of consciousness. Though idealism takes varied forms, the common conception underlying them is that the ultimate reality is spiritual in nature. For the present purpose, the idealistic theories may be classed into the following three groups. These groups differ from each other mainly as regards the conception of individual selves and the worldly phenomena. Śaṅkara's monism holds that individual selves and the worldly phenomena are delusive, having no existence, as against Brahma, and *Brahma* is the only reality which exists and which is immutable. The distinctive feature in Śaṅkara's idealism is that he denies change and difference in both the physical and the psychical worlds. But no philosophy can afford to ignore the explanation of the perceived world. The differences in the psychical and the physical realms are facts of our experience, and they cannot be passed over unexplained. For this Śaṅkara introduces the conception of *māyā*, but the situation permits him to grant for *māyā* only status of delusion which he also assigns to the perceived world. The second group deviates from Śaṅkara's position as regards the conception of *māyā*. Rāmānuja is not satisfied with the delusive status of *māyā* as assigned by Śaṅkara and thinks that *māyā* is a real power of *Brahma.* It gives rise to a creation of real selves and a real world. Difference and change are real characteristics of the world and are not delusive both physically and psychically. As Aurobindo observes. "both of these lines of thought start from one reality; but one ends in universal illusionism while the other in universal realism."[1] Hegel and the Neo Hegelians, for whom the differences and appearances of the visible world are not delusive, may also be included in the second group. It does not matter much whether the ultimate reality is of the nature of consciousness or thought, for both the cases, may be held to cover only a partial identity of the soul. Thought, if taken only literally is not the only form of consciousness, hence Hegel's thought must mean something more than what we generally mean by thought. In the same way the psychologist will object to the contention that consciousness alone is the form of existence of the psyche. The Jaina is also of opinion that thought is a mode of the knowledge-attribute and consciousness does not represent all the attributes of the soul, though it represents the essential nature of the soul. Whatever may be the form of idealism it must start with the fact of consciousness and somehow derive matter from it. Berkeley may be said to belong to the third group which stands between the two aforesaid groups. Berkeley does not derive the material existence from spirit but holds that the ideas themselves are so read that one is deluded to think that there is an external world. Berkeley agrees with Śaṅkara in holding that the spiritual reality does not transform into matter but differs from him in holding that the differences are true in the psychical sense. He agrees with Rāmānuja and Hegel in denying the immutability of the spiritual principle; but differs from them in assigning no reality to the world of matter.

Unlike materialism the basic conception of idealism is the emanation of matter from a spiritual principle. The positions of idealism and materialism may, in this respect,

1. Aurobindo: *Divine life*, vol. II, p. 185

be held to be interchanged. The former begins with spirit and the latter, with matter; but both of them come to the same world which includes both spirit and matter. So the entire criticism which was levelled against materialism finds application in case of idealism also. The transformation of consciousness into matter must suffer from the same fallacies which proved to be an obstruction in the way of materialism. Moreover, when the conscious principle is admitted to possess both the capacities for conscious and material transformations, it must not be held to be only conscious, for consciousness is only a form of manifestation of the underlying principle. Thus, like materialism, idealism also reduces itself to neutralism—a position to which any theory believing in the mutual transformations of consciousness and matter must lead.

Śaṅkara's View of the Soul

Śaṅkara's position may be held to be only a little different from what has been said about idealism so far. He tries to evade the aforesaid fallacy by introducing the principle of *māyā* in his system. In order that the creation of the world may not be real he assigns only an empirical reality to *māyā* and its workings. For the world of matter and individual souls *māyā* is held responsible in such a way that the *Brahma* is left out unaffected by it. As a matter of fact in a philosophy of absolute spirit there is no room for any other element. The absolutism and the immutability of spirit allow no status of existence to *māyā*. The difficulty is two fold. We cannot say that *māyā* is there, because in that case it will be the dualism of *māyā* and *Brahma*. We cannot say that *māyā* is not there, because, then, we shall not be able, to explain the world. To steer clear of the above difficulties Śaṅkara develops the conception of levels of existence and resorts to the logic of view-points. He holds the truth of *māyā* only at the empirical level, while *Brahma* is true at the transcendental level. Śo *māyā* does not come out to be absolutely unreal; and *Brahma* does not show himself to be absolutely real. There are levels of existence where both are held to be real. If such is not the position of Śaṅkara he has done no good to his system by introducing the principle of *māyā.* If *māyā* and distinctions both are admitted to be phenomenal, then it is like the birth of a horse's horns from the ass's horns. Samantabhadra says that no empirical truth can be established without the necessary transcendental reality behind.[1] No phenomena can be true, if it is based on something which is only phenomenally true. A.C. Ewing observes: "If the appearance-self is conceived as only a part of the phenomenal world, to make all phenomena dependent on it would be like that a man had built the house in which he was born."[2] A phenomenon to be possible must touch reality somewhere. Moreover on the contention of Śaṅkara himself the absolute reality and the phenomenal reality must agree in being a reality at least, or the phenomenal reality will not deserve the title of reality at all. There must be a type of reality which can be predicated both of *Brahma* and *māyā.* When *māyā* has something real in its nature and can stand parallel to *Brahma,* it becomes a case of dualism.

All proofs for the existence of *Brahma* must start from the facts of our experience, for the absolute is totally out of our ken. If the facts of our experience are absolutely unreal, then the inferences based on them will carry no validity. Advaita Vedānta must posit some reality in the facts of the empirical world, and they must not be taken to be totally delusive. Such a position will land us in a region of relativism holding the truth of both the absolute and the empirical worlds. Samantabhadra observes: "*Advaita* (monism) is not possible without *dvaita* (dualism) just as *ahetu* (non-cause) cannot be had without a *hetu* (cause). If *advaita* is established on the ground of a *hetu* or reason, then there is the dualism of the *hetu* (reason) and the *sādhya* (the thing to be established). If it is established without a reason, then

1. Cf. Samantabhadra: *Āptamīmāṁsā,* verse 44
2. A.C. Ewing: *Fundamental Problems of Philosophy,* p. 100

dvaita can also be proved simply by making a statement."[1] Malliṣeṇa contends "If *māyā* is existent, two entities are proved. If it is non-existent how can it generate the empirical world? If *māyā* generates the world-process in a delusive way, then it is like calling the same woman a mother and a barren lady."[2]

The true value of idealism lies in its emphasis on the spiritual side of existence and its ethical import. Dr. Deva Raj mentions that idealism negates the existence of the external world to arouse the spirit of renunciation. He also quotes the view of Vitthaleśa upādhyāya that Advaita Vedānta holds the universe to be delusive so that a spirit of renunciation may be awakened among the disciples.[3] A parallel view is upheld by the Jaina thinker Kundakunda. He adopts an ethical viewpoint and draws a distinction between the self and the non-self. The self is certainly distinct from *pudgala* (matter), but, as he propounds, it cannot also be identified with psychical functions like anger, pride, etc. According to Kundakunda the psychical functions can be attributed to a soul only from the empirical *(vyavahāra)* view-point which has been condemned as false *(mithyā)* by him. The falsity of the Jaina empirical view-point is not like the falsity or *māyā* in Advaita Vedānta. Advaita Vedānta wrongly accepts the falsity of *māyā* in the region of metaphysics; Jainism, on the other hand, confines this falsity to the region of ethics beyond which the truth of the empirical world is as integral to the Jaina theory of existence as that of the transcendental world.

Berkeley's View of the Soul

Berkeleyan idealism starts with the facts of perception. In our perception what we get of the external things is nothing but our own ideas. On this ground Berkeley

1. Samantabhadra: *Āptamīmāṁsā*, verse 26, 27
2. Malliṣeṇa: *Syādvādamañjarī*, p. 52
3. Cf. *Pūrvī aur Paścimī Darśana* (Hindi), p. 178

establishes his dictum, 'esse est percipi'. For him the world is there but it is only a group of ideas in our mind. Thus existence and perception are identified in his philosophy. Perceptions must inhere in something, while the so-called facts of the external world, being reduced to perceptions themselves, do not require a separate substratum. Thus for Berkeley the souls are the only reality in the world.

Berkeley holds that mind perceives its own perceptions by means of perceptions so one perception can be said to have another perception for its object. Now going backwards we may seek for the objects of previous perceptions. The series must end at one or the other stage in the reality of the external world as the objects of our perceptions; or the perceptions will be totally contentless. Berkeley's perceptions are like apperceptions of psychology which cannot originate, unless objects as distinct from the mind are presupposed. Dr. Haldar points out: "The error of materialism is to ignore the subject for which objects exist, and the error of Berkeley is to ignore the object in relation to and in distinction from which subjective processes are possible."[1] Berkeley is right in his assertion that knowledge consists of ideas, it can never be of the nature of things. So, if the external world at all exists it must be known in terms of ideas. Berkeleyan position does not disprove the existence of the external world, it simply establishes that, whether the external world exists or not, it must be known in terms of ideas. From this contention it also follows that the absence of knowledge of a thing is not a sufficient proof for its non-existence. A.C. Ewing remarks: "The idealist argument does not prove that matter could not exist independently of mind....The argument therefore is far from proving that whatever we know depends for its existence on our or some other mind's knowing it, nor does it even prove that every thing existent is knowable or known."[2] Berkeley believes in the existence of other minds; but what he can apprehend of these minds is nothing other

1. H.L. Haldar: *Neo Hegelianism,* p. 90
2. A.C. Ewing: *Idealism—A Critical Survey,* pp. 15-16

than the ideas about them. His own admission of the existence of other selves pre-supposes that there is something real behind the ideas. Dr. Haldar again remarks: "Berkeley's statement that matter as unrelated to mind is inconceivable simply means that matter always exists in relation to mind, not that it is ideas of the mind."[1] H.A. Pichard also says: "Existence of things is not their perception. Berkeley simply means that esse of things involves percipi. With this foundation he starts and then identifies existence with perception thus destroying the foundation itself."[2] A.C. Ewing emphasizes the necessity of the external world as "to know is to know something, and this something cannot be just our knowing....If we eliminate the reality thought about, the thoughts are the thoughts about nothing."[3] Knowledge and objects of knowledge cannot be identified, though there is a close relationship between them. The Jaina posits knowability in all the objects that exist, existence and knowability always go together. Vidyānandin says: "That which is not known by the perfect one (*Arhant*) is not knowable and hence is not existent."[4] But like Berkeley the Jaina does not mean the knowability of objects as comprehended by the mundane soul whose capacity is limited in various ways. Thus he is able to save the existence of the world, even when it is not perceived by many souls. Berkeley's dictum is destructive not only to the external world but also to the world of selves, as has been pointed out by Hume. Hume makes use of the same premises to disprove the existence of the soul, which Berkeley used to disprove the existence of the external world. Berkeley deprives the objects of their forms of existence, and Hume does the same with the selves. In his hands not only the other selves are reduced to ideas, but the percipient himself becomes merely a cluster of ideas. Thus Berkeley has not

1. H.L. Haldar: *Neo Hegelianism*, p. 89
2. H.A. Pichard: *Thinking and Experience*, p. 156
3. A.C. Ewing: *Idealism—A Critical Survey*, pp. 27-55.
4. Vidyānandin: *Āptaparīkṣā*, verse 95

been able to defend his position on the ground of his dictum.

Rāmānuja, Hegel and Bradley on the Soul

Rāmānuja, Hegel and Neo Hegelians are unanimous in holding the principle of difference and variation as intrinsic to the fundamental reality of the universe. Rāmānuja expounds the theory of real creation and holds *māyā* to be a real power of the *Brahma.* "For him the word *māyā* stands for God's power of creating wonderful objects."[1] Concerning the nature of Hegelian reality Collingwood says: "Nature for Hegel is real, it is in no sense an illusion or something which we think to exist when what really exists is something else; nor is in any sense a mere appearance, something which exists only because we think it. It really exists, and exists independently of any mind whatever.[2] Green also thinks: "If idealism is to be a tenable theory, it must make room for movement and change, novelties and fresh developments in the universe as it exists not merely for us but for God."[3] Bradley admits the reality of variations and differences even in the Absolute.[4] The position of this group of the idealist thinkers is quite distinct from that of Śaṅkara and Berkeley and it may be taken to be a reversion of the position of the materialists. If the material world is a real creation or a real emanation from spirit, then matter must be held to be a manifestation of the ultimate spiritual reality. As already mentioned in this respect Neutralism holds a better position than materialism or idealism.

By admitting reality to be ultimately spiritual we can, at most, mean the supremacy of spirit as against matter. It can not be taken to mean the negation of matter or its emanation from spirit. In face of the fact that the world of matter is a

1. Datta and Chatterji: *An Introduction to Indian Philosophy,* p. 472
2. R.G. Collingwood: *The Idea of Nature,* p. 12
3. H.L. Haldar: Neo Hegelianism, p. 34
4. Cf. *Ibid.*, p. 242

real creation, the conception of the ultimate spiritual reality finds little meaning. Spirit and matter become mutually reducible to each other, they are the manifestations of a principle whose nature cannot be said to be absolutely spiritual or material. Spirituality and materiality are its part characteristics. Hence to assign ultimate reality to one, and not to the other does not seem logically consistent. We cannot agree with Edward Caird who holds: "Nature as a systematic totality of inter-related things presupposes a spiritual principle of unity of which it is the necessary manifestation."[1] We cannot also agree with Bradley who thinks: "This ultimate reality is a single all inclusive suprarelational experience."[2] We have seen that difference is a real implication of reality; and so reality cannot be merely a unity. Unity and difference must be the two implicates of reality. If unity and difference are held to appear in the process of manifestation and are not intrinsic to the very constitution of reality, then, in Bradley's philosophy, it is vain to ascribe difference and appearance to the Absolute. Reality must include both unity and difference. Like the Jaina, these idealist thinkers must uphold the theory only as a relational and partial view of reality. We must distinguish between contexts in which reality can be held to be an idea or an object distinct from the percipient's ideas. Unless these contexts are allowed an equal status of truth the inconsistency involved cannot be got rid of. Thus even the conception of ultimate spiritual reality does not help us in explaining the world of matter. An ultimate reality can, at most, mean a form of existence most valuable in a particular reference-system, and the admission of such a reality can never mean the negation of other forms of existence.

1. H.L. Haldar: *Neo Hegelianism*. p. 93
2. *Ibid.*, p. 215

Neutralism as a Theory of the Soul

Between the extreme systems of materialism and idealism stands the theory of neutralism advocated by Bertrand Russell. Antagonism of mind and matter has proved an obstacle both to the idealist and the materialist. Neutralism is a theory which aims at minimising the opposition of mind and matter. "Recent developments have affected these traditional attitudes towards mind and matter in rather a peculiar way. In the first place matter, under the influence of modern physics, has been growing less material....In the second place mind, under the influence of modern psychology, has become progressively less mental. Mind and matter having lost most of their salient characteristics, the difficulty of bringing them under a common formula is correspondingly diminished, but this result is achieved not by merging either into the other, but by deriving both from a fundamental stuff of which the universe may be supposed to be composed. To this stuff Mr. Russell gives the name of 'neutral particulars', the word neutral being intended to convey the fundamental character of the particulars, and the fact that they are in themselves neither mental nor material"[1] Neutralism, by virtue of the position it hods must resort to something which is different from both mind and matter. Its success of overcoming the antagonism of mind and matter lies in the formulation of the theory of neutral particulars. Russell himself observes: "The stuff of which the world of experience is composed is, in my belief, neither mind nor matter but something more primitive than either. Both mind and matter seem to be composite."[2] The theory implies two things. Firstly the original stuff of the world does not possess the characteristics of mind or matter, and secondly it exists in the form of particulars. Neutralism does not negate the opposition of mind and matter but derives the two from the same original stuff. Mind and matter remain distinguished

1. Joad: *An Introduction to Modern Philosophy*, p. 30
2. Bertrand Russell: *Analysis of Mind*, p. 10

in their process of manifestation. The only difference between neutralism on one hand and materialism and idealism on another is that the former assigns neither consciousness nor unconsciousness to the basic reality while the latter two posit one or the other characteristic in the basic reality. The neutral particulars stand in opposition to both consciousness and unconsciousness, hence neutralism will have to explain a double opposition. Thus this theory, while solving the opposition of mind and matter, raises the problem of opposition between the neutral particulars on one hand and mind and matter on the other. Besides, neutralism leads to one more difficulty. By denying consciousness and unconsciousness both of the basic reality it reduces itself to the conception of a featureless entity or pure being. We fail to understand the nature of an entity which is neither conscious nor unconscious, Actually speaking, a totally featureless entity cannot be said to exist. Idealism and materialism hold a better position than neutralism, in this respect, because the basic reality in idealism and materialism has a positive characteristic and can be supposed to exist. The Jaina thinks that whatever is not present in reality as an attribute cannot come into existence as a manifestation of reality. Hence the Jaina will find it difficult to extract materiality or mentality from Mr. Russell's neutral particulars. These particulars present another difficulty on account of their discrete existence. The world stuff has been conceived in the form of particulars so as to facilitate their various arrangements. "The particulars are arranged in different contexts. Taken in one context and arranged in a certain way, they form the subject matter of psychology; taken in another context and arranged in another way, they form the subject-matter of physics."[1] The particulars, being discrete by nature, will not be able to generate the phenomenon of the unity of consciousness, just in the same way as materialism failed to bring about the same effect from the discrete atoms of matter.

---

1. Joad: *An Introduction to Matter,* p. 30

Continuum Theory of Reality and the Soul

The difficulty just referred to has been apprehended by A.N. Whitehead, Samuel Alexander and Northrop who replace the neutral particulars by a continuum. Northrop says: "Aesthetic continuum is a great mother of all creation."[1] All phenomena of the empirical world result from a process of differentiation of the original continuum. This continuum theory holds the same position as neutralism with the exception that the continuum is not discrete like the neutral particulars. The variations we see in the world, have emerged on account of the process of differentiation, and in ultimacy it is supposed that the continuum is totally featureless. Thus the continuum theory has to face the same criticism as levelled against the theory of featureless or pure being. This theory certainly succeeds in establishing the unity of consciousness from the continuum, but its triumph in generating the discreteness and difference is not equally remarkable. If continuity and discontinuity both are born of the same entity, then the capacity for the two must be presupposed to be inherent in it. Neutralism extracts unity from the discrete particulars, and the continuum theory extracts differences from the unity of the continuum. The flaw in the above two theories lies in the fact that they attempt to derive something from the basic reality but do not posit necessary capacity for such derivation in their reality.

Now something may also be said about the process of differentiation. This process must presuppose something positive to make a start. It cannot start in a totally featureless entity, for in that case the question, what is differentiated?, stands meaningless. Differentiation, therefore, can only mean the flow of manifestations of the intrinsically inherent attributes of the underlying reality. And we have already seen that the same substratum cannot have the attributes of consciousness and unconsciousness, hence the differentiation

1. Northrop: *Meeting of East and West,* p. 343

in the form of mind and matter from the same continuum is not possible. Whether we make use of the process of arrangement or the process of differentiation, the problem stands unsolved. The belief in the existence of neutral particulars subject to no process of arrangement and in the existence of continuum undifferentiated is unwarranted. We do not understand why a part of reality should remain unarranged and undifferentiated, while the rest is incessantly undergoing the same process. We may conclude that neither the theory of neutral particulars nor that of the original continuum can be said to have explained the existence of the soul or matter in the universe.

Hume's View of the Self

Berkeleyan dictum of 'esse est percipi' was carried to its logical extreme by Hume. He applied it in case of the self also and thus negated its existence. He observes: "for my part, when I enter most intimately into what I call myself, I always stumble at some particular perception or other, of heat or cold, light or shade, love or hatred, pain or pleasure. I never catch myself at any time without a perception and can never observe anything but the perception."[1] Thus for Hume the self became simply a cluster of ideas or perceptions, as the external world was for Berkeley. Barkeley could find nothing in the perceptions of the external world, which could have proved its existence; but he safeguarded the existence of the self without which the perceptions of the external world could not have been possible. Hume, on the other hand, could see nothing in the perceptions of the self which could have proved the existence of the self itself. If the reality of the external world is negated on the ground that we get nothing but perceptions about it, then Hume does no mistake in negating the existence of the self on the same ground. The main idea underlying Berkeleyan and Humean thesis is that the substance of the

1. Hume: *The Philosophical Works of David Hume*, vol. I, p. 312

external world and the self is not perceived by us, and hence both of them are held to be non-existent. Hume also thinks that the impression and the idea are individuals distinct from each other, and their mutual connection is determined by a uniting principle which he describes as a 'gentle force'. The laws of association which play an essential part in his philosophy are based on this gentle force.

Yogācāra on the Soul

The Yogācāra School of Indian philosophy propounds a view similar to that of Hume on the ground of simultaneous apprehension *(sahopalambha)* of the objects and their cognitions. "There is a series of momentary cognitions apprehending themselves. We are directly conscious of our cognitions and cannot, therefore, deny their reality. These congnitions are self luminous. They do not apprehend external objects which are non-existent."[1] It is again said: "There are two streams of cognitions in the psychic continuum of an ordinary individual *ālaya-vijñāna* (self cognition characterized by ego-consciousness) and *pravṛtti-vijñāna* (object cognitions as blue, yellow). *Ālaya-vijñāna* is the mind *(citta)* and manifold presentations (*pravṛtti-vijñānas*) are transformations of *ālaya-vijñāna*,"[2] The connection among the discrete cognitions is explained by formulating the principle of *vāsanā* which runs parallel to the Humean conception of the gentle force. As regards the functioning of the principle of *vāsanā* Dr. J.N. Sinha observes: "a leaves behind a trace à and it modifies the next sensation b' which leaves a trace b' and so on. This is the hypothesis of subconscious impressions or *vāsanās* and their transformation to succeeding psychoses (*vāsanā saṅkramaṇa*) to account for connection among discrete momentary sensations and ideas."[3] Thus we see that there is not much of difference between the Yogācāra and Humean views of the self.

1. J.N. Sinha: *Indian Realism*, p. 1
2. *Ibid.*, pp. 33-34
3. *Ibid.*, p. 61

A Criticism of Hume and the Yogācāra

Hume reduces the external world and the self to a group of ideas and impressions because what he comprehends of them is only a cluster of mad ideas and impressions. In the same way the Yogācāra establishes the monism of discrete cognitions on the ground of non-distinction between objects and their cognitions. We are directly aware of the ideas and perceptions which imply the existence of something beyond themselves. The truth of this implication is questioned by both of them because it fails to establish itself independently of the ideas and perceptions. Hume and the Yogācāra both are right so far as they establish the reality of the impressions, ideas and cognitions; but they have not been successful in negating the existence of the external world and the self with the same amount of consistency. The rule of simultaneous apprehension is not potent enough to negate what is other than the cognitions. It simply proves that the cognition and the object are apprehended simultaneously, and thus involves the duality of the cognition and the object cognized. The right conclusion from the concept of simultaneous apprehension of the object and its cognition is that both of them exist, we cannot negate one at the cost of the other. The Yogācāra must seek for the negation of the objects and the self elsewhere, and he may prove his thesis only by holding the implication of objectivity in our cognitions to be a delusion. Hume has denied the same because he fails to get any impression upon which the idea of the self and the world could have been based. The impressions and ideas of touch, taste and colour which we associate with the external world and those of knowing, feeling pain or pleasure which we associate with the self are not held to be the ideas about the external world and the self. Hume wants to have an impression of the self and the external world distinctively of these impressions and ideas which imply the various forms of their existence. If there is a substance of matter, it must exist in the form of colour, taste and touch. If there is substance of the self, it must exist in the form of knowing and feeling pain or pleasure. Nothing can exist independently of the forms which its existence is likely to take; and nothing can be known independently of the forms of knowledge which comprehends it. If the substances is deprived of all its forms of existence, it becomes non-existent and the possibility of its knowledge is also destroyed. So Hume is right in holding that he does not get any impression of the self and the external world as distinct from the impression of colour, taste, knowing and feeling. Had there been any other way of apprehending the substance of the self and the external world, it would have been possible to deny them on the aforesaid ground. Colour, taste, knowing and feeling, being the forms of existence of some entities, imply the entities themselves. The self, in cognizing the external objects and other selves, cannot identify itself with them, for in that case the problem of cognition itself vanishes. It must cognize them through its own perceptions about them. The very rule of simultaneous apprehension and the available impressions of the psychical and the physical worlds go to establish the reality of the self and the external world. Besides, the cognition of the Yogācāra and the impressions and ideas of Hume are, by nature, such as imply the fact of externalization which must be accepted as a true implication. If the implication of externalization is held to be false, we fail to find reason why their other implications should be held to be true. In the words of Malliṣeṇa. "If the blue object perceived were a mere form of cognition, then it would have been perceived as I am blue and not as this is blue."[1] For Hume and the Yogācāra neither the external world nor the self is true, hence the perception of the blue can neither be designated as 'this is blue' nor as 'I am blue'. So we are left with no form which can be assigned to the cognitions and the impressions—a fact which is totally contradictory to our experience.

---

1. J.N. Sinha: *Indian Realism*, p. 61

Neither Hume nor the Yogācāra propounds the philosophy of delusion. The unity they derive from the discrete cognitions and ideas is a fact of experience. Hence *vāsanās* or subconscious impressions must not be unreal, nor the laws of association contentless. As for the Yogācāra there exists nothing but cognitions, *vāsanās* cannot be distinct from the cognitions. So Dr. Sinha says: "*vāsanā* or disposition is only the latent power of cognition."[1] Now when the cognitions are momentary they must be totally destroyed every moment with all their capacities. *Vāsanās,* as a power of the cognition, is, therefore, also destroyed along with the cognitions every moment. Thus *vāsanā* as a power of cognition fails to determine any connection among the cognitions. A cognition does not leave behind any residue which could have been taken to work as a connecting link between two cognitions. "The preceding cognition cannot impress the succeeding one before it comes into existence, and the succeeding cognition cannot be impressed by the preceding ones, since it is destroyed."[2] Quoting Keśava it is again said that "the preceding cognitions cannot "perfume or madalize the succeeding cognitions"[3] Haribhadra has rightly said: "Without a connection with other elements a *vāsanā* cannot be generated, just as no perfuming of oil is possible in the absence of smell of flowers etc. There must be something distinct from the cognitions to perfume the cognitions. This something is *karma* for us (the Jaina), and the *vāsanā* is not a consistent conception if interpreted in any other way."[4] "By introducing the concept of '*santāna*' nothing fresh is mentioned. If it is identified with the series of momentary cognitions, its distinct existence is not established. If it is distinct from the series, it must be real. Then again it can be either permanent or momentary. If it is momentary, it is again on the same level with the momentary

---

1. *Ibid.*, p. 108
2. *Ibid.*, P. 125
3. *Ibid.*, p. 265.
4. Haribhadra: *Śāstravārtāsamuccaya (Bandha),* verses 102, 103

cognition. If it is permanent, it is the soul in disguise of another name."[1] Dr. Sinha again observes: "The Yogācāra argument involves a hysteron proteron. The variety of subconscious impressions which form a beginningless series is due to a variety of perceptions of external objects. Perceptions are causes of sub-conscious impressions. Subconscious impressions are not the causes of perception."[2] Another inconsistency of the principle of *vāsanā* is seen, when the problem of the unity of the individual self is raised. When cognitions are mutually distinct like the loose leaves of a book, they can be attached to any series as the loose leaves can be placed in any of the books.[3] The problem is 'what is that which determines the unity of a particular series of cognitions and obstructs the coexisting cognitions of different persons from being connected in the form of a single series? The Yogācāra explains this by admitting a causal connection among the cognitions of a particular series. He cannot uphold the theory of efficient cause because the cognitions are momentary. Then the only way of effecting a causal connection among the cognitions is that the preceding cognitions perfume the latter ones—a position which has already been found untenable. Vidyānandin observes: "If the dictum of causal agency is established on the ground of the identity of the cognition-series, then there is the fallacy of mutual dependence between the preceding and the succeeding cognitions, The identity of the cognition-series is based on the truth of the causal relation. and the truth of the causal relation is based on the identity of the cognition-series. There is no other way out."[4] Cognitions and ideas, being absolutely distinct, cannot enter into relationship with each other and therefore they cannot yield any unity whatsoever. If Hume's ideas and impressions are also discrete like the cognitions of the Yogācāra, the same

1. Malliṣeṇa: *Syādvāda-mañjarī*, p. 246
2. J.N. Sinha: *Indian Realism*, p. 206
3. M.C. Jain: *Tattvārtha-cintāmaṇi*, vol. p. 288
4. Vidyānanda: *Ślokavārtika*, verses 183-184

criticism may be levelled against his view of the self and the external world. The gentle force of the uniting principle is only a force of the passing ideas and impressions themselves, hence it must disappear every moment along with them. To bring about any effect this force must be connected with at least two ideas one following the other. But this is not possible in Human philosophy, or he will have to accept the truth of the connecting principle along with that of impressions and ideas. The Jaina upholds the truth of substance behind the changing modes to establish a unity. Substance is really the connecting principle behind the varying modes. The question of its direct perception should not arise, as the modes are the very forms of its existence. The truth of the soul and the self is proved by the fact that without such a conception we fail to account for the individuality and the unity of perceiving minds. The laws of association can simply show the mode of behaviour which the ideas and impressions follow. They cannot be a substitute for the principle of unity among them. Thus the impressions must be held to imply distinction and unity simultaneously. At the same time they must not be only transitory, there must be a side of their existence which evinces permanence and durability. The impressions are mutually distinct in one of their aspects of existence, and constitute a unity in another. Such a position can be consistently held only in a non-absolute philosophy. That aspect of the existence of impressions which evinces unity and permanence is the substance of the soul behind the impressions. Thus the gentle force in the impressions and ideas and the principle of *vāsanā* imply the existence of the substance of the soul.

The Psychological View of the Self

The distinctions drawn between purposive and mechanical behaviours lead to the same conclusion that self consciousness occupy a position distinct from that of matter. It is only the behaviouristic school of psychology which identifies consciousness with behaviour. But it is doubtful that behaviourism has been able to explain the phenomenon of consciousness. At most it can give us a clue to other's consciousness. The feeling of pain accompanied by a certain behaviour is not only a behaviour. Though this fact is difficult to verify in case of others, yet it can be definitely experienced in one's own case. One can easily distinguish between a feeling of pain and the attendant behaviour in one's own case. The correct behaviouristic response is not all of the conscious life but this response is accompanied by a feeling of being conscious. In face of the fact that the correspondence between the psychical phenomenon and the bodily behaviour is not perfect and invariable we cannot reduce consciousness to behaviour. On the ground of Helm Holtz's discovery J.C. Flugal affirms: "....the speed of transmission along the motor nerve of the frog was about ninety feet per second and for the sensory nerves of a man something between 50 and 100 feet per second. It shows that man's body does not instantly obey his mind. Thought and movement follow one another at an appreciable interval, instead of being practically simultaneous as has previously been thought"[1] This leads to the conclusion that behaviour and consciousness are not one. Jung also thinks: "A psychology that treats the psyche as an epiphenomenon would do better call itself brain physiology and remain satisfied with the meagre results that such a psycho-physiology can yield. The psyche deserves to be taken as a phenomenon in its own right."[2] Mc Dougall has well remarked: "I believe that the mind has a nature and a structure and functions of its own which cannot be fully adequately described in terms of structure of the brain and its physical processes."[3] These psychologists not only oppose the identification of consciousness with the brain or the behaviour but also do not like to hold the stuff

1. J.C. Flugal: *A Hundred Years of Psychology,* p. 90
2. Jung: *Contributions to Analytic Psychology* (translated by M.G. and Carry F. Baynes), p. 6
3. Mc Dougall: *An Outline of Abnormal Psychology,* p. 480.

of the mind to be discrete. Mc Dougall again observes: "On really impartial and unprejudiced consideration of the problems, it does appear that no aggregation of elements or bits of conscious stuff, or of conscious processes call them sensations or ideas or what you will, can produce a self conscious ego, a self directing being aware of itself and its continuing identity over against other similar selves and the physical world."[1] The psychologist cannot advance a step without presuming the existence of psychical or mental dispositions into which the unity of the mind is analysed. Two things are implied by the psychological theory of mind. Firstly the mind constitutes a distinct category, and secondly it is a unity which on analysis yields a diversity. "The central mystery of life and mind", as McDougall thinks, "can be solved only by going behind the most elementary psychical phenomena to the life movement which determines all the psychical manifestations."[2] Again it is said that the "mental structure is that enduring growing frame work of mind which we infer from the observed manifestations of mind in experience and behaviour."[3]

We are able to comprehend only the functions of the mind, the structure has been taken to be a fact derived from the observed functions. The mental structure is constituted of the mental dispositions, and, at the same time, it displays a unity which is absent in the material structure. Unless this unity is intrinsic to the very nature of mind, the psychological view cannot be distinguished from the views of the Yogācāra and Hume. The unity of the mind must show difference at the same time. It must be held to be an entity in which unity and difference are obtained simultaneously. This is the entity which lies behind the elements in the structure of the mind. Thus mind is found to imply the concept of substance. Though the substance of the mind is different from that of matter. C.R. Jain observes: "Cognition and emotion cannot inhere in nothing, nor can

1. Mc Dougall: *An Outline of Abnormal Psychology*, p. 480.
2. Mc Dougall: *Instinct and Personality*, p. 51.
3. J.S. Ross: *A Ground Work of Educational Psychology*, p. 36.

volition be the function of a non-entity. Hence they must be the states of a something which exists, consequently of a substance."[1] The psychical functions may be taken to be the modes of the substance of the soul, while the facts of the mental structure may be taken to embody an analytical view of the same entity. B.L. Atreya observes: "In the zeal to acquire the status of an exact science psychology has really lost its soul and has been wasting much of its time in aping the lower sciences of Mathematics, physics and chemistry, which are built on a Method which fails in the field of psychology unless supplemented by another which is peculiarly its own."[2] So long as psychology does not take the soul as the most fundamental principle behind the structure and the functions of the mind, it remains to be an incomplete science of the psyche. The psychical functions and structure must be supposed to have a substantial basis. C.R. Jain observes: "Nothing that exists can exist, or be the abode of qualities, independently of a substantive basis. The mind, too, must, therefore, be a substance."[3] Psychology cannot base the reality of mind on something which is not conscious in itself. Nothing less than a conscious substance can account for the mental structure and the mental functions. According to Bausfield "the basis of memory is not recorded in the protoplasmic structure but in immaterial psychic structure. Such a structure involves the conception of a substance of which it is built....Psychoplasm in our vocabulary stands for the immaterial substance of which the psychical structure is built."[4]

Dualistic Theories of the Soul and the Position of Jaina Dualism

Mind and matter are the facts of common experience. Whether we make a start with spirit or with a neutral

---

1. C. R. Jain: *Key of Knowledge,* p. 44.
2. B.L. Atreya: *An Introduction to Para Psychology,* p. 1.
3. C.R. Jain: *Jaina Psychology* (1934), p. 2.
4. Mc Dougall: *Modern Materialism,* p. 103.

entity, we shall have to explain the existence of mind and matter in the world at one or the other stage. Dualism of mind and matter is a common problem for all the thinkers. We have already seen that neither mind nor matter can be held to be a delusion. They are the real objects of our knowledge. This brings us to the dualistic systems of philosophy. According to them mind and matter are distinct entities and one cannot be reduced to or derived from the other. Mind or soul is characterized by consciousness, while matter is unconscious. Such a theory is maintained by a number of philosophers both in the east and the west. The main ground upon which the validity of dualistic systems is based is the antagonism held between mind and matter. The weakness of the systems other than dualism lies in the fact that they fail to assign a common origin to mind and matter. The only alternative before us is to accept two distinct substrata to account for the mental and the material manifestations. Descartes held mind and body to be diametrically opposed, and his was an extreme type of dualism. The value of his dualism is assessed as "that it left nature free for the mechanical explanations of natural science. Mind is eliminated from nature and given an independent territory of its own."[1] Descartes maintains such a position by holding absolute distinction between the two substances. But we have to consider the implications of absolute distinction and opposition in every respect; that is, one must oppose the existence of the other. Absolute distinction and opposition can find meaning, only when one entity is existent and the other, non-existent. Hence Descartes' soul and matter cannot be said to co-exist, or there is no absolute opposition and distinction between them. To be mutually distinct mind and matter both must have something which is not intrinsic to the other. As human personality is not mind alone or matter alone, mind and matter must agree with each other along with their differences and consequently enter into a relationship.

1. Thilly: *A History of Philosophy*, p. 255

Collingwood says: "Descartes also felt the need that his mind and matter must be somehow connected."[1] This connection cannot be maintained if absolute distinction and opposition are upheld. Thus the position of a dualist amounts to partial difference and partial agreement between mind and matter—a view advocated by the Jaina. "Lord Risabhadeva", says Nemicandra, "has taught us the dualism of soul (*jīva*) and non-soul (*ajīva*)."[2] For the Jaina the *jīva* and the *ajiva* are only partially different. In some respects mind opposes matter, while in others they agree with each other. This is the Jaina view of reality as distinction-cum-non-distinction.

The Nyāya and the Sāṅkhya systems of Indian philosophy start with the dualism of soul and matter. The *Nyāya* distinguishes between the substances of soul and matter and their essential attributes. In order that the soul and matter may enter into a relationship with each other or they may stand as members in the same cosmos, the distinction between them must not be taken to be absolute. The empirical self in the Nyāya philosophy is not simply the *ātman* but it is in its very root the union of the *ātman* and the *manas* which is one of the nine fundamental substances. M. Hiriyanna observes: "In other words, the self is the basis of psychic life, but that life is only adventitious to it. The necessary condition for the appearance of psychic features in the self is its association with the *manas.* For these reasons, it would perhaps be better to describe the two together as really constituting the self in the common acceptation of that term."[3] It means that the *ātman,* though it is distinct from the *manas,* is not absolutely opposed to it. The qualities of *dharma* (merit) and *adharma* (demerit) which get associated with the *ātman* in its mundane existence, are admitted to function in cooperation with the world of matter. It is the *ātman* itself, when qualified by *dharma* and *adharma,*

1. Collingwood: *The Idea of Nature,* p. 6
2. Nemicandra: *Dravyasaṅgraha,* verse 1
3. M, Hiriyanna: *Essentials of Indian Philosophy,* p. 90

which functions in cooperation with matter. Thus the soul of the *Nyāya* is not absolutely opposed to matter and other categories; and at the same time, they maintain their distinctions.

The absolute passivity of *puruṣa* in the Sāṅkhyan dualism does not find a consistent place in the system. Perhaps this is the point where the greatest weakness of the system lies. It is said of the Sāṅkhyan philosophy that "the system was originally purely naturalistic, and that the notion of *puruṣa* or spirit, for which there is really no need by the side of self-evolving and self-regulating *prakṛti,* was imported into it on the analogy of other doctrines."[1] To say that there is no need of *puruṣa* in the Sāṅkhṣyan system is to reduce it to materialism. As the Sāṅkhya thinks without the presence and attention of *puruṣa,* the *Prakṛti* could not have begun its dance. The conception of *puruṣa* is integral to the system, but the position of absolute passivity which is assigned to it creates difficulties. If the *puruṣa* is absolutely passive it is always the same for *prakṛti.* Then we shall not be able to explain the incessant variations in *prakṛti.* The process of the world is determined both by the *puruṣa* and the *prakṛti.* The presence of the *puruṣa* has to make its contribution to it. Hence the *puruṣa,* in spite of the fact that it is static, is somehow related with the *prakṛti.* Absolute unrelatedness of the *puruṣa* with the *prakṛti* is equivalent to the non-existence of the *puruṣa*. The Sāṅkhya has not been able to maintain an opposition between the *puruṣa* and *prakṛti* which must somehow be related with each other, as Cartesian dualism also required. Thus we again come to the same conclusion that the dualism of the soul and matter can imply only a partial opposition between them. As we have seen the Jaina is able to brush aside these difficulties of his way by conceiving distinction and non-distinction between the two entities in a non-absolute way. Jaina dualism admits of the contributions of both the soul and matter in the process of the world.

---

1. *Ibid.*, p. 128.

The Problem of the Relation between the Soul and the Non-soul

The greatest difficulty in the way of dualism is the problem of the mind-body relation. If the dualism of the soul and the non-soul is admitted, a relationship between them must also be accepted. Interactionism and parallelism are the two main theories of the mind-body relation. Interactionism holds: "Mind cannot act on body without giving rise, in the body, to a gain or loss of energy which is not balanced by an equivalent loss or gain. Without some interchange of energy between mind and matter, no interactionism is possible."[1] On the contrary parallelism holds that the two series of mental and material events are mutually independent, the members of one series are not determined by the members of the other series. "Parallelism also presupposes mind and body. It means that the mental process and the nervous process go on together and very concomitantly. But they do not interact and neither is dependent on the other for its existence....The parallelist asserts that the mental event is so connected with a concomitant brain process that both act together; they act together in such a way, that, from the ordinary point of view of empirical science, it is impossible to refer part of the effect to the one and part to the other. But both are so connected that neither can exist without the other, and neither can vary in any manner of degree independently of the other."[2] Thus interactionism upholds the mutual transformation of mental and bodily energies, and parallelism denies just the very fact but is anxious to maintain the concomitance somehow. The Jaina being a dualist must formulate some theory about the relation between the soul and the non-soul. Kundakunda says: "A substance cannot transform its attributes into those of

1. G.F. Stout: *Mind and Matter*, pp. 87, 88
2. *Ibid.*, p. 73.

another substance. All substances manifest by themselves."[1] Such a view is to be maintained, if the substances of the soul and the non-soul, are held to be distinct. The transformation of mental energy into material one can take place only by a process of transformation of the attributes and hence of substances. Without a transformation of substance we cannot think of a transformation of attributes, or a substance will lose its essential attributes. By denying the transformation of attributes of the soul and the non-soul the possibility of interactionism in Jainism is brushed aside. Such a position has led some philosophers to think that Jaina view of the mind-body relation is simply a parallelism. Dr. Radhakrishnan says: "Nor is Jainism aware of the conception of development according to which the body in its higher phases assumes new properties. It is obliged to rest content with the dualism of mind and body and stop at the psychological point of view. It cannot adopt the theory of interaction but has to accept the view of parallelism with all its difficulties."[2] Pointing out the difficulties of both interactionism and parallelism G.F. Stout observes. "Both parallelism and interactionism in their phenomenal form are indefensible. The parallelist goes astray in holding that, like parallel lines, mental and physical processes can never meet. But the advocate of interactionism does not assail his opponent's position of this weakest point. On the contrary he makes the same assumption himself. What he asserts is that though mind and matter never meet they none-the-less can and do act on each other."[3] It appears that no theory of mind-body relation can totally overthrow the implications of parallelism and interactionism, and at the same time none of them can be upheld to the negation of the other. Hence G.F. Stout gives a solution of the problem on the assumption that human personality is a joint effect of mind and body. He again observes: "The action of the mind is not

---

1. Kundakunda: *Samayasāra,* verse 385
2. Dr. Radhakrishnan: *Indian Philosophy,* Vol. I, p. 310
3. G.F. Stout: *Mind and Matter,* p. 91

action of the mind alone, but action of mind and body in one".[1] Our basic problem is how mind and body come to enter into such a close relationship; and in spite of explaining the relation it seems to have been presumed by Stout. According to him mind and body unite to give rise to human personality; and thus he leaves the problem of the mind-body relation unsolved. The opposition of mind and body still persists in the region where mind and matter stand as constituents of human personality. Such inconsistencies must arise, if an absolute distinction between mind and matter is maintained.

The Jaina on the Problem of Mind-Body Relation

The Jaina theory of mind-body relation is neither interactionism nor parallelism of the aforesaid type. The Jaina formulates the theory of *nimitta* (auxiliary) causation to explain the relation between the soul and the non-soul. It lays emphasis on the fact that the different substances work in coordination with each other, thereby maintaining their individuality and also helping each other's function. According to this theory there is no mutual transformation of the two substances or their attributes but the one, by accepting the *upakāra* (virtual action) of the other undergoes transformations in its own constitution. The nimitta theory of causation presupposes a capacity in both the soul and the non-soul by virtue of which the mutual *upakāra* becomes possible. The manifestation of the one is simply an occasion to the manifestation of the other, as the occasionalist held. His divine interference may be interpreted to be an inherent capacity of the substances themselves. Such a capacity must be presupposed to account for the close relation between the soul and the non-soul. This is perhaps the pre-established harmony between the two partially different substances as Leibniz thought. Jainism, though it does not accept mutual transformation of substances, never denies

1. *Ibid.*, p. 92

their mutual '*upakāra*'. Amṛtacandra ṣūri correctly remarks: "Matter undergoes modifications on account of the *nimitta* (auxiliary) causation of the modes of the *jīva;* and similarly the *jīva,* on account of the auxiliary causation of matter, undergoes manifestations"[1] Neither the *jīva* creates the attributes of karma-matter nor karma-matter creates those of the *jīva*. The manifestations of the two are determined by their mutual *nimitta* (auxiliary) causation."[2] Śuch a theory cannot be termed as interactionism, as there is no mutual transformation of the substances. It cannot also be termed as parallelism, as the two series cannot be held to be absolutely independent of each other. The two series are so constituted that they mutually accept the '*upakāra*' of each other. Now as the Jaina logic permits, interactionism and parallelism both can be held as consistent theories of the mind-body relation but only when governed by a suitable context. Parallelism and interactionism are the two views of the same event, obtained from the different angles of vision. Kundakunda in his *Samayasāra* propounds a view which does not take into consideration the virtual action done by the *ajīva*. He is, thus, able to isolate the series of soul manifestations determined independently of the *ajīva*. For this reason his view appears to be a parallelism. On the other hand if the *upakāra* or virtual action of the *ajīva* is taken into account, the two series of the soul and the non-soul manifestations are seen to be dependent upon each other. The Jaina will not like to hold or deny the truth of either absolutely. Actually speaking parallelism and interactionism are the implications of the relation that exists between the soul and the non-soul.

Conclusion

Thus according to Jainism soul and matter are two substances, neither of them being reducible to the other.

---

1. Amṛtacandra Sūri: *Puruṣārthasiddhyupāya,* verses, 12, 13
2. Kundakunda: *Samayasāra,* verse 87

Nor can they be traced to a common origin different from mind and body both. Both of them are possessed of capacities that enable them to admit of the *'upakāra'* or virtual action of each other. This allows a scope for an interplay between mind and matter. It is on account of the *nimitta* theory of causation, which is ultimately based on the non-absolute nature of reality that the doctrine of mind-body relation takes a tenable form. At the same time the Jaina theory of *nayavāda* reduces it to interactionism in one context and to parallelism in another. Thus none of these theories embody the whole truth about the mind-body relation, they are only the partial aspects of the whole truth. They cannot be held to be false, unless we mean by the formulation of the one the total negation of the other.

Chapter 4

The Soul and Consciousness

Introduction

The Jaina philosophy holds a very close relation between the soul and consciousness. From one point of view it thinks that the two are identical, While from another point of view it draws a distinction between the two. The soul is a substance as we have shown in the previous chapter; and consciousness is its differentiating characteristic. Where there is the substance of the soul, there is consciousness as its characteristic and vice versa. The soul and consciousness are always found together, it is only by way of abstraction that we can talk of consciousness distinctively of the soul. Nemicandra states that "consciousness is the very differentia of the *jiva.*"[1] There is no difference of opinion among the Jaina thinkers as regards the definitions of the soul. All such definitions refer to consciousness in one or the other form.

The Nyāya school of Indian philosophy opposes the above Jaina theory of soul and consciousness by holding consciousness as an adventitious quality of the soul. For the Naiyāyika consciousness does not characterize the soul; it is associated with the soul on account of the manas and the senses. Hence it is held that in the liberated state the soul loses the quality of consciousness. The Nyāya view of consciousness as an adventitious quality of the soul is found inconsistent in two ways. Firstly, if the soul and consciousness are absolutely distinct, they cannot be brought together to constitute a unity of the type which we require

1. Nemicandra: *Dravyasaṁgraha,* verse 3

between a substance and its attributes. The category of *samavāya* cannot unite them unless they in themselves are possessed of a capacity for unity. Moreover the category of *samavāya* itself is said to be distinct from both the categories of substance and attributes. Hence before effecting the unity of the substance and the attributes, it must be somehow united with them. If some other *samavāya* is required to connect it with other categories, then there will be an infinite regress. If the category of *samavāya* gets united with other categories by virtue of its own capacity, then the other categories may also be supposed to possess such a capacity. Vidyānanda points out: "If the soul is held to be conscious by its connection with consciousness, then why should substances like *ākāśa* (space) be not held to be conscious because of the presence of *samavāya*."[1] Actually speaking to account for the inherence of consciousness in the soul, something must be supposed in the soul itself; or the inherence of consciousness in other categories must be held valid. Secondly, if consciousness is distinct from the soul and requires the category of *samavāya* for its union with the soul, then it can be easily inferred that the soul in the *Nyāya* philosophy is really a featureless substance. We need not repeat the defects of such a position, as they have been pointed out while dealing with the conception of featureless reality.

Consciousness and Upayoga

The Jaina writers are unanimous in giving consciousness and *upayoga* as the differentia of the *jiva*. "The identity of the *jīva* is constituted of consciousness", says the author of the *Pañcādhyāyī*.[2] Umāsvāti gives *upayoga* as the defining characteristic of the *jīva*.[3] Kundakunda mentions consciousness and *Upayoga* as the constituents of the soul.[4]

1. Vidyānandin: *Tattvārtha-śloka-vārtika*, verse 188, p. 40
2. Rājamalla: *Pañcādhyāyī*, II, verse 192
3. Umāsvāti: *Tattvārthasūtra*, 2.8
4. Kundakunda: *Pravacanasāra*, verse 35

Devanandin says; "*upayoga* means a soul's conscious manifestation in the presence of external and internal causes."[1] The two fold definition of the soul emphasizes the same entity but in its different aspects. *Upayoga* and consciousness are the two sides of the same entity. *Upayaga* stands for consciousness as a function, while consciousness may be taken to be an element in the structure of the soul. Consciousness may be interpreted both as a structure and a function but *upayoga* refers to the functional side only. *Upayoga* gives us almost the same meaning as we get by being mentally active. Just as a mental activity is a fact of mental functioning and a mental capacity, a fact of mental structure; in the same way consciousness or *cetanā* may be taken as a fact of the soul's structure and *upayoga,* as a fact of the soul's function or *vṛtti.*

Identity of Consciousness

So far as *upayoga* and consciousness are held to be related with the soul as facts of its function and structure, the Jaina thinkers seem to be agreed; but as regards the identity of consciousness their opinions differ. Devanandin and Akalaṅka think that the meaning of the term *jīvatva* is consciousness.[2] *Jīvatva* refers to the totality of the *jīva's* attributes. Hence their views imply that consciousness cannot be identified with one or the other attribute of the *jīva;* nor can it constitute an attribute in itself. Commenting upon the meaning of consciousness Amṛtacandra Sūri says: "Consciousness means the general characteristic of the qualities of the soul. Consciousness is the identity of the soul, and the soul undergoes manifestations in its terms. It means that whatever is the soul's manifestation it must not go beyond consciousness."[3] In the '*Bhagavatī-sūtra*' *jīvātman* or the generality of the soul's attributes is taken to be

1. Devanandin: *Sarvārthasiddhi,* p. 89
2. Devanandin: *Sarvārthasiddhi*, p. 88
3. Akalaṅka: *Rājavartika*, 2.8.1

consciousness. Akalaṅka again mentions: "Consciousness is the general trait of all the qualities of the soul, on account of its absence in other substances they cannot be called *jīvas*. Its divisions are *darśana* (conation[1]) and *jñāna* (knowledge), etc., and the word consciousness applies to them collectively and also to bliss etc., which are its parts."[2] But Devasena, the author of the '*Ālāpa-paddhati*', enumerates consciousness along with *darśana* and *jñāna* as one of the special attributes of the soul.[3] For him consciousness is distinct from knowledge and conation and must not be held to be a general trait of all the attributes of the soul. Like Akalaṅka, Nemicandra also thinks that *upayoga* or consciousness is of two kinds. i.e., conation and knowledge. This view does not aim at establishing *upayoga* or consciousness as a general implication of all the manifestations of a soul. But Kundakunda mentions three types of *upayoga*, i.e., delusion, ignorance and non-abstention, when qualified by delusion.[4] Akalaṅka is of opinion that *upayoga* also applies to bliss.[5] In the 'Bhagvatī sūtra' *vīrya* (strength) has also been said to imply *upayoga*."[5] This leads to the conclusion that consciousness or *upayoga* is not limited to conation and knowledge only, and in itself it does not constitute an attribute or a mode. Consciousness is the generality (if not of all the attributes of the soul) of the attributes which distinguish the *jīva* from the *ajiva*. So also *upayoga* will mean the generality of the manifestations of such attributes. This shows that consciousness cannot be given a status of attributes in the structure of the soul; and

---

1. As we shall see that *darśana* is no part of the cognitive process and marks a precondition of cognition in the form of readiness on the part of the soul, conation has been given as the English equivalent of the term. J.L. Jaini also gives the same translation in his commentary on the *Gommaṭasāra*.
2. Amṛtacandra: *Tattvadīpikā-vṛatti of Pravacanasāra*, p. 173
3. Devasena: *Ālāpapaddhati*, p. 33
4. Kundakunda: *Samayasāra*, verse 96
5. Akalaṅka: *Rājavārtika*, p. 82
6. *Bhagavatī-sūtra*, p. 66.

knowledge and conation alone as generally understood, will not constitute the differentia of the *jīva*. "In the *Tattvārtha-sūtra* the definition of soul in the shape of *upayoga* is very liberal. It includes bliss and power in it."[1] On the contrary every attribute and its manifestation which evince consciousness can be held to be a differentiating element in the structure of the soul. There are other manifestations of the soul's attributes which are conscious but are not covered under conation and knowledge. The enumeration of consciousness as a distinct attribute by Devasena may be taken to mean an inclusion of the affective aspect of the conscious life. Affection, as modern psychology will also support the view, cannot be identified with conation or knowledge. Rājamala points to the same truth, when he says: "An attempt is made to include the affective side of the soul by introducing the consciousness of our actions and their fruitions."[2] Thus our conclusion is that consciousness is not equivalent to conation and knowledge as is generally understood; nor can it be an independent attribute of the soul. It is the general implication of a number of attributes of the soul.

Controversy Regarding Conation and Knowledge

Consciousness or *upayoga* has been said to be of two kinds, i.e., conation and knowledge. Both of them are prehensions (*grahaṇa*) of the objects by the subject. Nemicandra distinguishes between conation and knowledge by stating that conation is the prehension of the generality of the objects and knowledge is the prehension of the details (*ākāra*) of the object.[3] When the subject and the object come in contact, there is conation and then follows the comprehension of the object. Nemicandra further states: "The indescribable prehension by the soul of the mere

1. M.L. Mehta: *Outlines of Jaina Philosophy*, p. 45
2. Rājamalla: *Pañcādhyāyī*, II, verse 195
3. Nemicandra: *Dravyasaṅgraha*, verses 43, 44

presence of objects having general and particular qualities is conation (*darśana*)."[1] Thus the general characteristics of the objects are the subject-matter of conation, and the particular ones are, of knowledge. This view though most popular in Jainism, proves to be inadequate in two ways. Firstly when objects are universal-cum-particular, how does knowledge grasp only one part of reality and fails to prehend the other.[2] This will also mean that knowledge ever remains ignorant of the universals in the objects. Secondly as the universals and the particulars are only relatively true, there is nothing like absolute universal or absolute particular; and the subject-matter of conation and knowledge cannot be distinctively defined. It is the same entity which in one reference-system is held to be a particular, and, in another, becomes a universal. We may now think of the ultimate generality of the objects as the subject-matter of conation. If this generality is the subject-matter of conation, then one conation cannot be distinguished from another. At the same time a conation cannot be without its subject-matter. Jainism holds four types of conation, everyone being different from the others. If all types of conation arise from the same ultimate generality and in themselves have no details, their mutual distinction becomes a dogmatic assumption. In other words it does not seem consistent to hold that conation grasps simply the generality of the objects and knowledge, its particularity. Brahmadeva observes that conation prehends generality and knowledge prehends particularity is not a tenable view, because reality is universal-cum-particular.[3] Vīrasena modifies the view as the experiencing of the self is conation, and the comprehension of the external objects is knowledge.[4] He himself criticizes that if knowledge is admitted as having two capacities to apprehend self and

1. Nemicandra: *Gommatasāra* (*Jīvakāṇḍa*), verse 483
2. Nemicandra: *Dravyasaṅgraha,* verse 4
3. Brahmadeva: *Dravyasaṅgraha-vṛtti,* p. 80
4. *Dhavalā* (Com. on *Saṭkhaṇḍāgama* by Vīrasena) *Sat-prarūpaṇā,* part I, Vol. I, p. 383

not-self, then conation is reduced to a superfluous entity. He tries to solve the problem by stating that knowledge prehends things other than the self, conation prehends things identical with the self, and, therefore, the two cannot be the same.[1] From the above contention it is clear that the writer does not like to deviate from the general view that conation and knowledge are two distinct faculties of the soul. He establishes this distinction on the ground of a distinction in the subject-matter; and thereby he must mean that the self cannot be prehended by knowledge and the not-self, by conation. This view distinguishes conation from knowledge on subjective grounds, while so far they were distinguished on objective ones. In the commentary on the *Dravyasaṅgraha* Brahmadeva makes the pupil say: "If conation prehends the self and knowledge, the not-self, then the fault that knowledge does not know the self comes in."[2]

He solves the difficulty as against the *Nyāya* view by referring to the postulation of two distinct attributes of conation and knowledge in Jaina philosophy. He also mentions that from the non-distinctive view-point the same consciousness, when it prehends the self, is said to be conation and, when prehending the not-self, is said to be knowledge. This implies that, when the distinctive point of view is adopted, conation and knowledge must come out to be two distinct constitutive attributes; and, when the non-distinctive view is meant, consciousness absorbs not only conation and knowledge but all the special attributes of the soul. The identity of consciousness has been shown to be based on the generality of the special attributes of the soul. Conation and knowledge, being two different attributes of the soul, must determine two distinct flows of their modes. Neither conation nor knowledge can be said to be absent in a soul, whether liberated or mundane, even for a moment. Every moment of the soul's existence must evince modes of conation and knowledge simultaneously. The conclusion is

1. *Ibid.*, p. 383
2. Brahmadeva: *Dravyasaṅgraha-vṛtti,* p. 82

that simultaneous occurrence of conation and knowledge must be admitted both in the mundane and the liberated souls. This conclusion goes against the view that the two manifestations are successive in the mundane souls—a view unanimously maintained by the Jaina thinkers, but it follows logically from the two copresent attributes of conation and knowledge in the soul. This conclusion is in agreement with the view of simultaneous occurrence of conation and knowledge in the liberated souls.

Controversy of Successive and Simultaneous Occurrence of Conation and Knowledge

The identity of conation being difficult to define and the successive occurrence of conation and knowledge being admitted, the Jaina thinkers are divided among themselves on the problem of successive or simultaneous occurrence of conation and knowledge. "Regarding the occurence of them in an imperfect person, the Jaina thinkers are unanimous, in as much as all of them admit the impossibility of the simultaneous occurrence of apprehension and comprehension in an imperfect being. But in respect of the case of a perfect (omniscient) one, there is a controversy among them."[1] Umāsvāti, Kundakunda, Akalaṅka and Vijyānanda are unanimous as regards the simultaneous occurrence of conation and knowledge in the omniscient. Kundakunda has said that conation and knowledge operate simultaneously as light and heat are emanated by fire simultaneously.[2] Nemicandra has already been mentioned to hold the same view. The Jaina writers, without exception, are of one opinion about the successive occurrence of conation and knowledge in the mundane souls. They would explain this difference between the mundane and the liberated souls by assigning a hampered capacity to the

1. M.L. Mehta: *Jaina Psychology*, p. 51
2. Kundakunda: *Niyamasāra*, verse 159

souls under the influence of *Karmas.* Jinabhadra sees some inconsistency in the above view and holds that conation and knowledge are successive in the omniscient also. The argument advanced in support of the view is that "no two conscious activities can occur in the same soul simultaneously."[1] Under the situation Siddhasena tries to solve the difficulty by holding that conation and knowledge are identical. He bases his position on the argument that, as the conation-obscuring and knowledge-obscuring *karmas* are shed off simultaneously, the dawning of the perfect conation and perfect knowledge is also simultaneous. He accepts the distinction between conation and knowledge in all the stages preceding the perfect one. He concludes identity of conation and knowledge from their simultaneity in the perfect ones. Like Jinabhadra, Siddhasena also thinks that two conscious modes cannot be simultaneously found in the same soul, hence, for him, the identity of conation and knowledge in the only way out. All these views are found to be inadequate in one or the other way. We have seen that the general tendency of the Jaina thinkers is that conation and knowledge are two distinct attributes. Then it follows that the modes pertaining to the two attributes, must occur simultaneously, and we do not see any reason why conation and knowledge should not be found simultaneously in the mundane souls. Jinabhadra's view is untenable because by making conation and knowledge successive, there is a breach of the flows of knowledge and conation both. This would mean that there are moments when a soul can be found as devoid of either knowledge or conation. So neither conation nor knowledge will essentially belong to the soul. Besides it becomes unintelligible how a positive attribute should be held to suspend its function, however momentary this suspension may be. Siddhasena's view runs totally against the traditional view that conation and knowledge are two distinct attributes. He can uphold his position only when there is one single faculty behind both conation and knowledge. We

1. *Viśeṣāvaśyaka-bhāṣya*, verse 3096

have seen that consciousness does not stand only for conation and knowledge, but refers to all the special attributes of the soul. So consciousness cannot be held to be a faculty determining modes of conation and knowledge. For argument's sake let there be one common faculty behind conation and knowledge. It would yield only one mode, and conation and knowledge can be held to be the implications of the same mode. Then the aforesaid two implications of the same mode must be simultaneously found in all souls, mundane and liberate. So this view, in a way, amounts to Śiddhasena's view of simultaneous occurrence of conation and knowledge. If consciousness is a single faculty of the soul, the conception of two distinct *karmas,* i.e., conation-obscuring and knowledge-obscuring becomes superfluous, because every mode of the soul with respect to consciousness, whether determined by the former or the latter *karma* will distinctively imply what will be called conation and knowledge. The same difficulty has been pointed out by Brahmadeva in his commentary on the *Dravyasaṅgraha.* Dr. N.M. Tatia mentions that the *karma* theory is one of the old tenets of Jainism,[1] and it gives two categories of *karmas* to obscure the faculties of conation and knowledge. Hence this theory may also be taken as a evidence against the non-distinction of conation and knowledge.

Brahamdeva's Solution of the Controversy

Brahmadeva gives a solution of the controversy. He attempts to reconcile the views of Nemicandra and Vīrasena. He explicitly refuses the view that generality is apprehended by conation and particularity by knowledge, for generality and particularity both constitute the identity of a real. He adopts the scripture-point of view (*siddhāntābhiprāya*) and the logic-point of view (*tarkābhiprāya*). From the former view point conation means the first attempt in the form of

1. N.M. Tatia: *Studies in Jainism,* p. 30 (footnote)

perception of the self which is the cause of generation of succeeding knowledge. After conation the detailed comprehension of the external things is knowledge. Then follows the conclusion that if conation apprehends self and knowledge not-self, then knowledge must not know the self. Brahmadeva solves the difficulty by admitting two distinct attributes of conation and knowledge in Jainism. The self knows itself by the conation-attribute, and the not-self by the knowledge-attribute. From the non-distinctive point of view consciousness is one; while from the distinctive point of view self-apprehending attribute is conation and the other-apprehending attribute is knowledge. Another fallacy is pointed out in holding this view, i.e., the external things are no subject-matter of the faculty of conation. Then he explains the problem from the logical viewpoint which is mainly concerned with the contention made by the opponents. According to it conation and knowledge are held to be two attributes, one apprehending the self and the other, the not-self. From the common view-point the general perception of the external things has been termed as conation, and the perception of special features has been called knowledge.[1] Thus Brahmadeva has emphasized both the identity of conation and knowledge and their mutual distinction. From the non-distinctive point of view, as we have seen, not only conation and knowledge are identified but all the special attributes of the soul are similarly effected. It means that there is some community of traits between conation and knowledge for which they can be integrated into one consciousness. But it never means that their distinction is thereby annihilated. The level which admits of a distinction among attributes must hold the mutual distinction of conation and knowledge; and if so, a distinction must be caught in their own identity. Conation and knowledge being two attributes, they can have their modes simultaneously. While drawing the above conclusion the only difficulty in our way is that two conscious activities

1. Cf. Brahmadeva: *Dravyasaṅgraha-vṛtti*, pp. 81-83

cannot take place simultaneously in the same soul as pointed out by Haribhadra. On this very ground the simultaneous occurrence of conation and knowledge is denied even in the liberated souls.[1] We must remember that conation and knowledge alone do not constitute consciousness, but many more such attributes fall under consciousness; and, being distinct attributes, all of them must be held to have their modes simultaneously and all of them must be called conscious, being modes of conscious attributes. There is no inconsistency in having the modes of conation and knowledge simultaneously. The same mental activity is characterized by conation, cognition and affection which do not require different moments of time for their manifestation. What is contained by the soul as attributes must be seen as modes in every moment of its existence. Siddhasena's view that conation and knowledge are identical cannot be held in face of the facts which support their distinction. Yāśovijaya attempts to reconcile the conflicting views of the Jaina thinkers by stating that Jinabhadra resorted to pure *ṛjusūtra* (analytic stand-point) and Siddhasena to the *saṅgraha* (collective) standpoint which obliterates distinction.[2] Dr. N.M. Tatia concludes his discussion with the view of Yāśovijaya,[3] and Dr. Mehta[4] follows almost the same line of discussion and draws the same conclusion. The adoption of collective and analytic view-points does not solve the difficulty satisfactorily, for both the distinction and the non-distinction of conation and knowledge are emphasized at the analytic level of thought. The collective view-point does not go to prove the identity of conation and knowledge at the level of attributes. Our problem was whether we could distinguish between conation and knowledge as attributes of the soul, and Yāśovijaya's solution has nothing to do with conation and knowledge as attributes of the soul. Mostly the Jaina

1. Haribhadra: *Āvaśyakaniryukti,* verse 973
2. Yośovijaya, *Jñānabinduprakasa* p. 48
3. N.M. Tatia, *Studies in Jainism,* p. 79
4. M.L. Mehta: *Jaina Psychology* p. 56

writers are in favour of establishing a distinction between conation and knowledge, but the difficulty arises as regards the identity and subject-matter of conation.

Meaning of Conation

The Jaina writers generally believe that conation always precedes knowledge. In other words every iota of knowledge must be grounded on conation immediately preceding it or by way of a chain of cognitions ultimately grounded on conation. Hence conation will mean the first psychic stage which determines the process of knowledge. Knowledge is also a continuity of the cognitive process having various stages; and the Jaina does not like to make conation a member in the cognitive process. Conation is determined by a different faculty of the soul, so it has its own identity distinct from that of knowledge. H.H. Price has observed: "Again from the side of the mind, the consciousness of a surface is but the first stage in the consciousness of a material object....Now this consciousness of the object is not acquaintance (as the consciousness of the red something is) nor is it any other kind of knowing. It is but provisional acceptance, partly determinate and partly indeterminate, and it is subject to correction throughout, it may well turn out that some or all these characteristics do not really belong to the object or even that it does not exist."[1] Herbert Warren mentions that "before we know a thing in a detailed way, there is a stage where we simply see, hear, or otherwise become conscious of it in a general way without going into its ins and outs. We simply know it as belonging to a class. This is the first stage of knowledge. It may be called detailless knowledge or indefinite cognition. If this stage is not experienced, there can be no knowledge of the thing."[2] Bradley also thinks: "What comes first in each of us is

---

1. H.H. Price: *Perception*, p. 106
2. H. Warren: *Jainism*, p. 29

rather feeling, a state as yet without either an object or subject....Feeling is immediate experience without distinction and relation in itself. It is a unity, complex but without relations. And there is here no difference between the state and its contents, since, in a word, the experience and the experienced are one. And a distinction between cognition and other aspects of our nature is not yet developed. Feeling is not one differentiated aspect, but it holds all aspects in one."[1] Modern psychology distinguishes between the physical stimulation and sensation. The psychosis consequent upon the first contact between the mind and the object marks the beginning of the perceptive process. "The simplest mind we can legitimately conceive is, then, one which would respond to a sense impression not by merely having a sensation, but by an act of knowing; this act we could only describe as becoming aware of something there, an object in space, no matter how completely undefined the nature of the object as thought of and the nature of its spatial relations. Such a mind, of simplest possible structure, must be conceived as consisting of one cognitive disposition linked with a single conative disposition. Such a mind would respond to every sense impression that affected it at all (no matter what its nature) with simple awareness of something there and a vague undirected impulse of appetition, of striving towards the object."[2] It appears that this elementary process of perception is not distinct from knowing. Sometimes a similar view which identifies conation with the indistinct apprehension of the object, technically known as *vyañjanāvagraha* in Jaina philosophy, is also maintained.[3] But the general opinion of the Jaina thinkers is that conation forms no part of the cognitive process. Vādideva Sūri is of opinion that conation marks a stage prior to that of *avagraha* (indeterminate sensuous knowledge). It is like the stirring of consciousness on the contact between

1. Bradley: *Essays on Truth and Reality*, p. 194
2. Mc Dougall: *An Outline of Psychology*, p. 260
3. Indracandra: *Epistemology of Jaina Āgamas* (unpublished), p. 558

the soul and the object.[1] The two divisions of conation into occular and non-occular ones is a clear evidence of the fact that it involves the use of the senses. Unless the contribution in the form of sense stimulation is accepted, we cannot distinguish among conations dependent upon various senses. This goes against Vīrasena's position that conation means consciousness turned soulward as nothing of the soul can be prehended through the senses.

According to Śaṅkara indeterminate perception is purely non-relational apprehension which apprehends the mere being. We have already seen that mere generality, being a relative term, cannot be the subject-matter of conation, for, then, all conations will be indistinguishable. Hence Rāmānuja seems to be more consistent when he holds that 'Indeterminate Cognition is neither the apprehension of mere existence, nor the cognition of a qualified object and its qualifications unrelated to each other, as the Nyāya-vaiśeṣika recognizes. On the contrary, it apprehends an object attributed by some qualities.'[2] To bring the above contention in agreement with the Jaina view it must be said that whatever is held to be indeterminate cognition by the various thinkers is, in no way, a form of knowledge. It is determined, as Jainism holds, by a faculty different from that of knowledge. Call it the consciousness of the surface, the sensation and the indeterminate cognition, it must not belong to the series of knowledge. The very fact has been emphasized by the Jaina by recognizing two attributes of conation and knowledge in the soul. He distinguishes between the first step in knowledge from conation, not only with respect to their succession or simultaneity but with respect to their identity. This justifies the Jaina conception of the two types of *karma,* i.e., conation obscuring and knowledge obscuring; otherwise one knowledge obscuring-*karma* would have been sufficient to manifest all the stages of knowledge from the elementary to the higher ones. The

1. Vādideva: *Pramāṇa-naya-tattvāloka,* 2.7.
2. M.L. Mehta: *Jaina Psychology,* p. 45

thinkers already quoted seem to be inclined to include conation as a very elementary stage in the cognitive process. It must be noted that 'conation is the indescribable prehension by the soul of the mere presence of objects having general and particular qualities.'[1] Brahmadeva also holds conation to the devoid of details,[2] but it cannot be taken to mean that it prehends nothing of the objects. Whatever conation prehends must pertain to the object itself. It is a sort of readiness or inclination on the part of the soul to comprehend an object, and is not identified with the comprehension of the object. This readiness or inclination must have some object towards which the prehension is directed. This very identity of conation, when we begin to describe it, takes a tinge of knowledge. Hence it can be described by the terms like general apprehension, the consciousness of the surface, etc.; but it is always a pre-stage of the process of knowledge and can never be identified with knowledge. The generality which can be said to be apprehended by conation is not the ultimate generality, but the generality of a system to which the object belongs. As that effort in the form of conation has very little to do with the external object, it can be taken to be confined to the self itself. Perhaps this aspect of conation seems to have been emphasized by Vīrasena.

Conation and Knowledge as Attributes of the Soul

Now the situation we have reached so far makes the problem of identity of conation and knowledge fall to the ground, except only when a collective view point is meant. Conation and knowledge, being two distinct attributes, must have distinct simultaneous modes. And this interpretation is quite in agreement with the concept of simultaneous occurrence of conation and knowledge in the omniscient ones. No Jaina writer is in favour of the view that the flow

1. Nemicandra: *Gommaṭasāra (Jīvakāṇḍa)*, verse 483
2. Brahmadeva: *Dravyasaṅgraha-vṛtti,* p. 80

of knowledge can be broken at any stage in the history of the soul's life, nor does the Jaina theory of attributes permits such a conception. On the same ground the flow of conation must also be held to be continuous. Thus the problem of successive occurrence of conation and knowledge does not at all arise. Then the conception of their successive occurrence, in the mundane souls, must yield such a meaning as would not imply the breach of their flows. It appears that the Jaina writers are making their statement from the object-point of view. It means that conation and knowledge both cannot be directed towards the same object. Once the conation has given a start to the process of knowledge, it becomes unintelligible that it persists in the same form throughout the process of knowledge. But at the same time the function pertaining to conation cannot be suspended. It would mean that in the mundane souls conation and knowledge find their direction to different objects. The contention that two conscious activities cannot take place simultaneously has already been meted out. Modern psychology also holds that no psychosis is purely conative, cognitive or affective; it can, at most, show a dominance of one or the other aspect. Mc Dougall remarks: "But it is generally admitted that all mental activity has these three aspects, cognitive, conative and affective; and when we apply one of these three adjectives to any phase of mental process, we mean merely that the aspect named is the most prominent of the three at that moment.'[1] A psychosis according to the Jaina philosophy of the soul, is a collective mode of the soul based on a number of attributes. Hence it must show a comprehence of conation, cognition and affection. Cognition and affection with respect to an abject must coexist; but cognition of an object and cognition of a feeling with respect to the object cannot coexist, because they are the modes of the same attribute. So also we must distinguish between conation and knowledge of conation, the latter belongs to the series of knowledge. Considered

1. Mc Dougall: *An Outline of Psychology*, p. 266

subjectively, conation and knowledge must be held to occur simultaneously even in mundane souls. In the omniscient souls, there being nothing to obscure the two faculties, both conation and knowledge are free to have their full manifestations. Then the effort towards knowing becomes natural, and conation, in a way, may be perceived as being absorbed in knowledge, thus leading to theory of non-distinction between conation and knowledge.

The Problem of Objectless Consciousness

Now the concept of objectless consciousness may be considered. Akalaṅka has distinguished between two forms of consciousness, i.e., the knowledge-form and the knowable-form. The knowledge-form is like the surface of a mirror, when it has nothing to reflect.[1] Haribhadra also thinks:" Knowledge is of the nature of enlightenment. When it is objectless, it enlightens itself."[2] This leads to the conception of objectless consciousness. Consciousness, when it is prehending something, is intelligible as having a form agreeing with the form of the object prehended. The problem is whether the Jaina theory of the substance of the soul will admit of the possibility of objectless consciousness. If it is an objectless consciousness, it would mean that it is a consciousness which prehends nothing. This means that the function of the soul with respect to consciousness is suspended. Consciousness must manifest every moment of its existence, and it can manifest only by being conscious of something. It is also implied by the Jaina theory of substance that every mode concerning an attribute comes into existence by exhausting the entire capacity related with the attribute, there is no residue of a capacity over and above the mode it has determined. Thus every mode of consciousness is an embodiment of the total capacity behind it. The entire capacity gets actualized in the mode. So consciousness is

1. Akalanka: *Rājavārtiaka*, p. 34
2. Haribhadra: *Sāstrvārtāsamuccaya*, verse 19

actualized every moment and its actualization takes place by being conscious of something. Thus in Jaina philosophy we do not come across a consciousness having no objects. Mitchell states: "There is no experience that is experience of nothing; when conscious I am always conscious of a definite something or other and this is called the content of my experience or consciousness."[1] The objectless consciousness is like holding a piece of matter as having colour which is neither white, red, black nor of any other shade. B. Russell rightly remarks: "There can be no consciousness which is not of something."[2] W.T. Stace also thinks, "Pure awareness is not an activity. It is purely passive;[3] and the Jaina dynamism of substance cannot accept passivity in case of any of the attributes. Hence we can conclude that the conception of objectless consciousness is untenable.

Meaning of Knowledge

"Knowledge actually exists only as a number of psychic events in the minds of the knower.[4] Knowledge is a manifestation of the soul with respect to its comprehending capacity. The cognitive function of the soul is determined by its knowledge attribute. It is a prehension of the objects with their details. A prehension of the details of objects is known as the 'sākāragrahaṇa' which is generally taken to signify the cognitive process. The term ākāra, when applied to matter, certainly implies spatiality; but, when applied to knowledge, it can only mean the distinctive nature of the flow of the knowledge-attribute. The area of a field is spatial, but the knowledge of this area can never be called spatial. Samantabhadra states: that the knowledge of Lord Mahavira behaves like a mirror with the objects of the three

---

1. Mitchell: *Structure and Growth of Mind*, p. 11
2. B. Russell: *Analysis of Mind*, p. 289
3. W.T. Stace: *Theory of Knowledge and Existence,* p. 81
4. *Ibid.*, p. 14

worlds including the alokākāśa.[1] It is likely to make us misconceive the Jaina theory of knowledge. It never means that the objects are reflected in the soul and the soul comprehends these reflections. The metaphor is meant to suggest the absence of attachment, aversion and delusion in the knowledge of the perfect ones. In other words knowing becomes a natural function of the soul with no preference whatsoever for the objects, just as the mirror reflects the objects that come in front of it. The ākāra theory of knowledge holds that the *ākāras* or reflections of objects are there in the precipient's mind; and it is for this that he is able to distinguish one cognition from another. This theory is different from presentionism which does not allow any reflections to come between objects and their cognitions. It holds that objects are directly cognized by the soul. Representationism recognizes the contributions of the mind towards the enrichment of the impressions received by the senses. The theory of knowledge becomes most unsatisfactory when the term *ākāra* is interpreted to imply spatiality. Spatiality is not the only characteristic of the objects which may be said to be reflected in the soul. Not all characteristics of the objects can yield spatial reflections. Our mind is able to comprehend much more than mere spatiality about the objects. Moreover, if the *ākāra* theory is upheld, knowledge will reflect only what is present, and the past and the future will be totally out of reach. For the Jaina, who also holds knowledge to be a *sākāra* (with details) prehension of the objects, *ākāra* means a distinctive feature of a mode comprehended by the knowledge attribute. The truth of presentationism and representationism lies in the fact that knowledge is constituted of two components: one which the mind receives from outside and the other which it contributes from its own side. The one sidedness of the former component reduces the soul to a tabula rasa, as

---

1. Samantabhadra: *Ratnakaraṇḍa-śrāvakācāra*, verse 1. In Jainism space is held to be infinite. All the substances are found only in a part of space beyond which it is called the *alokākāśa*.

Locke held. The two components taken together give a better picture of knowledge. A.C. Ewing has correctly remarked: "Here I should just say that representative theory would be more correctly expressed as being the view that we do not perceive the objects directly, but that we do not perceive them directly in the sense as we perceive directly the sensory data (sensa) which we use in perception of physical objects."[1] The knowledge-attribute of the soul so functions that it is ready to receive something from outside and contribute something from its own side. It is equivalent to say that mind is not passive in receiving impressions, but it manipulates on what it receives. The Jaina advocates a similar theory of knowledge by formulating two types of capacities for *matijñāna* (sensuous knowledge) and *śrutajñāna* (perceptual knowledge). Thus the Jaina theory of knowledge includes elements of both the theories of presentationism and representationism. It should be remembered that in the cognitive process neither the mind need be transformed into objects nor objects, into the mind. Objects are simply an occasion for the generation of knowledge about them in the soul. The Jaina theory of knowledge may take various forms in accordance with the Jaina theory of substance. Thus knowledge may be held as an attribute, a manifestation of an attribute, an everchanging series of cognitions, a process, an activity and also as an entity in itself. These are the partial descriptions of knowledge, and may be found consistent in a suitable context. None of them taken absolutely can give a full picture of the soul with respect to its knowledge-attribute, all of them describe the same entity in its various aspects. The process of knowledge is constituted by the momentary modes of the knowledge attribute, and so it may be looked upon as a series of cognitions. When these modes are perceived along with the unity of the attribute behind, knowledge may be considered to be a process. As an element in the structure of the soul, knowledge may be seen to be a potentiality. It can also be

1. A.C. Ewing: *Idealism—A Critical Survey,* p. 288

held to be an activity if viewed in its functional aspect, knowledge is an activity of the soul with respect to its knowledge-attribute. If knowledge is considered in isolation from its substratum, it may be taken to be an entity in itself.

From Berkeley's dictum of '*esse est percipi*' we drew the conclusion that knowability and existence go together. The soul has a capacity to comprehend things, and things are such as can be comprehended. On account or these capacities the relation of knowledge between the subject and the object is made possible. If an object is known by the soul, then, according to the Jaina the object is not transformed into the soul. Such a transformation is denied by Berkeley and the Jaina both. The former to avoid this transformation reduced the objects to perceptions. The implication behind the Berkeleye theory was that mind can prehend only what is mental, hence its own perceptions. The Jaina is also agreed to the view that perceptions and cognitions are spiritual affections; but, in order that they may be the perecptions and cognitions of the objects which are different from the perceiving mind, they must somehow be connected with the objects. In the same way the appearances, as Kant held, may be interpreted in two ways. Appearances as forms of our comprehensions may be looked upon as mental affections. They may also be seen as the partial aspects of the objects themselves, as they are caused by the objects. A. Chakravarti observes: "The apperarance is just the appearance of reality and the reality cannot exist apart from and independent of its appearance which is but its manifestation. The contradiction between reality and existence is but the result of mental abstraction, and as such has no basis in a genuine metaphysics."[1]

The Sensum Theory of Knowledge and Its Criticism

It has been a common problem how an entity different from knowledge can determine the process of knowledge.

1. *Samayasāra* (Com. in English by A. Chakravarti), Introduction, p. XXXIV

This very difficulty has led to the view that there is something lying between the subject and the object in the process of knowledge, and this something is the direct object of our knowledge. B. Russell thinks that. "Things immediately known are sense data as colour, smell, etc. Sensation is the awareness of the sense-data"[1] This sensum or sense datum is the direct object of our perception. As regards the identity of sensum Dawes Hicks says "The sensum is a particular existent but a particular existent of a particular kind. It is not a physical existent; and there is no reason for supposing that it is a mental existent; in the sense of being either a state of mind or existentially dependent on mind. It resembles physical entities, as ordinarily conceived, in having spatial and other characteristics usually ascribed to physical entities, it resembles mental entities in being private to the individual pecepient."[2] H.H. Price also says: "When I am in a situation which is described as seeing something, touching something, hearing something, etc., it is certain in each case that a certain patch, or a pressure, or a noise exists at that moment and that I am acquainted with this colour, patch, pressure or noise. Such entities are called sense data, and the acquaintance with them is called sensing."[3] Price also holds that the sensum is a third kind of entity which is neither mental nor physical.[4] It should not be taken to mean that the sense data have no features, a new type of feature is assigned to them. "Sense data are neither physical nor mental but they are vital in the sense in which breathing and digesting are vital. Hence they must inhere in some sense organ...The concluson then would be that sense data are neither psychical, nor cerebral, but psychocerebral."[5] This leads to the view that the sense data constitute an entity different from mind and matter both, but have some

1. B. Russell: *Problems of Philosophy*, p. 17
2. G. Dawes Hicks: *Critical Realism*, p. 48
3. H.H. Price: *Perception*, p. 18
4. *Ibid.*, p. 18
5. *Ibid.*, pp. 121 and 133

specialities. In the very beginning the difficulty was how a mind can apprehend matter which is non-mental. The sensum theory solves the difficulty by postulating an entity which is not matter. But the sensum, being still different form the mind, the difficulty does not seem to disappear. If mind can apprehend the sensum directly in spite of all the differences of the latter from the former, then it can also be held to be apprehending matter equally directly. By calling the sense data psychocerebral the problem of the unity of the psychic and the physical is not solved but is presented in a different way. On the other hand we do not have any evidence to prove the independent existence of the sensum except the pseudonecessity created by the sensum theory. By holding that the sense data are different for each individual an indirect attempt is made to make them mental, for only the mental can be said to belong singularly to the mind in the true sense of the term. On the other hand G.E. Moore questions the independence of the sense datum from the objects. He says: "If what was seen were merely coloure sensation and what was touched were only a tactual sensation and both were merely mental or physiological states, the one could not be identified with the other. The sense data are, therefore, somehow, connected with the physical object."[1] Thus the identity of the sense datum is required to be reduced to mind on one hand and to the objects on the other. The theory does not successfully lead to an independent identity of the sensa. A right implicaton of the sensum theory may be that the precess of knowledge is bipolar. It admits of contributions made by the subject and the object both. In the absence of either of them knowledge will not be possible.

The Three Termed Theory of Perception

The three termed relation theory of knowledge holds that 'the sensed qualities in sensed space and time are

1. D.M. Datta: *The Chief Currents of Contemporary Philosophy,* p. 375

related to the physical object, not directly as common sense supposes, but indirectly by way of the observer.'[1] This may be taken to mean that, if something is not perceived, it cannot be held to be related with its qualities—a position upheld by Berkeley. The observer comes in not to effect the relation between the things and their qualities, but to effect a knowledge of the entities known and their relations. The same author again observes that "the colour of the rose, to be sure, is a function of the observer, but it is equally surely a function also of the character of the rose."[2] Such a view is grounded in a confusion between an entity and its perception. The colour is certainly a function of the rose, but the function of the observer is not colour but the perception of the colour. Again the correct implication of the theory is that perception is a bipolar process being constituted partially by the observer and partially by the object perceived. It never means that perception negates the contributions made by the object or the observer. The third term finds no place in the process, but it is the same as the second term qualified by the first. The Jaina does not need a third term in the process of knowledge. No object of knowledge is required to change itself into a mental entity for its comprehension. Mind need not assimilate an object into its own constitution to have a knowledge of the object. The knowledge of the object is an affection of the soul in relation with the object. The knowing capacity totally belongs to the soul. The objects are possessed of knowability, and they simply become an occasion for the generation of knowledge. The seeing capacity resides in the soul, but it is only actualized in the presence of the object. The capacity of the soul to know objects and the knowability of the objects are the two basic conceptions upon which the Jaina theory of knowledge stands. Thus according to Jainism only the object and the observer are the terms in the process of preception, the differences in perceptions of the same object

---

1. Northrop: *Meeting of the East and West*, p. 78
2. *Ibid.*, p. 443

by different percepients are accounted for by the differences in the perceptual capacities of the selves. Māṇikyanandi observes, "The order in the process of knowledge is determined by the destruction subsidence[1] of the obscuring *karmas.*"[2]

Mati and Śruta Types of Knowledge

Our senses play an important part in the process of knowledge. They stand between the soul and the objects. The types of knowledge like the tactual, visual, olfactory, gustatory and auditory are mainly determined by the instrumentality of the senses. Devanandi states that the soul, being incapable of comprehending objects by itself, accepts the assistance of the senses.[3] The knowledge which is so determined has been called the *matijñāna* or sensuous knowledge. Along with it there is another type of knowledge which does not directly require the object but makes use of the knowledge already attained. The Jaina names it as the *śrutajñāna* or the perceptual knowledge. The characteristics of this type of knowledge have been variously described. Umāsvāti says: "*Matijñāna* must proceed *śrutajñāna.*"[4] Sensuous knowledge is a precondition for perceptual knowledge. Again Nemicandra says: "*Śruta* or perceptual knowledge is the knowledge of another object (arthāntara) than one (known by the sensitive knowledge). Necessarily it is preceded by sensuous knowledge." Thus perceptual knowledge[5] is held to be not only distinct from sensuous

1. In Jaina philosophy the personality of a living being is the joint effect of the forces generated by the self and the *karmas.* When some of the obstructing *karmas* are in a state of subsidence and some others are in an operative state, the soul is said to be in a state of destruction-subsidence, *kṣayopaśama)*
2. Māṇikyanandin: *Parīkṣāmukhasūtra,* 2.8
3. Devanandin: *Sarvārthasiddhi,* p. 61
4. Umāsvāti: *Tattvārthasūtra,* 1.20
5. Perception always involves the use of the apperception masses of the perceiver, though such a use appears only when one has experienced sensation. Sensation and perception are mutually

knowledge but its subject-matter is also different from that of the latter. Perceptual knowledge must mark a transcendence over the sensuous knowledge, though the former cannot make a start without the latter. Our actual process of knowledge consists of these two types. B. Russell locates non-sensational elements in perception and contents; "When we perceive any object of a familiar kind, much of that which appears subjectively to be immediately given is really derived from past experience."[1] The distinction he draws between knowledge by acquaintance and knowledge by description, may be identified with the distinction between the sensuous and the perceptual types of knowledge of Jaina philosophy. W.T. Stace seems to hold a similar view, when he thinks: "The mind starts from a certain fundamental data, which we call the given and it builds upon these data the whole fabric of knowledge by means of constructions and inferences between constructions."[2] The close relation between sensuous and perceptual types of knowledge and the precedence of the former are again recognized as "knowledge is everywhere tied to the given. That is the first principle of epistemology."[3] Sensuous knowledge is certainly the first step in the process of knowledge, the rest being inferred from or constructed on it.

The transcendence in perception on the given has been generally accepted, and sensation being a very elementary process of cognition such a transcendence becomes inevitable in the process of knowledge. Now the problem is whether the process of inference and construction can start on perception itself. We fail to see any obstruction in such

---

distinguished on account of the intervention of the apperceptive masses in the process of knowledge. According to the Jaina when an extension of knowledge on the ground of sensuous knowledge is effected, it becomes perceptual knowledge (*śruta jñāna*). It is why the terms 'sensuous and perceptual' have been taken as equivalent to *mati* and *śruta* of the Jaina philosophy.

1. B. Russell: *Analysis of Mind,* p. 81
2. W.T. *Stace: The Theory of Knowledge and Existence,* p. 45
3. *Ibid.,* p. 47

a transcendence. Akalaṅka accepts the truth of the aforesaid contention but reduces the previous peception to the status of sensuous knowledge in a derivative sense.[1] Hence as regards the identity of the *śruta* or perception we can affirm that it is a knowledge constructed on or inferred from another knowledge. So far we were concerned with the sensuous and perceptual types of knowledge, but Jainism recognizes three more types under the genus direct knowledge.[2] Now the problem is whether transcendence over direct types of knowledge is possible or not. Perceptual knowledge is possible only where there is a field for transcendence. As *kevalajñāna* or the perfect knowledge leaves nothing unknown, no advancement over it is possible. Hence we cannot think of perceptual knowledge built on the perfect knowledge. The other two types of knowledge, i.e., the *avadhi* or clairvoyance and the *manahparyaya* or telepathy allow scope for further extension, and so it seems possible that perceptual knowledge can be built upon them. It is possible that the Jaina writers would have taken the aforesaid two types of direct knowledge as sensuous knowledge though in a devivative sense, as they have done in case of perceptual knowledge itself. Where the direct knowledge does not penetrate, the perceptual knowledge can do so but in an indirect way. In other words the facts apprehended by direct knowledge may be utilized as a ground for further infrences and constructions.

Generally the process of our knowing is constituted of the sensuous and the perceptual elements. Haribhadra observes: "The *mati* and *śruta* are found in the same self and they penetrate each other."[3] Akalaṅka also maintains: "*Mati* and *śruta* do not leave each other. Where there is *mati* there is *śruta* and vice versa."[4] The science of psychology tells us that our sensations are every moment supplemented by our

1. Akalaṅka: *Rājavārtika,* 1.20.10
2. Umāsvāti: *Tattvārthasūtra,* 1.9.
3. *Nāndisūtra* (com. by Haribhadra), p. 57
4. Akalaṅka: *Rājavārtika,* p. 47

apperception masses to facilitate the actual process of our knowing. Not only this but the apperception masses also enrich our perceptions. This very clearly shows that sensuous and perceptual types of knowledge are distinct and accompany each other.

Siddhasena Divākara holds a different view in this connection. He thinks: "If *śruta* is admitted as a distinct category form *mati,* then there is the fault of redundancy and unwarranted extension."[1] Yaśovijaya holds the same opinion. According to him "The conception of *śruta* as separate from *mati* is futile in as much as the function of the former can be adequately fulfilled by the latter."[2] Akalaṅka raises the same question as "*Matī* and *śruta* are identical, because they accompany each other, they are found in the same locus, and they are not distinguished from each other."[3] He, then, offers a criticism of the aforesaid view as "On this very ground the distinction between *mati* and *śruta* can be maintained. Mutual accompaniment is possible only of those that have their distinct identity.... How can one that is prior be non-distinct from that which is posterior.... Apprehension effected by *mati* is different from the one effected by *śruta* though they may apprehend the same object."[4] The conclusion which Akalaṅka wants to draw is that *mati* and *śruta* must be held to be distinct. We have already seen that knowledge by description and knowledge by acquaintance, the given and the knowledge which transcends the given cannot be identified. Kant also recognized the rational and the empirical elements in our knowledge. We find very little evidence in favour of the views of Siddhasena and Yaśovijaya. If a synthetic view-point is adopted then not only *śruta* and *mati* become identical, but all types of knowledge merge into one

---

1. Siddhasena: *Niścayadvātriṁśikā* p. 12
2. N.M, Tatia: *Studies in Jainism,* p. 61
3. Akalaṅka: *Rājavārtika,* 1.9.21
4. *Ibid.*, 1.9.22-25
5. *Ibid.*, 1.9.22-24

generality. We cannot obliterate the distinction between *mati* and *śruta* at the level where Umāsvāti enumeretes five types of knowledge.

Pratyakṣa or the Direct Types of Knowledge

Besides the sensuous and the perceptual types of knowledge most of the Indian systems of philosophy accept the possibility of the *pratyakśa* or the direct type of knowledge. Umāsvāti divides all cognitions into two groups, i.e. direct and indirect. The first two, i.e., the sensuous and the perceputal types are indirect, and the rest are direct.[1] Etymologically the term *pratyakśa* means that which is determined by the soul itself, hence it is independent of the non-soul.[2] A more lucid meaning of *pratyakśa* is again given as "*pratyakśa* is the detailed apprehension which is independent of the senses and the manas and is free from faults."[3] As our knowledge is limited to sensuous and perceptual types only, our experience provides almost no evidence in favour of direct knowledge. Northrop imagines of an experiment in which all sensations are reduced to a minimum. He gives the result of the experiment as 'the report is that one is left with one of the most emotionally overwhelming aesthetic ineffable experiences, with no sense either of self or of objects.'[4] The Nyāya Vaiśeṣika gives almost a similar description of his yogi-pratykśa which functions without admitting the instrumentality of the senses. The researches of para psychology have been found very hopeful towards the establishment of direct knowledge. The phenomena of clairvoyance, clairaudiene, telepathy and psychometry make us think of the possibility of direct comprehension, independent of the senses. 'The phenomena of extra sensory perception (which includes clairvoyance

1. Umāsvāti: *Tattvārthasūtra,* 1.9.12
2. Akalaṅka: *Rājavārtika,* 1.12.2
3. *Ibid.,* 1.12.1
4. Northrop: *The Meeting of the East and West,* p. 369

and clairaudience) is in direct contradiction to the assumption of all the psychologists that there can be no sensory knowledge without the use of sense organs and that all knowledge of the external world comes to us through the gate ways of senses.'[1] H.H. Price also observes: 'The evidence for telepathy and clairvoyance is both abundant and good, and the evidence for precognition—the most paradoxical, perhaps, of all the supernormal phenomena is very considerable.'[2] Mc Dougall observes: 'The ancient belief in clairvoyance seems also in a fair way established. Further, precognition and foresight or events that lie in the future is also under experimental investigation that seems to promise positive results.[3] He at another place, very hopefully asserts; 'In my view the evidence for telepathy is very strong, and I foretell with considerable confidence that it will become stronger and stronger the more we investigate and sift the evidence.'[4] Though we do not get decisive evidence in favour of the direct type of knowledge still there is nothing which may obstruct its possibility. Jainism thinks that knowledge is an essential attribute of the soul and the limitations to its pure function are due to causes alien to the soul's structure. In sensuous knowledge the limitation is so effected that the instrumentality of the senses becomes necessary. With further attenuations of the obstructions it is also possible that the soul may refuse the instrumentality of the senses and tend to attain its self-determined function.

Avadhi and Manaḥparyaya Types or Direct Knowledge

Jainism includes three types under direct knowledge. They are clairvoyance (*avadhi*), telepathy (*manahparyaya*), and perfect knowledge (*kevala-jñāna*). All of these can

---

1. B.L. Atreya: *An Introduction to Para Psychology*, (2nd edition), p. 11
2. H.H. Price: 'Questions about Telepathy and Clairvovance', *Philosophy*, October, 1940
3. Mc Dougall: *Riddle of Life*, p. 235
4. Mc Dougall: *Religion and Science of Life*, p. 80

comprehend things independently of the senses. Rājamalla explains the *praktyakṣatā* or directness of knowledge as 'Directness in clairvoyance and mental knowledge is due to its origination independently of the senses.'[1] They are mutually distinguished with respect to their capacity to penetrate the objects and the scope of their subject-matter. *Avadhi* has generally been so described, because it is limited and has been called *sīmā-jñāna* (bounded knowledge) in the scriptures.[2] Telepathy, being inferior to perfect knowledge, also has limitations, though they are different from those of *avadhi.* The aforesaid description of *avadhi* does not enable us to distinguish it from telepathy. As these two types of knowledge are separately enumerated in the Jaina scriptures, we have to look for their distinctive features. About telepathy Akalaṅka says: "The term *manas* means the object which is in the other's mind. What is that entity which is in other's mind? It is the subjective (knowledge) form of the pot, etc. The knowledge obtained by approaching such an object from all sides and effected by the purity of the self, is *manaḥparyaya* or telepathy.'[3] Nemicandra says; "That which knows the thought of, not thought of and half thought of manifold objects is called the *manaḥparyaya.*"[4] Dr. Radhakrishnan mentions very clearly that "*manaḥparyaya* is the direct knowledge of the thoughts of others, as in telepathic knowledge of other's minds."[5] "When a person has overcome hatred, jealousy etc. (which create obstacles that stand in the way of knowing other's minds), he can have direct access to the present and past thoughts of others. This knowledge is called *manaḥparyaya* (entering a mind)."[6] So far the conclusion is that telepathy is mainly the knowledge of the thoughts of a person, and not simply of

---

1. Rājamalla: *Pañcādhyāyī*, verse 699
2. Nemicandra: *Gommaṭasāra* (Jīvakāṇda) verse 370
3. Akalaṅka: *Rājavārtika*, p. 44
4. Nemicandra: *Gommaṭasāra* (*Jīvakāṇḍa*) verse, 438
5. S.Radhakrishnan; *Indian Philosophy*, Vol. I, p. 295
6. Chatterjee and Datta: *An Introduction to Indian Philosophy*, p. 86

the objects of his thoughts. But the thoughts must comprehend some objects, so telepathy, by comprehending thoughts, knows the objects of such thoughts also. Telepathy is mainly concerned with the thoughts present in other minds; but as these thoughts cannot exist without comprehending their objects, telepathic knowledge is not unconscious of the objects of such thoughts. If the objects of the thoughts about them are known without comprehending the thoughts themselves, it will not be a piece of telepathy. To be brief, we must not identify the comprehension of the thoughts about things with the comprehension of the things themselves. Akalaṅka perhaps, seems to emphasize this distinction between the object and the cognition of the object by mentioning the term '*bhāva-ghaṭādi*'(knowledge-form of the pot, etc.) in his commentary. This implication becomes very clear, when Nemicandra distinguishes between two kinds of telepathic knowledge. "Simple telepathy knows the material objects of all the three times thought by the present soul. Complex telepathy knows what had been thought in the past and will be thought in future."[1] Present thoughts are comprehensible by simple telepathy, and the thoughts that have passed away and those that will come into existence in future are known by complex telepathy. The dictionary meanings of clairvoyance and telepathy as 'faculty of seeing mentally what is happening or exists out of sight' and 'action of one mind on another at a distance through emotional influence without communication through senses', also suggest that the former is confined to material (*rūpī*) objects while the latter extends to the mental impressions or thoughts of others.[2] Thus thoughts are the subject-matter of telepathy.

A different view about telepathy is upheld in the Bhagwatīsūtra. It states that the *manaḥparyaya jñāna*

---

1. Nemicandra: *Gommaṭasāra* (jivakaṇda), verse, 441
2. The Conscise Oxtord Dictionary of Current Engiish, pp. 203 and 1259

comprehends only the substance of the *manas*[1]—a material sense like the other five senses.[2] Jinabhadra agrees to the above view and says: "A person possessing the faculty of telepathy perceives the states of the mind substance directly, but cognizes the external objects thought by the mind only through inference. The above view has been strengthened by Hemacandra as "It is a unanimous fact that for one who is not omniscient, it is impossible to perceive a non-material object directly. Hence, it must be admitted that one possessed of the power of telepathy knows the object thought by others only by way of inference, and not directly."[3] Umāsvāti states that the subject-matter of *avadhi* is matter while that of *manaḥparyaya* is an infinitesimal part of the same.[4] *Avadhi* and *manaḥparyaya* both are concerned with material substances, but the latter is able to prehend finer and subtler forms of matter. Akalaṅka, in his commentary, enumerates those modes of the *jīva* which result from the operation, subsidence and destruction-subsidence of the *karmas* as material. He does not include the natural and destructive types of the manifestations which are immune from material effect,[5] Thus *avadhi* may also be admitted to comprehend such manifestations of the *jīva* which result from its association with matter; and, hence *manaḥparyaya* should be held to comprehend still subtler manifestations of the *Jiva* which result from *karmic* association. As the thoughts of others are destructive-subsidential

1. Jainism recognizes the sense of *manas* along with the five senses. It is a physiological organ made of a special type of matter called *manovargaṇa*. As regards the subject-matter of *manahparyaya* the Jaina thinkers are divided into two groups. One group holds that *manahparyaya* knows the material of the *manas*, and from this knowledge it infers the knowledge of thoughts in others' minds; The other group holds that *manahparyaya* comprehends directly the thoughts in others' minds.
2. *Bhagvati-sūtra*, p. 71
3. *Viśeṣāvaśyaka-bhāṣya*, 814
4. Umāsvāti: *Tattvārthasūtra*, 1. 27-28
5. Akalaṅka: *Rājavārtika*, p. 88

manifestations of the Jīva, they are comprehensible, on the ground of Akalaṅka's agrument, not only by *manaḥparyaya* but also by *avadhi.* All the Jaina writers are unanimous as regards the comprehensibility of the thoughts of others by *manaḥparyaya,* they differ in holding such a comprehension as direct. If *avadhi* and *manaḥparyaya* are concerned only with material substances, we do not know how the problem of the comprehensibility of other's thoughts has come into existence. It is no use saying that the knowledge of other's thoughts is inferred from the knowledge of the substance of the mind, because, then, such a knowledge would be called *śrutajñāna.* It cannot also be held that the subject-matter of *manaḥparyaya* is only the substance of the *manas*, because it is not the only infinitesimal part of the substance known by *avadhi.* There is a view that the substance of the *manas* is comprehensible by *avadhi* also. It is said that 'the person possessing *avadhi* cognizes the mind substances, but the person possessing *manaḥparyaya* intution knows the self-same objects in a more lucid form.'[1] Then it must be held that in the *manaḥparyaya* alone the comprehensions of the mind-substance rises to a stage where the thoughts of others can be inferred. In the same way Akalaṅka may be taken to mean that the capacity to comprehend other's thoughts appears only in a soul that has attained telepathy. *Avadhi* is not capable to comprehend thoughts in others' minds, being a lower type of attainment than *manaḥparyaya.*

From the above discusssion it also follows that *avadhi* and *manaḥparyaya* must be held to be distinct types of knowledge. Being the subclasses of direct knowledge they cannot be non-distinct. Just as sensuous knowledge and perceptual knowledge yield two types of experience, though they may comprehend the same object, so also clairvoyance and telepathy, in spite of comprehending the same object, will yield different types of experience. The five types of knowledge have been so devised mainly because the experiences yielded by them are mutually distinct. Their

---

1. Tatia and Mookerjee: *A Critique of the Organ of Knowledge*, p. 38

directness and indirectness being dependent ultimately upon the fact that they are able to generate the experience exclusively with the soul and without the help of the intervening senses. Different categories of *karmas* are enumerated to obscure the faculties of *avadhi* and *manaḥparyaya;* and hence *avadhi* and *manaḥparyaya* must be admitted to be mutually distinct. Degrees of manifestation are contained in *avadhi* as well as in *manaḥparyaya* but for that reason no new class is formulated. There is some difference between the two types of cognition yielded by *avadhi* and *manaḥparyaya*. Being deterimined by the destruction-subsidence of some karmic forces, they cannot be said to be perfectly direct in spite of the fact that they do not make use of the senses at all; but, on account of the vividness they carry with them they are classed with the direct types of knowledge.

Kevalajñāna or the Perfect Knowledge

Now we come to the last named type of knowledge, i.e., the Kevalajñāna. As Jainism holds the manifestation of the soul with respect to the knowledge attribute takes subtler and subtler forms with the weakening of the obstructing *karmas,* so a stage can be conceived where the knowledge-attribute manifests in full effulgence. Samantabhadra remarks: 'Faults and obscurations are totally destroyed in some soul because of degrees in their destruction like the destruction of the internal and external dirt on account of the proper causes. The subtle future, past and distant things like the fire, etc., which can be known must be directly comprehensible by some one. This establishes the possibility of omniscience.'[1] Vidyānanda writes: 'Knowledge attains its highest limit in some soul because of its manifestation in degrees like the magnitude in space'[2] The same anthor establishes the possibility of the total

1. Samantabhadra: *Āptamīmāṁsā*, verses 4 and 5
2. Vidyānandin: *Tattvārthaślokavārtika*, 1. 29. 28

eradication of *karmas* on the ground of the absence of the causes of bondage and the presence of the cepacity for shedding them off.[1] Prabhācandra also comments on the subject as 'There is a soul comprehending directly all the entities of the universe because its nature is to comprehend them and because along with this there is the destruction of obstructions. That which has the nature of comprehending something along with the possibility of the removal of obstructions, comprehends that directly, as the visual knowledge free from the obstrúctions of darkness, etc., comprehends colour (*rūpa*). There must be some soul which, along with the nature of comprehending all things, enjoys the removal of all obstructions.'[2] The author of the *Pramāṇa-mīmāṁsā* gives the same proof for the possibility of omniscience. 'Knowledge attains its final form as there is its gradual development.'[3] C.R. Jain observes 'Consciousness being the very nature of the substance of soul, and all things being knowable by nature, omniscience, full and perfect, must be predicated in respect of the essential nature of each and every individual.'[4] Vādideva Sūri observes: 'when consciousness has the power of comprehending all the objects, then, on the removal of the *karmas* why will it not see all the objects?'[5]

The above statements may be analysed as under. Firstly the soul is held to possess the capacity of comprehending the totality of the universe. This implies the comprehensibility on the parts of the objects, i.e., no entity is such as would refuse to enter into the knowledge-relation with the conscious self. Secondly, this capacity of the soul is obscured by the *karmic* forces and thus result the limitations of the conscious manifestations. Thirdly, there is the possibility of the removal of the obstructions.

---

1. Vidyānanda: *Āptaparīkṣā*, p. 1
2. Prabhācandra: *Nyāyakumuda-candrodaya*, p. 91
3. Hemacandra: *Pramāṇa-mīmāṁsā*, 1.1. 16.
4. C.R Jain: *Key of Knowledge*, p. 95
5. Vādideva: *Nyāya-viniścayavivaraṇa*, III, verse, 24

The first of the three components of the argument for omniscience has already been established in the previous chapter. The remaining two components are concerned with the relation of the soul with the *karmic* forces—a topic to be discussed later on under *karma* phenomenology. (See chapter 8). Here, we simply accept the truth of this relation as granted. Perfect knowledge is not something thrust from without into the nature of soul; but it is the pure function of the soul with respect to the knowledge-attribute. This brings us to the Cartesian theory of innate ideas which means that the soul must be imbued with all forms of cognitions. 'What the real object is, what it is when stripped of the qualities the senses ascribe to it, we can know only by clear and distinct thinking. If we cannot derive true knowledge from sense experience, if genuine knowledge is the result of certain basal notions and principles, these must be inherent in the mind itself, innate, or *a priori*.'[1] Jainism may be said to believe in the theory of innate ideas but such ideas, being modes of an attribute, are contained in the soul only potentially. There are no ready made ideas stored up in the constitution of the soul. When the soul is left to itself, its function becomes self-determined; and ideas concerning all the objects emerge in it. This conclusion is based on the truth that the nature of an entity is never detrimental to its identity. Considered subjectively the *kevalajñāna* or the perfect knowledge represents the purest form of knowledge. The term *kevala* implies independence from all sorts of aids....Thus *kevalajñāna* is distinct from all those types of knowledge which are determined by the destruction-subsidence of the *karmas*.[2] The idea implied is that perfect knowledge, in its identity, is not identical with clairvoyance and telepathy. Considered objectively, the *kevalajñāna* has been said to be embracing all the substances and their modes.[3] H. Joachim thinks: 'Omniscience, we may admit,

1. Thilly: *A History of Philosophy*, p. 259
2. Akalaṅka: *Rājavārtika*, 1.9.7
3. Umāsvāti: *Tattvārthasūtra*, 1. 29.

must be the knowledge of everything, and in the infinite experience nothing can be lost. Every fact and every feeling (every thing in any sense real) as an element in that experience, is invested with the timeless necessity which defies change or destruction....In this sense past and future are no less and not otherwise than the present there is no difference between the trivial and the important,"[1] The knowledge possessed by a perfect soul would, then, consist in the knowledge of all that its own nature is capable of revealing; it would, to a very large extent, not be knowledge of things actually existing, but of the forms of all things as lying in the womb of possibility."[2] No details are superfluous and redundant for omniscience. Another characteristic of omniscience, which may be seen to follow from the above dicussion, is that the omniscient being must comprehend all the things simultaneously. When the soul possesses the capacity to know everything, it must know all the things simultaneously, for there is nothing to obstruct such a function of the soul. Like a mirror it must reflect all that comes under its span. Hence omniscience must mean the simultaneous knowledge of all the knowables of the world.

Arguments Against Omnīscience and their Refutation

The Mīmāṁsaka opposes the possibility of omniscience on the ground of its non-perception by any means of comprehension. Prabhācandra summarises the opponent's view as "Let there be the omniscient being. Whether he knows all the things of the past, etc., in their own forms, or in terms of something in the present. If the former alternative is held, omniscience cannot be direct, because its object is not present..... In the second case omniscience becomes a delusion, for it comprehends things in a different way from their existence."[3] Besides Prabhācandra gives a number of

1. H. Joachim: *The Nature of Truth*, p. 111
2. C.R. Jain: *Key of Knowledge*, p. 401
3. Prabhācandra: *Nyāya-kumuda-candrodaya*, p. 88

doubts against the theory of omniscience. A few are given here. It is impossible to entertain cognitions, in one and the same soul, of the mutually opposing entities like the cold and the hot. If the omniscient being knows everything in one instant, he will become unconscious the next moment. The omniscient, when he knows attachment and aversion of others, must become himself overwhelmed by them.[1] Very often a doubt is raised that, when perfection in one department of knowledge is found to be practically impossible, the problem of omniscience is totally out of question.

The Jaina tries to meet the situation on the ground of his basic theory of the soul. If one is able to know the absence of omniscience in all times and at all places, he himself must be an omniscient being. In other words one cannot deny the possibility of omniscience without the risk of self-contradiction. Mutual opposition of entities existing simultaneously or in succession is no obstruction in the way of their comprehension. They must be known as they are found to exist. As regards the knowledge of past and future events Amṛtacandra Sūri states: 'Just as on the picture wall the traces of things past, future and present are seen clearly at the same moment, in the same way they are perceived on the wall of consciousnes.... just as the traces of the past and future events are present, in the same way the cognitive traces of the past and future modes become present.'[2] Moreover the non-existence of the future and the past events is meaningful only with respect to the present, but they are existent with respect to their own times. Memory always relates to things which are non-existent with respect to the present. "The past and future are perceived by the omniscient not as present, but as past and future."[3] So his knowledge is never objectless and cannot be called a delusion. It is wrong to say that the omniscient will become unconscious

1. Prabhācandra: *Prameyakamala-mārtaṇḍa*, p. 72
2. *Pravacanasāra (Tattvadīpikā-vṛtti* by Amṛtacandra), p. 50
3. M.L. Mehta: *Jaina Psychology*, p. 112

the next moment, because he has comprehended all in the previous moment. This will be possible only when the objects and their cognitions are wiped out of existence the next moment. As the series of cognitions and objects extends infinitely, such a situation will never arise. Knowledge and feeling of aversion and love being two different manifestations of the soul, knowledge will not always be followed by them. Omniscience is generated only when the liability for such feelings completely ceases. Hence the question of the omniscient's being tainted by love and averson does not arise. The last question against the possibility of omniscience simply limits the span of discursive knowledge. It has nothing to do with the direct type of knowledge which advances in quite a different way from that of the indirect types. It is true that one cannot exhaust all the contents of the universe by one's sensuous and and perceptual types of knowledge; but it is also impossible to put a limit to the heights of knowledge the human beings may attain.

Self Consciousness

Omnicience being established the next problem is whether it will have the self also as its objects. On one hand if self is an exception to perfect knowledge, *kaivalya* loses its title. The nature of the Jaina theory of omnisicence implies that the self must know itself. Just as external things are known in terms of their attributes and modes, so also the self will be known in terms of its own attributes and modes. Maṇikyanandi observes: "The comprehension of the self takes place when consciousness is directed towards the self."[1] Such direction of consciousness will not be found to be impossible, if the self if taken as unity of its attributes and modes. Self consciousness must mean the consciousness of the attributes and modes of the self. It is vain to seek for the identity of the self, as distinct from the feeling of love or

1. Māṇikyanandin: *Parīkṣāmukhasūtra:* 1.6

hatred, as Hume did. According to Jaina philosophy, as we have seen, the soul is not absolutely distinct from its attributes and modes. Hence self consciousness must mean the consciousness of the soul's attributes and modes. The Mīmāṁsā School of Indian Philosophy, which divides itself into the Bhātta and Prabhākara schools, maintatins that the conception of self consciousness is untenable. The Bhātta thinks that, when we know an object, we are not conscious of the knowing self. The knowledge of the self is inferred from the knownness of a cognition. For the Prabhākara self consciousness is impossible, for the self cannot be the subject and the object of the same act of knowledge. The phenomenon of self consciousness may be interpreted in two ways. We must note that, from the analytical point of view self does not stand only for knowledge, it is much more than knowledge. So the conception of self consciousness yields two meanings. Firstly, it may mean the consciousness of the states of the self by the self's own cognitions. Secondly, it may also mean the comprehension of the cognitions themselves by the self. But such a comprehension must take place in terms of the modes of the knowledge-attribute. Hence self consiousness would mean the cognition of the cognitions themselves. The Nyāya school holds that cognitions are not known by themselves but by other cognitions. This is the first meaning of self consciousness. Psychology distinguished among emotions, cognitions and many other states of the psyche. The comprehension of its own emotions by the self does not present a difficulty. We can cognize our own emotions. If various capacities of the soul are recognized, this type of self consciousness becomes quite compatible. Expounding Śankara's view A.C. Mookerjee observes: "Self consciousness is the consciousness of the self as mediated through the conciousness of the objects, and as this mediation is impossible when there is no object, there is, consequently no consciousness in the absence of the objects."[1]

1. A.C. Mookejee: *Nature of Self,* p. 226

This is very likely to lead to the conclusion that self consciousness can exixt only as mediated or in terms or consciousness of its objects. Dr. Radhakrishnan has remarked: "We become aware of our own self, as we become aware of love or anger, directly by a sort of the identity with it.... Śaṅkara says that the self knowledge which is neither logical nor sensuous is the presupposition of every other kind of knowledge. It alone is beyond doubt, for it is of the essential nature of him who denies it."[1] The Jaina and Descartes both establish the existence of the self on the ground of self consciousness. Jean Paul Sarte thinks: "Consciousness then comes into existence as consciousness of something with awareness of this consciousness.... I am conscious of being a waiter because I am not only wholly and solely a waiter, but happen to get my existence by separation from a waiter, not a journalist, not a diplomat."[2] So our conclusion is that cognitions must be self conscious cognitions. The charge of infinite regress is generally levelled against the Nyāya view, because the series of cognitions, for their comprehension, must be extended infinitely. Some cognition must he held to be self conscious. If so, we fail to understand why the very first cognition should not be held to be self conscious. As regards the cognition of cognitions themselves Vidyānanda says: "If cognition is unconscious, how can it effect the consciousness about its object:"[3] Māṇikyanandi also holds: "Who does not think the comprehension, which makes us conscious about its objects, as conscious like a lamp"[4] Akalaṅka does not like to distinguish between the consciousness of an object and the consciousness of this consciousness.[5] The phenomenon of self consciousness is denied on the ground that the self cannot become its own object which is the meaning of self

1. S. Radhakrishnan: *An Idealistic View of Life,* p. 139
2. Blackham: *Six Existencialist Thinkers,* p. 112
3. Vidyānandin: *Tattvārthaślokavārtika,* 1.9.38
4. Māṇīkyanandin: *Parīkṣāmukha-sūtra,* 1.11.12
5. cf. Akalaṅka: *Rājavārtika,* 1.10.4

consciousness. Just as an acrobat cannot climb on his own shoulders, in the same way the self cannot know itself. The subject cannot accept itself as an object and so the soul also cannot became an object of its own knowing. We should remember that the above conclusion is based on an example which embodies only a partial truth. The Jaina holds that just as a lamp enlightens objects and itself simultaneously so also the soul comprehends the objects and itself at the same time.[1] The lamp does not require another lamp to enlighten itself, and this shows that the subject can become an object of itself. Knowledge is also an entity of a similar type, hence it must be held to enlighten itself and its objects. When enlightenment of itself and the objects is the very nature of the soul, consciousness as well as self consciousness must emerge as consequent functions. Prabhācandra says: "...nothing can be contradictory to its own nature or identity, or the enlightenment of the objects and itself must also be held contradictory."[2] We have to probe deep into the nature of the soul to see whether it contains anything which may obstruct self consciousness. No such obstruction is seen in the way of consciousness of the self in terms of its attributes and modes. On the contrary the Jaina is of opinion that "in knowng there is the comprehension of the subject, the instrument and the process like that of the object."[3]

However Vidyānanda distinguishes between two aspects of knowledge. He says: "If it is said that knowledge comprehends objects and the self by the same identical nature or *dharma,* then there will be the inconsistency of the activity in the self, for that which is knowable, i.e., the soul is held to be absolutely non-distinct from the knower. There is no fault for those who hold the non-absolute theory of distinction."[4] The idea is that if the soul is held to be

1. cf. Māṇikyanandin: *Parīkṣāmukha-sūtra,* 1.11
2. Prabhācandra: *Nyāya-kumuda-candrodaya,* p. 187
3. Māṇikyanandin: *Parikṣāmukha-sūtra,* 1.9
4. Vidyānandin: *Tattvārthaśloka-vārtika,* p. 125

absolutely a knower it cannot become an object of its own cognition. The Jaina thinks that a number of traits can be distinguished in the knowledge attribute as they are distinguished in a momentary mode. The cognition of the self and the cognition of the objects may be held to be due to two traits of the same mode of the knowledge attribute. Vidyānanda stresses the point that the traits determining self-consciousness and object-consciousness are different, and thus he saves the Jaina position from the inconsistency of the activity in the self. Prabacandra also maintains the same view and states: "From the view-point of comprehension there is no distinction between the nature of an entity and the entity itself. From the view-point of enlightening the self and other objects there is a distinction."[1] As a matter of fact self-consciousness and object-consciousness are the two aspects of the same cognition, and one implies the other. On this interpretation Akalaṅka's view of non-distinction between consciousness and self consciousness can be consistently held. When the self is the object of our knowledge, the subject and the object constitute one unity which would imply distinction in the region of traits.

1. Prabhācandra: *Nyāya-kumuda-candrodaya*, p. 189

Chapter 5

Structure of the Soul and Extension

Form of the Soul's Existence

The problem of the existence of the soul may be considered chiefly in two ways. Firstly, the soul may be thought to exist with its dimension, whether finite or infinite. This form of the soul's existence was generally upheld both in the east and the west. As regards the other form of the soul's existence the view is based on the concept that dimensions cannot be applied to it. This very problem takes another form when interpreted in terms of space. It becomes the problem of extension or inextension of the soul. The latter view is not as old as the former one. It appears that the theory of non-spatiality of mind did not develop till Descartes. In the east the idea of non-spatiality of that soul seems to have developed on its ubiquitous nature.

Meaning of Extension

Descartes distinguishes between the essential natures of the soul and matter. He holds that "extension solely belongs to matter, and consciousness is an exclusive quality of the soul. Extension and consciousness cannot coexist."[1] It is again said that "Extension is length, breadth and thickness, hence extension and space are identical."[2] We must remember that, while affirming extension of matter or soul, we mean that the dimensions belong to matter or the soul itself. The dimensions are intrinsic to the structure of the

1. Thilly: *A History of Philosophy*, p. 254
2. *Ibid.*, p. 253

substances which are measured by means of them. This measurement is expressed in terms which smell spatiality, and this is the only community between extension and space. A piece of matter is seen to occupy space. It means that what are called length, breadth and thickness belong to matter itself. In the same way if the soul is supposed to possess extension, extension must belong to the soul itself. Thus the theory of extension of the soul is not very much based on the theory of space. We are required to show that the features which extension implies are also seen in the structure of the soul. We may begin with extension in case of gross matter and go to its most highly attenuated forms. In case of the soul extension may be supposed to be subtler than that which could be conceived of the most attenuated form of matter. This is only a way of approach to the soul's extension and cannot give us an exact idea about it. Dealing with the Jaina view of extension it is observed: "It should be borne in mind, however, that a soul's occupying space simply means its presence in the different parts of space and not filling space like a body. A material body fills a part of space in such a way that while it is there, no matter can occupy it. But a soul's presence in a particular space does not prevent another soul's presence there; the two souls may be present at the same place, the Jainas point out, just as two lights can illumine the same area."[1] This distinction between the spiritual and the material extensions is only partially true as the Jaina holds that the capacity of offering resistance belongs only to a part of matter,[2] but in the present context the above account may be taken to be a satisfactory one because the souls offer resistance neither to matter nor to other souls. By affirming extension both of the soul and matter the Jaina emphasizes the fact that extension is a necessary implication of a substance. An atom of matter is said to be unextended, but by inextension the Jaina does not mean the negation of space-occupation

1. Chatterjee and Datta: *An Introduction to Indian Poilosophy,* p. 107
2. Kundakunda: *Pañcāstikāya,* verse, p. 7

but what he means is the space-occupation of the smallest possible magnitude. Inextension as an antithesis of extension will mean the non-existence of a substance. According to the Jaina no substance is without extension; it can, at most, be unextended in the above sense.

Extension in Case of Attributes

A substance is a unity of its attributes and modes. The constituents in a substance can be analysed and conceived as abstracted from their subtratum When matter with its attributes is considered as a substance, extension becomes one of its necessary accompaniments. When the attributes are considered in abstraction from the substance, the idea of extension loses its consistency. We can say that a piece of red cloth is four inches in length; but the statement that red as abstracted from cloth possesses a length becomes meaningless. Similarly in case of the soul, the substance responsible for the generation of consciousness is extended, while consciousness as abstracted from the substance of the soul refuses to enter into any spatial relation. We cannot say that a thought is to the right or to the left of some other entity, but the soul whose thought is meant can be characterized by such spatial relations. In this connection G.F. Stout remarks: "I would rather say that thinking and willing as such do not themselves enter into spatial relations, and I would say the same of perception and appetite, and of desiring and imagining. Subjective processes including all forms and processes of feeling, attention and conation are not themselves extended, do not occupy places, do not stand in relation of position, distance and direction relatively to each other or anything else"[1] The abstractive process of thinking has a similar effect both on the soul and matter. It is only in a derivative sense that a quality can be said to be extended.

---

1. G.F. Stout: *Mind and Matter*, p. 158

Extension and the Mental Structure of the Purposivist School of Psychology

For the Jaina the ideas of substance and extension do not seem to be incompatible. The soul as a substance must be held to possess extension. Hence where extension is denied of the soul, its substantiality is also questioned. The Yogācāra may assign no extension to cognitions, because there is no idea of substance behind his cognitions. But the purposivist school of psychology marks an advance on the Yogācāra position by introducing the concept of the structure of the self. Mc Dougall thinks: "I believe that the mind has a nature and a structure and functions of its own which cannot be fully and adequately described in terms of structure of the brain and physical process."[1] Again it is said: "Mental structure is that enduring, growing frame work of mind which we observe from its observed manifestations in experience and behaviour."[2] The mind in the purposivist school of psychology is not only a group of functions, but it implies a structure. The physical functions are the manifestations of the mental structure. Thus there is a dualism of structure and functions in purposive psychology. On one hand we see that the principle of the psyche is distinguished in structural, functional and temporal aspects; and thus is brought very close to the substance of the soul; while on the other hand its difference from the substance of the soul is maintained by affirming non-spatiality of it. Thus the position of the purposivist school lies between the views of the Saṁvedanādvaita of Buddhism and the substance-view of the soul.

Criticism of the Above View

Jainism conceives every entity in its four aspects termed collectively as the '*Svacatuṣṭaya*'. They are the structural, the functional, the temporal and the spatial ones. Psychology

1. Mc Dougall: *An Qutline of Abnormal Psychology*, p. 48
2. *Ibid.*, p. 41

in-case of its psyche, accepts the first three, and drops the last one. It must do so, because its structure has not yet attained the status of a substance. In this respect it adheres to the abstractive process of thinking. The process of abstraction takes place in such a way that the former abstractions look like facts of structure with respect to the latter ones. When our vision is limited to such abstractions only, the question of their spatiality does not arise. The complexes and dispositions themselves are the functions of some entity behind them, and, hence, in themselves, they cannot be held to be spatial. The mental structure which is based on complexes and dispositions must also be non-spatial. These abstractions must be ultimately dependent upon something substantially true. This substantial reality is the very foundation upon which the entire edifice of the mental structure is built. Just as the principle of *vāsanā* was reduced to the principle of the soul, so the principle of unity and integration of the mental structure must get transformed into the substance of the soul to provide a solid foundation for psychology. The position concerning the psyche which Mc Dougall has developed suggests the fourth aspect of the *svacatuṣṭaya* of Jainism. Spatiality or possession of some magnitude is a necessary implication of existence which, in terms of Jaina philosophy, is a compendium of origination, decay and permanence, the characteristic of a substance. We have already seen that psychology has to presume something substantial like the psychoplasm as a substrate for the elements of the mental structure. This substrate being recognized that truth of the self or the soul with its spatiality follows like a corollary.

Nyāya, Sāṁkhya and Vedānta on the Soul's Extension and Their Criticism

The *ātman* of the Nyāya and the *puruṣa* of the Sāṁkhya schools are all-pervasive categories. By this they must mean their presence everywhere in the universe. This can never mean a negation of extension in the soul, but on the contrary it is a clear admission of an infinite magnitude of the soul. A substantial reality must possess a finite or an infinite magnitude. Advaita Vedānta never aims to deny extension at all the levels of existence. Extension is affirmed of the objects, though at a lower level. It must be affirmed of the subject at the same level, because one individual becomes an object with respect to another individual. Thus Advaita Vedānta only partially opposes the view of an extended soul. The idea of one grand soul suggests more of an infinite dimension than inextension of the *Brahma.* Sometimes it is said that from the transcendental view-point *Brahma* is a spaceless entity. In this connections A.C. Mukerjee supports Śaṅkara's view and maintains that "Objects of knowledge have temporal determinations, but that for which these temporal relations have a meaning cannot be in time. It is in this sense an eternal presence."[1] Following the same chain of reasoning it can be added that the objects of knowledge have spatial determinations, but that for which these spatial relations have a meaning cannot be in space. It is in this sense a universal presence. Thus the timelessness and spacelessness of *Brahma* is maintained only from the transcendental view-point. The same argument may be further extended as 'The objects of knowledge have structural and functional determinations, but that for which these determinations have a meaning cannot itself have a structure and a function.' In this way not only temporarity, spatiality, structure and function is denied of *Brahma,* but in the same breath even existence can also be denied of it. Actually speaking the argument does not lead to Advaita Vedānta's absolutism of *Brahma* but to nihilism. The neti (not this) of *Brahmādvaita* never means that there is nothing positive in *Brahma. Brahma* to be positively something must be a substance, though an unchanging one. Then spatiality must be affirmed of it, though it may be an infinite spatiality.

If the soul is held to be extended, then the problem is what magnitude can be consistently assigned to it. Generally

---

1. A.C. Mukherjee: *Nature of Self. p. 133*

three answers have been given to the question. The Nyāya and the Sāṅkya hold the soul to be of infinite magnitude. For Rāmānuja and the Bhāṭṭa Mīmāṁsaka it is infinitely small. The Jaina view stands between the aforesaid two extremes. Nemicandra says: "The *Jīva* is coeval with the body it inhabits."[1] As the physical body is changeable, so the size of the soul must be held to be variable. Prabhācandra observes: "The soul is felt as I in the forms, I aṃ happy, I am sad and I know a *ghaṭa* (pot)' in the organism itself, not in the organisms of others, or in the intermediate space."[2] Yośovijaya also states: "The soul is coeval with the body, because its qualities are seen as pervading the body."[2] Individual consciousness is seen bound with the organism and is due to the presence of the soul in it. So the soul must be held equally extensive with the body. The mundane existence of the soul is determined by its association with the *karma-śarīra* which is coeval with the soul. The soul, the *karma-śarīra* and the physical body must all be held of the same magnitude. The extension of the soul beyond the physical organism seems to be superfluous, for no consciousness whatsoever is experienced outside the organism. According to Rāmānuja "the all pervasive nature of the soul which the Upaniṣads describe cannot, therefore, be taken, in the literal sense. The real sense of the pervasiveness of the soul is that the soul is so subtle (*sūkṣma*) that it can penetrate every unconscious material substance."[4] Akalaṅka has also observed: The soul is coeval with the body, it is not only knowledge. From the view point of knowledge it is all pervasive, it is not all pervasive absolutely."[5] If the soul is held to be extending outside the body, then consciousness must be felt there; but such a conclusion is not confirmed by our experience. If it is held

1. Nemicandra: *Drayasaṅgraha,* verse p. 2
2. Prabhācandra: *Prameya-kamala-mārtaṇḍa,* p. 171
3. Yośovijaya: *Nyāyāloka,* p. 49
4. Chatterjee and Datta: *An Introduction to Indian Philosophy,* p. 484.
5. Akalaṅka: *Svarūpasambodhana,* verse 5.

that the part of the soul coextensive with the body becomes conscious and the rest remains unconscious, then the unity of the soul and experience becomes inexplicable. This view leads to not only the divisions of one continuous substance of the soul, but reduces a part of the soul to an unconscious entity.

Almost the very criticism may be given against the view of atomic extension of the soul. The only advantage of the two extreme views is that they are free from the difficulty of assigning variable magnitudes to the soul. The Jaina has to face this difficulty. His general solution in the words of Umāsvāti is that "the *jīvas* take a variable magnitude by expansion and contraction of the *pradeśas*."[1] The Jaina presupposes a capacity for expansion and contraction in the soul. It is on account of this capacity that the soul is able to contract and expand.

Some Objections Against the Jaina View of the Soul's Extension

The above explanation as given by the Jaina creates newer difficulties. Dr. Radhakrishnal remarks: "According to Śaṅskara the hypothesis of the soul having the same size as its body is untenable, for, from its being limited by the body, it would follow that the soul, like the body, is also impermanent, it would have no final release....We may grossly conceive the soul as capable of becoming bigger or smaller by addition or substraction of parts. New particles will be constantly carried in and old particles will be getting out, so that we can never be sure that the same soul continues for any length of time."[2] From another angle of vision the same difficulty has been pointed out by Sushilkumar Maitra. He observes: "If it be said that the soul is capable of contraction and expansion like the light of a lamp, then it will follow that the soul is susceptible of

1. Umāsvāti: *Tattvārtha-sūtra,* 5.17
2. S. Radhakrishnan: *Indian Philosophy,* vol. I, p. 311

modification and is non-eternal, which will strike at the very root of the Law of *karma,* so that merit will go unrewarded and demerit unpunished."[1] Mainly the criticism is against the soul's capacity for cortradiction and expansion. We should remember that for contraction and expansion subtraction and addition of particles is not the only way, they can take place by a process of interpenetration and mutual extirpation of parts—a theory which the Jaina propounds. The number of *pradeśas* or the supposed units, in the constitution of a soul, is constant,[2] and the magnitude of the soul varies not by diminution or addition of the *pradeśas* but by their interpenetration and mutual extirpation. Such a criticism can be justly levelled against the complex-theory of the self, because the mental structure endures by an addition or a subtraction of the complexes. This charge against the Jaina theory is not a novel one. Akalaṅka observes: "If the soul possesses a capacity for contraction and expansion, it becomes impermanent. It is not so, because from the view-point of expansion and contraction as modes generated by the *karma-śarīrī* the soul may be held to be impermanent."[3] Again he writes "If on account of parts the soul is held to be mortal, it is not so because the soul does not leave its immaterial nature."[4] In the process of contraction the *pradeśas* or the parts of the soul penetrate each other and in expansion the process is reversed. Thus there is no addition to or subtraction from the structure of the soul, and the substance of the soul is perfectly saved. Still there is some change in its modal aspects. The non-absolute philosophy of the Jaina can well maintain, the permanence of the soul's substance through its functional variations. This situation does not present a moral difficulty. If the soul were held absolutely permanent, there would have been no action for moral judgement. If the soul were absolutely impermanent, merit must have gone unrewarded and

1. S.K. Maitra: *Fundamentals of Indian Metaphysics and Logic,* p. 99
2. Umāsvāti: *Tattvārtha-sūtra,* 5.8.
3. Akalaṅka: *Rājavārtika,* p. 458
4. *Ibid.,* 5.16.4

demerit unpunished. These are the difficulties of the absolute systems of philosophy. The Jaina, being a non-absolute thinker, is able to steer clear of the extreme positions. From the substance view-point the continuity of the soul is maintained and from the modal point of view change and actions are made possible.

Dr. J.N. Sinha interprets the Jaina theory of the soul's extension in such a way that the soul cannot be said to be extended or unextended. He observes: "The soul is a spiritual principle. So it is non-spatial or un-extended. But it is considered to be an extensive substance (*astikāya*) because it illumines the whole body with its consciousness like the light of a lamp which illumines the whole room which it occupies. The soul has no physical expansion. It has spiritual manifestation. It pervades the whole of body by spiritual manifestation. Just as a piece of red ruby placed in a cup of milk imparts its lustre to the milk, so the soul residing in a body imparts its consciousness to the whole body."[1] The last sentence of the above quotation appears to embody the contents of a verse from Kundakunda's *Pañcāstikāya*.[2] Kundakunda never means that the soul is an unextended substance. On the other hand he clearly admits extension of the soul in the same work.[3] It is wrong to hold that the soul is said to be extended on account of its association with the body. Nemicandra is of opinion that extension has been affirmed of matter only in a derivative sense, because the atoms of matter possess the minimum extension.[4] We may distinguish between the extensions of a soul and a molecule of matter, but such a distinction cannot lead to the inextension of the soul. Jainism is quite definite in assigning extension to the soul, and we cannot agree with the view of the above critic that "Jainism is undecided as to spatiality or non-spatiality of the soul"[5]

---

1. J.N. Sinha: *A History of Indian Philosophy,* Vol. II, p. 236
2. Kundakunda: *Pañcāstikāya,* verse 33
3. *Ibid.,* verse 109
4. Cf. Nemicandra: *Dravyasaṅgraha,* verse 26
5. J.N. Sinha: *A History of Indian Philosophy,* Vol. II., p. 221

Conception of Pradeśas in the Soul

We have seen that the Jaina is able to solve the difficulty regarding contraction and expansion of the soul by introducing the concept of *pradeśas* or units of the soul. "A *pradeśa* means that extension of space which is occupied by an atom."[1] Hence a *pradeśa* of the *Jiva* means a soul-unit occupying a *pradeśa* of space. It is also held that a *Jiva* is one substance.[2] Hence the difficulty is how a *Jiva* can have *pradeśas* and be one substance at the same time. Akalaṅka solves the difficulty in two ways. Firstly he holds that the soul being a partless entity, the conception of *pradeśas* in the structure of the soul is only concessional.[3] Actually speaking there are no such units in the soul; but for the sake of measuring its extension they are supposed in it. Such parts in the soul's extension can be distinguished with respect to various units of dimensions like a distance which can be measured in terms of miles, furlongs, yards, etc., without disturbing its unity. Secondly it is also affirmed that the conception of *pradeśas* in the soul is not concessional, i.e., such *pradeśas* are there in the *Jiva*.[4] An extended substance must admit of a distinction among its *pradeśas*. Without such a distinction extension itself becomes meaningless. The partlessness of the soul is suggestive of its perfect unity, but, being an extended substance, it must admit of a distinction among its parts. The latter aspects of the soul enables us to give an explanation of the process of contraction and expansion of the substance of the soul. Contraction takes place by interpenetration of the soul's *pradeśas* and expansion in the same way, takes place by a process reverse of the former up to a maximum where interpenetration is totally absent.

1. Akalaṅka: *Rājavārtika*, 5.8.4
2. Umāsvāti: *Tattvārtha-sūtra*, 5.6
3. Akalaṅka: *Rājavārtika*, 5.8.10
4. *Ibid.*, 5.8.11

Conclusion

According to the Jaina theory of substance not only the soul but all the substances must have some extension, finite, infinite or atomic. Inextension does not imply negation of extension, for that would mean non-existence; but it means an extension of an infinitely small dimension. Mere subsistence cannot do. It is meaningless whithout presuming existence which is conceived in its four aspects, i.e., the structural, the functional the temporal and the spatial. Extension becomes a necessary accompaniment of existence. Variability of a soul's magnitude, which is perceived through the variability of the organism of the living beings, can be explained only by affirming extension of the soul.

The Jaina theory of the soul requires that the soul must be one substance and, at the same time, must be distinguishable in respect of its *pradeśas.* We are to see whether the Jaina has been able to combine the above two conceptions into one i.e., the conception of the soul. As a substance the soul is one, but the *pradeśas* are the divisions of the substance of the soul. If the soul units are admitted in the structure of the soul, it will become composite. The soul-units will have to be granted a status of distinct substances which will lead to the difficulty of the unity of consciousness. So the substance of the soul must be one and continuously extended. Then, as the Jaina must mean, the soul-units must be an ascription made with some standpoint in view. The soul-units are meant to measure the magnitude of the substance of the soul. We have seen that the soul's capacity for contraction and expansion leads to interpenetration of the soul-units. This means that the conception of the soul-units may also be taken as a measure of the density of the soul's substance. When the same soul is said to occupy organisms of varying magnitudes without any diminution from or addition to its substance, its density must be held to be varying. Dr. Umesh has pointed out that the soul of the Jaina has not been able to get rid of the material associations which the Jaina affirms by admitting *pradśas,* and hence parts, in the soul.[1] The idea of the density[2] of the soul must be taken by him as contributing towards the same inconsistency. We have distinguished between spiritual and material extensions, and in the same way spiritual density must be distinguished from the material one. If a substance is extended its density also becomes a necessary accompaniment. The extension and the density of the soul's substance may be held to vary approximately in the inverse ratio. These very facts have led Akalaṅka to admit that the soul-units may be held to be real but they never imply the division of the soul's substance.

---

1. Umesh: *Bhāratīya darśana,* (Hindi) *p. 132*
2. The term 'density' when used in case of the soul seems to be inappropriate, as it is very closely connected with material bodies. Where the theory of interpenetration of matter is not accepted, affinity of atoms in the rigid body is taken to be the meaning of its density. But were the above theory is upheld density will also refer to the copresence of the atoms at the same space point. Spiritual density, according to the Jaina theory means the compresence of the soul-units, because the soul is a continuous substance. This meaning of density well applies to the spiritual dentity, as the souls contract by interpenetration of their *pradeśas.*

Chapter 6

Bliss as an Attribute of the Soul

Statement of the Problem

No psychic act can be said to be purely cognitive, conative or affective. It shows all the three characteristics simultaneously with the allowance that it may be dominated by one or the other. A psychic act, thus, is a unity of cognition, conation and affection. This is the synthetic view of a psychic act. But, when an analytic view-point is adopted, the distinction among the various constituents of a psychic act must have a meaning. Just as conation (*darśana*) is distinguished from cognition (*jñāna*) on the attributive level, so also affection must be distinguishable at the same level. Now the problem is whether feeling or affection stands parallel to cognition or it is an aspect of cognition.

Feeling as Distinguished from Cognition

In our own experience the states of feeling and cognition are clearly distinguished. "If I were merely a thinking being, if my soul were not somehow intimately conjoined with my body, I should, for example, know that I am hungry, but not feel hungry."[1] Knowledge of hunger and feeling of hunger are different and distinct from each other. At this stage we do not want to consider how feeling is generated. It will be sufficient for our purpose if we are able to draw a distinction between cognition and feeling. It is possible that we may have a cognition of a feeling and a feeling about a cognition; but this cannot establish the identity of the two. The very

---

1. Thilly: *A History of Philosophy*, p. 256

fact that a feeling is cognized and a cognition can be left proves the separate identity of the two. "Feeling is an intermediate state of consciousness that occurs between cognition and conation. It is related to both knowledge and will. On one hand, cognition serves as the stimulus for feeling, while on the other, feeling stimulates will. In a different way, feeling can be considered as the effect of cognition, and at the same time as the cause of conation."[1] The conception of sense-feeling does not at all identify it with sensuous perception on the ground of the community of the instrumentality of senses. The senses, as the Jaina recognizes, are not only the instruments of cognition; but they are also the instruments of conation. They can also be held to be the instruments of affection. Just as the sensuous and perceptual types of knowledge must be tied to the given directly or indirectly, so also "the physical and mental pleasures are both of the sensory type, they depend on the functioning of the senses or on the recollections of the functioning of the senses. The same is the case with pain. It is either actual or imagined, that is, the product of memory or imagination in a train of thought. Beyond the senses neither pleasure nor pain is able to extend."[2] Knowledge and feeling differ in their appearance also. Feeling appears in the form of pleasure or pain while knowledge appears in the form of experience of an object. Feeling is the object of liking or disliking as the case may be, knowledge in its pure state is above these subjective considerations."[3] Thus feeling is a distinct phase of mental life, and it must have some structural truth behind it. It means that the affective manifestations of the self must be determined by some dispositions lying in the structure of the self. To use Jaina terminology the soul must have some capacity to bring about the affective manifestations, just as the cognitive manifestations are determined by the knowing capacity of the soul.

---

1. M.L. Mehta: *Jaina Psychology*, p. 113
2. C.R. Jain: *Jaina Psychology*, p. 26
3. Indracandra: *Epistemology of Jaina Āgamas*, p. 211

Bliss as an Attribute in the Structure of the Soul (Rājamalla's View)

The Jaina thinkers seem to be divided into two groups as regards the indentity of the affective faculty of the soul. Rājamalla says, "In the soul there is a self-established and immortal attribute of bliss. Being disturbed by the destructive type of *karmas* it has become invisible....It is true that the *jīva* has the attribute of bliss like the attributes of cognition, etc. It becomes disturbed in the form of pain on account of the operation of eight kinds of *karmas*."[1] He also denies the thesis that bliss is an attribute of other attributes like knowledge, because the *Tattvārtha-sūtra* says that the attributes inhere in the substances, but in themselves they do not have any other attribute."[2] "Undisturbed bliss is the power of the *jīva* inhering in its substance. Its disturbance is due to the destructive type of *karmas*."[3] "Pain as a whole taking place in a moment is also thought to be a disturbed manifestation of the attribute of bliss."[4] Herein the writer seems to be very explicit in affirming bliss as a distinct attribute of the soul. Pain and pleasure arise on account of the soul's association with the *karmas*. This attribute of bliss when left to itself, produces what C.R. Jain designates as spititual pleasure. Now we are able to appreciate the use of the term '*sukha*' or bliss in the sense of feeling by the Jaina writers. Devasena in his Ālāpa-paddhati also enumerates bliss as a special attribute of the *jīva*.[5] This very attribute takes the form of pleasure or pain, when disturbed by the *karmic* agencies. Aurobindo remarks: "Pleasure can become pain or pain pleasure, because in their secret reality they are the same thing differently reproduced in the sensation and emotion."[6] Thus the faculty of bliss is the same as the

1. Rājamalla: *Pañcādhyāyī*, II, verses 313 and 1107
2. *Ibid.*, verses, 1105 and 1106
3. *Ibid.*, verse 327
4. M.C. Jain: *Tattvārtha Cintāmaṇi*, I, p. 412
5. Devasena: *Alāpapaddhati*, p. 33
6. Aurobindo: *The Divine Life*, p. 339

faculty of feeling, the nomenclature being borrowed from the free manifestations of the mentioned faculty.

Bliss as Non-Distinct from Knowledge

(Views of Akalaṅka, Amṛtacandra, Jayasena and Śrutasāgara Sūri)

Akalaṅka holds that bliss is identical with knowledge.[1] Amṛtacandra Sūri observes that bliss and knowledge are the nature of the soul, and bliss is non-distinct from knowledge.[2] Jayasena comments: "The material cause of the infinite bliss, which is desirable from all points of view, is the simultaneously all-comprehensive perfect knowledge; and the sensuous knowledge, being incapable of simultaneously apprehending all its objects, is not the caue of bliss."[3] Śrutasāgara Sūri admits very clearly the non-distinct identity of bliss from knowledge and conation. He says: "Bliss is a mode of knowledge and conation, hence it is not destroyed (in the liberated state)."[4] The distinction of bliss from knowledge may be conceived in two ways. Firstly they are mutually distinct as attributes of the soul—a view held by the author of the *Pañcādhyāyī*. Secondly bliss and knowledge can be distinguished as implications of the same attribute. The view that establishes the identity of bliss and knowledge must distinguish them at least as traits of the same attribute or mode. The view of Śrutasāgara Sūri is the most startling one, as it admits bliss as the mode of two attributes, i.e., conation and knowledge.

Criticisn of the above Views

We may begin our criticism with a consideration of Śrutasāgara's view. He must mean that some modes of

1. Akalaṅka: *Rājavārtika,* p. 642
2. Amṛtacandra: *Tattvadīpikāvṛtti of Pravacanasāra,* pp. 27 and 69
3. Jayasena: *Tātparyavṛtti of Pravacansāra, p. 74*
4. Śrutasāgara: *Tattvārtha-vṛtti*, p. 320

conation and knowledge are forms of bliss, while others are cognitive and conative. As a mode of the same attribute conation and bliss or cognition and bliss cannot be copresent. This will lead to the breach of the series of conations and cognitions—a position which is contradictory to the Jaina conception of reality. Hence to call bliss a mode of conation or cognition is not a tenable view. The other writers are not so clear as Śrutasāgara Sūri in this respect. Hence the only alternative left is that bliss may be admitted as a trait of the manifestaions of the knowledge attribute. We have already shown that there is a distinction between feeling and cognition. Moreover the disproportionate co-existence of bliss and knowledge suggests that bliss and knowledge are not determined by the same faculty of the soul. It seems reasonable that a distinct faculty must be postulated to determine the affective manifestations of the soul. The author of the *Pañcādhyāyī* expresses his view as 'The non-distinction of pleasure and pain from knowledge is also not unproved, for pleasure and pain, being conscious, are not found elsewhere expect with knowledge."[1] Bliss and cognition may be looked upon as identical from some point of view, but their identity as a single attribute is not consistent. Rājamalla has once accepted the distinction between knowledge and bliss at the attributive level, so he cannot establish their identity at the same level. We have seen that consciousness is a general implication of the special attributes of the soul. Knowledge, conation, bliss all are conscious attributes and for this reason they cannot be held to be identical. Taking a synthetic view of the self not only bliss is identical with knowledge as held by Akalaṅka, Amṛtacandra and Jayasena, or it is identical with knowledge and conation both as held by Śrutasāgara Sūri; but all of them can be held identical with one another and ultimately forming one unity wherein these attributes can be distinguished. The Jaina, being a non-absolute thinker, will easily accommodate all these views, but he has to assign

1. Rājamalla: *Pañcādhyāyī*, II, verse 14

proper contexts and levels to make his view difinite and consistent. Hence we are in a position to conclude that feeling is due to a distinct faculty of the soul. This faculty is responsible for the generation of the states of pleasure, pain and bliss.

Pleasure and Pain as Manifestation of the Faculty of Feeling

Pleasure and pain are not the natural manifestations of the substance of the soul. They are the distorted and limited forms of the soul's capacity for feeling. This distortion and limitation, as the Jaina thinks cannot be self-caused. There must be something other than the self to generate the states of pain and pleasure. This would mean that pleasure and pain presuppose some alien agency for their generation. The Jaina conceives the agency of the *karmas* for this purpose. "The blissful manifestations of the soul disappear being disturbed by the destructive types of *karmas*."[1] "The attribute of bliss takes the perverted form on account of the eight kinds of *karmas*."[2] Just as sensuous and perceptual types of knowledge are not natural manifestations of the soul and are caused by the destuction-subsidence of the *karmic* energies, so also pleasure and pain stand on the same level requiring destruction-subsidence of some *karmic* energies for their generation. This *karmic* agency distorts the feeling faculty so as to give rise to the states of pleasure or pain. Environmental factors occupy the same position as in case of sensuous or perceptual knowledge. This necessitates the instrumentality of senses in the process of affection. Senses are channels not only of cognition but also of conation and affection. The physical senses work as pieces of apparatus for receiving the stimuli. The soul is trebly prepared to receive them with its faculties of conation, cognition and

1. Rājamalla: *Pañcādhyāyī*, II, verse 313
2. *Ibid.*, verse 1107

affection. Just as the perceptual knowledge is tied to the given or presupposes the sensuous knowledge, so also the sense feeling must be there so as to give rise to emotional types of feeling.

The Distortion of The Faculty of Feeling by Karmas

The author of the Pañcādhyāyī accepts, at one place, the agency of all the eight kinds of *karmas* and, at another place, only of the four destructive kinds of *karmas* for the generation of pain and pleasure.[1] It is also admitted in the Jaina scriptures that omniscient lord attains infinite bliss in the presence of the four non-destructive types of *karmas.* This appears to contradict one of the aforesaid statements. Let us suppsoe that all the *karmas* are obstructive to the manifestation of the faculty of bliss. Then, how can the omniscient lord be said to attain infinite bliss, when four types of *karmas* still cling to his soul? Infinite bliss cannot exist along with pleasurable and painful feelings. To say that pleasurable and painful feelings are there, but the lord is not deluded by them does not seem to be a consistent interpretation of facts. Feeling, as painful and pleasurable, is a state which is not immune from delusion. Feeling and delusion go together, except when feeling assumes a natural form in the absence of the agency of the deluding *karmas.* "The Jaina doctrine of *karma* does not give any explanation as to why the omniscient who is free from all attachment and aversion, does not give up all suffering and happiness. Because of the presence of his physical body he has to suffer or enjoy is not a satisfactory answer, inasmuch as despite the presence of the body he does not cognise through the media of the physical organs so also he may not experience any feeling.... Moreover the concealed cause of all pleasantness and unpleasantness is in the shape of passions and emotions. In the absence of passions and

1. Rājamalla: *Pañcādhyāyī*, verses 327 and 1107

emotions, pleasure and pain have no meaning."[1] Nemicandra observes; "Because in the omniscient lord attachment, aversion, and knowledge depending on senses are destroyed, he does not suffer from the sense generated pleasure or pain caused by the operation of *sātā-vedaniya* (pleasure-generting *karma)* or *asātāvedanīya* (pain-generating *karma)*."[2] Then the problem is whether all the types of *karmas* or the destructive ones only are responsible for the distortion of the faculty of feeling.

Vedanīya and Mohanīya Karmas together Generate Pleasure and Pain

Akalaṅka says: "The sātā-vedanīya type of *karma* brings about the attainment of the bodily and the mental pleasures in the states of life like the celestial one by its operation. That whose fruition is of the form of many kinds of pain is due to the *asātā vedanīya*."[3] This clearly means that the *vedanīya* type of *karma* plays a very important part in the generation of the phenomenon of feeling. The omniscient lord has not been able to shed off the *vedanīya* type of *karma*. Then why should we not presume the existence of painful or pleasurable feeling in the omniscient lord? The position is explained by making the function of the *vedanīya karma* dependent upon that of the other *karmas* specially the *mohanīya* (deluding) one. The identity of the *vedanīya karma* has been explained as "the *vedanīya karma* disturbs the *jīva* like a destructive type of *karma* on account of the power of the *mohanīya karma*."[4] The feeling determining *karma* in itself is not very destructive to the faculty of bliss, but, when supported by the deluding *karma* it works like a destructive kind of *karma* producing the feelings of pain and pleasure. We are to find out some reason for the strange identity of

1. M.L. Mehta: *Jaina Psychology*, p. 114
2. Nemicandra: *Gommaṭasāra* (*Karmakāṇḍa*), verse 273
3. Akalaṅka: *Rājavārtika*, 8.81 and 2
4. Nemicandra: *Gommaṭasāra* (*Karmakāṇḍa*), verse 19

the *vedanīyas karma* which causes its enumeration once among the destructive *karmas* and then also among the non-destructive *karmas.* The reason seems to be purely a psychological one. If an attitude of liking or disliking is absent, the self will not accept the things as objects of feeling. As these attitudes are determined by the deluding *karma,* the *vedanīya karma* must presuppose the *mohanīya karma,* for its function, and in the absence of the latter the former must become quite ineffective. This makes the generation of pleasure and pain dependent upon two kinds of *karmas,* i.e., the *vedanīya* and the *mohanīya.*

Both Destructive and Non-Destructive Types of Karmas as Responsible for Generation of Pleasure and Pain

We have still to find out reasons why the four destructive *karmas* and also all the eight *karmas* have been said to distort the faculty of feeling. In producing the feelings of pain and pleasure the *vedanīya karma* has a direct hand, but its nature is such as it becomes ineffective in the adsence of the *mohanīya karma.* This accounts for the presence of infinite bliss even when the *vedanīya karma* has not been totally eradicated. At the same time all the *karmas* have a negative effect upon the soul, each of them brings about some sort of impairment of the soul. In the presence of the deluding *karma* all the eight *karmas* contribute towards the distortion of the soul's capacity for feeling. It is why no one partcular *karma* has been assigned this function. It is in this sense that all the eight *karmas* have been said to obscure the faculty of feeling. From this it also follows that in the absence of the *mohanīya karma* no distortion of the feeling faculty of the soul is possible. The destructive types of *karmas* bring about an impairment of a serious type, and the *mohanīya karma* is included in this group. The knowledge-obscuring and the conation-obscuring *karmas* hit directly some of the most important attributes of the soul. When their function is reinforced by the deluding *karma,* the impairment of bliss takes very serious forms. When such serious impairments of bliss are concerned we may hold the view that only the destructive types of *karmas* are said to obscure the faculty of feeling. The *mohanīya* and other kinds of *karmas* cause the various impaired manifestations of the soul. The potency of the *vedanīya karma* lies in the fact that it generates the feeling of pleasure and pain in respect of the above referred manifestations. Again it is said that in order to attain *kevalajñāna* the deluding *karma* is first destroyed, and, then, allowing an interval of time though very short, the remaining three destructive *karmas* are simultaneously destroyed."[1] This allows a stage where the deluding *karma* is absent while the other destructive *karmas* are present. As the *vedanīya* is ineffective in the absence of the *mohanīya,* infinite bliss must result in this-stage also. The truth of this conclusion seems to be affirmed nowhere, but it follows from the order of destruction of *karmas* as held by Umāsvāti, so either we should accept the presence of bliss in this stage or find out some causes for lower types of its manifestation. As regards the obscuration of the faculty by the *karmas,* it is not to be seen there because *mohanīya karma* has been eradicated and the other *karmas* have become ineffective (only with respect to the faculty of feeling) on account of the absence of the deluding *karma.* Still the Jaina is not prepared to accept the presence of infinite bliss in this stage. The situation may be explained as follows. The destructive type of faith appears much earlier than the dawn of perfect knowledge, and gradually goes on being perfected. Its imperfection in earlier stages is not due to the faculty of faith but is caused by the imperfect knowledge, to which faith must be applied. In the same way the imperfection of bliss in the above referred stage is also due to the non-attainment of perfect knowledge. It is in this sense also that the destructive *karmas* are held to be obstructive to the manifestations of bliss. Thus we come to the conclusion that all the eight *karmas,* the four destructive *karmas* or the *vedanīya karma* when supported by the *mohanīya*

1. Cf. Akalaṅka: *Rājavārtika*, 10.1,1

karma are responsible for the generation of pleasure and pain.

Bliss as an Unobstructed Manifestation of the Faculty of Feeling

In the perfect stage where obstructions due to *karmas* are totally eliminated, the soul does not accept the instrumentality of the senses. So the faculty of feeling also becomes free from sensuous dependence and associations. Feeling then advances by itself and is the maximum enjoyment of the unobstructed manifestations of the soul's faculties. It is the realization of the soul by itself in respect of *ānanda* or the bliss attribute. Bliss must be different from the feelings of mundane souls, and in this sense we can say that the emancipated souls neither enjoy pleasure nor suffer pain. If a faculty of feeling were absent in the soul, the states of pleasure and pain would also have been impossible. Pure bliss, pleasure and pain all agree in being states of feeling. The presence of pleasure and pain in the lower stages presupposes some alien disturbances in the soul. Pleasure and pain are said to be posivive states only because they are based on a positive faculty of the soul. This is why the Jaina does not agree with the Naiyāyika and the Sāṁkhya who hold a total cessation of feeling in the stage of liberation. He agrees with Advaita Vedānta in this respect, because it holds the supreme soul to be existent, conscious and blissful. While dealing with Advaita Vedānta it is said, "The fleeting pleasures which we have in wakeful and in dream can be understood as the fragmentary manifestation of the joy or bliss which forms the esssence of the self"[1] We also see in the philosophy of Ranade that bliss does not take only a dominant position in the absolute but existence and consciousness are reduced to the status of mere means for the attainment of bliss. Existence and consciousness are not found idependently of bliss. In Ranade's philosophy

1. Chatterjee and Datta: *An Introduction to Indian Philosophy*, p. 459

emphasis is laid on bliss which includes existence and consciousness.[1] It may be taken to mean that bliss is a distinct element in the soul's structure, but it cannot lead to the negation of other elements. Really speaking the soul is a plurality of such faculties and negation of anyone of them will not be its faithful description. The Jaina cannot reduce bliss to knowledge or vice versa merely on the ground that the two are seen together. The reduction or inclusion of any one faculty of the soul into any other should be taken to mean the dominance of the latter over the former which a system of discourse may require. Bliss as a faculty of feeling is present both in the mundane souls and the liberated ones.

1. Sangama Lal Pandey: *Ranade kā Tattvadarśana, (Hindi)* Allahabad University, 1958

Chapter 7
Plurality of Souls

Statement of the Problem

The problem of plurality of souls may be considered in its two aspects. Just as the truth of consciousness on its functional side is not disputed, so also the truth of plurality of souls on the functional side should not be questioned. No two persons feel as one. Not only the physiological structures of two persons are seen distinct, but also their mental structures repel each other. Plurality of souls or centres of conciousness like consciousness itself, is a fact of our experience. Every system of philosophy has to accommodate and explain the concept of the plurality of souls. Lord Haldane rightly remarks: "The self that knows is distinguished from other selves by the details of experience, by its own peculiar surroundings, by its history, by contents stored in memory, of which it is aware if they are reflected on and so made an object for its thinking.... What is it that makes me and my friend and animals separate animals? It is our own separate organism and their histories and their individual experience."[1] The Jaina is of opinion that the souls are not only functionally distinct, but they are so structurally as well. In other words, for the Jaina, the substance of one soul is not identical with that of any other soul. It is mainly on the basis of the individual experience that the individuality of the souls is admitted.

1. Haldane: *Reign of Relativity*, p. 151

The Naīyāyika and the Sāṅkhya on the Pluratity of Souls

The Nyāya and the Sāṁkhya schools of Indian philosophy maintain the plurality of selves along with their ubiquitous nature. They base their conclusion on the distinctness of experience of two individuals. This will mean that the souls penetrate each other without offering even the least resistance and maintain their individuality. The distinctness of experience in all its three aspects i.e. the conative, the cognitive and the affective is clearly felt. In no way the experiences of two persons are seen to be the same. Negatively if there were only one soul, it would have been difficult, to account for experiences of different individuals. The basic unity of the one soul could not have taken a form of plurality at any stage of its existence. The substance of the individual souls being distinct, the fact of the plurality of souls is a natural conclusion both on its structural and functional sides. Expounding the views of the Nyāya-Vaiśeṣika M. Hiniyanna observes: "The selves are many; and, although they are all pervading, their capacity to know, feel and will is originally manifested through the physical organism with which each of them is associated for the time being. The very disparity in the circumstances characterizing the lives of beings is regarded as an index to the fundamental distinction of their selves. This difference, being intrinsic, continues in the state of release also; and, though all other differences between any two selves disappear when both have been released, there will be the *viśeṣas* then, as in case of atoms, to distinguish them from each other."[1] The Jaina is in perfect agreement with the *Nyāya* view and strengthens his position by holding that the unity of a substance can never be disintegrated by any means. The soul is one individual both in its mundane and liberated states. The Sāṁkhyan plurality of *puruṣas* is also based on the individuality of experience. The death, birth, thinking and activity of different individuals are

---

1. M. Hiriyanna: *The Essentials of Indian Philosophy,* p. 191

mutually distinct.[1] This very fact, according to the Sāṁkhya, leads to the plurality of selves.

The Views of Descartes, Berkeley, Kant and Leibniz about the Plurality of Souls

The Cartesian dictum 'cogito ergo sum' does not only establish the truth of the soul as distinct from the body but is also a sufficient proof for its singularity. The phenomenon of doubt, more generally that of thinking and perception, is different from individual to individual. So on this distinctly perceived empirical ground Descartes proves the plurality of souls. The existence of other minds is not proved simply by an analogy. Correct responses from others like those which I make to some stimuli are a clear proof of the existence of other minds. I receive some facts from others and verify them for myself as correct. This proves the possibility of thinking outside me. In my case I feel that what I call the conscious activities are not possible without a soul within my organism. This becomes the major premise of the syllogism which leads to the existence of other souls. Berkeley reduces all existence to perceptions, and, by arguing that perceptions cannot inhere in nothing, he safeguards the position of the soul. The perceptions being individual, plurality of the souls becomes a necessary conclusion from his dictum 'esse est percipi'. He holds: "Spirits, then, are active indivisible substances, ideas are innert, fleeting, dependent things which subsist not by themselves, but are supported by or exist in minds or spiritual substances. We comprehend our own existence by inward feeling or reflection, and that of other spirits by reason."[2] In the philosophy of Leibniz the soul is born of a plurality of monads. Along with the distinction among the individual souls, he upholds the plurality of the elements, the monads, which constitute the soul. He gets his individual soul from

1. Īśvarkṛṣṇa: *Sāṅkhya-kārikā*, verse 18
2. Thilly: *A History of Philosophy*, p. 309

the monads by a process of integration. The process of integration terminates with the evolution of the queen monad—which may be taken to be the birth of the individual soul. This process of integration takes place at many centres giving rise to a plurality of queen monads. Kantian philosophy, so far as it is an objective idealism, must allow scope for plurality of souls. Kant thinks that we are not able to know things-in-themselves, but know them only as they appear to us. In the same manner the soul may also be comprehended as it may appear to us. The notion of the thing-in-itself is there to support the appearances we comprehend. Kant is very sure about the existence of the noumena. The psychic functions of others are also subject to our perceptions, hence there must be some noumena to support our perception of other selves. Watson observes: "...a noumenon is not a special kind of object for our understanding, namely, as intelligible object; on the contrary it is problematic whether there is any understanding that could have such an object before it. Such an understanding would not know its object discursively by means of categories, but intuitively in a non-sensuous perception; and how this is possible we cannot form even the faintest conception. Still, in conception of a noumenon our understanding gets a sort of negative extesion; for in calling things in themselves noumena, and viewing them as not objects of sense it rather limits the sensibility than is limited by sensibility."[1] Kant mainly emphasizes the unknowability of the noumena by sensuous knowledge but is never seen to oppose a pluralistic attitude towards the conscious and the unconscious worlds. He agrees, in this respect, both with Berkeley and Descartes. The plurality of appearances must depend upon the plurality of the noumena, or the necessity of noumena will become utterly obsolete reducing Kant's philosophy only to a form of subjectivism.

1. Watson: *The Philosophy of Kant*, p. 133

Idealism and the Plurality of Souls

Regarding the problem of the plurality of souls the idealistic school of philosophy divides itself into two groups. The first group consist of the Śaṅkarites. Śaṅkara's idealism is distinguished from that of others by the fact that it holds differences to be mere delusions. So the plurality of souls, for Śaṅkara, is not a true conception but is only a delusion. Śaṅkara distinguishes between the empirical and the transcendental levels of existence and holds the truth of the plurality of souls at the former only. He marks a difference from the views of other idealist thinkers by admitting both the existence and the perception at the empirical level as delusive. These levels of existence and perception being determined by *māyā* Śaṅkara's success wholly depends upon the conception of *māyā.* The second group consists of those idealists who hold the truth of differences. Rāmānuja, Hegel and the Neo Hegelians may be taken to belong to it. They think that there is the plurality of selves in the world, but it is derived from the same monistic principle.

Hegel, Bradley and Rāmānuja on the Pluratity of Souls and their Criticism

On account of the affinity between the Jaina conception of the plurality of souls and the views of the thinkers belonging to the second group it is desirable to consider the views of the thinkers of the latter group first. In Hegel's philosophy we see that, in spite of the great import of difference, there is an inclanation towards monism and unity of thought. It is why we see a reaction against this tendency in Bradley who holds the truth of differences even in the Absolute. If differences are affirmed of the absolute, the position must lead to the plurality of souls equally consistently. Bradleian view of the absolute just opposes the conception of the merging of differences into the unity of the absolute. Bradley never comes to the conclusion that the absolute is a mere unity. Unity and difference are seen to live upon each other, neither can exist in isolation from the other. For Rāmānuja creation is a real act of God, and difference is not a delusion. He is said to hold: "These texts do not mean to deny the reality of many objects, but only teach that in all of them there is the same *Brahman,* on which all are dependent for existence, just as all gold articles are dependent on gold."[1] Exposing the views of Rāmānuja M. Hiriyanna observes: "They (souls) are infinite in number, each being fundamentally distinct from others as shown by the differences in their experiences. Each has its own imperfection, such as ignorance and suffering. Each is atomic. They are different from God, and not only from one another, but the difference is not absolute as in case of matter, for they have features like sentience and bliss (though qualified) common with God."[2] For this group of idealists the plurality of souls or centres of consciousness is an accepted fact. The only point the Jaina would like to dispute is their origination from a unitary spiritual principle. We have already considered problem in all its three aspects, i.e., when the common origin this is held to be matter, spirit or some neutral stuff in Chapter 3. The individuality of consciousness presupposes the individuality of a structure behind it. This structure must be distinct from individual to individual. Hence the common origin must be conceived as giving rise to such distinct structures. It is not intelligible how a unitary indivisible structure can give birth to a plurality of structures. It is why all the pluralists hold a substantial distinction among such structures. The basic argument for the plurality of souls, mostly in all the pluralistic systems, starts with the functional distinctions, and from them we can infer the structural distinctions, behind them.

---

1. Chatterjee and Dutta: *An Introduction to Indian Philosophy,* p. 472
2. M. Hiriyanna: *Essentials of Indian Philosophy*, p. 192

Advaita Vedānta and Plurality of Souls

S.S. Suryanarain Śāstri criticizes the Sāṁkhyan conception of the plurality of souls as 'The Sāṁkhyan demonstration of a plurality of spirits applies properly to the materially constituted empirical selves, not to the pure unchanging *puruṣa.* The Sāṁkhya arguments proceed on the varying incidence of birth and death and the varying endowment of sense organs, etc. But birth and death do not happen to the *puruṣa,* nor does the *puruṣa* have sense organs...the plurality of empirical selves is all that the Sāṁkhyan arguments require."[1] This criticism will certainly apply to the empirical selves, if the Sāṁkhya also admits the reality of the transcendental self as conceived by the Advaitin. For him the empirical self is not false as it is for the Advaitist. According to the Sāṁkhya the plurality of *puruṣas* is besed on the variability of proportion of the three *guṇas.*[2] Hence the plurality of selves, which is established at one level of existence must also be true at another level. By saying that the plurality of selves is empirically true the Sāṁkhyan position cannot be refuted, because the distinction between the transcendental and the empirical truths does not stand the test. Such a distinction is maintained on the postulation of *māyā* which, being absolutely unreal, stands perfectly ineffective. If we assign any reality to *māyā,* it becomes a dualism of *Brahma* and *māyā*. The aforesaid argument, can carry some weight, only if the truth of *māyā* can be held with all its unreality. Actually speaking the plurality of selves is well established on the ground of individuality of experience. Vidyānanda criticizes the thesis of Advaita Vedānta as "The perception of the one spirit is also delusive, because the experience of the self as one in the form of a delusion is also had in dreams, etc. If it is held that, as consciousness in general is always uncontradicted and is always free from delusion, then the general

---

1. *Sāṅkhyakārikā* of *Īśvarkṛṣṇa* (Edited by S.S.S. Śāstrī), Introduction. p.XIII
2. *Ibid.*, p. 22 (verse 18)

consciousness of different individuals will also become consistent, being self consciousness with respect to others like my consciousness. Just as you are not aware of the consciousness of others, so also others do not have the consciousness of your existence. This culminates in complete void. If you want to prove your existence, then on the ground of others' consciousness, the plurality of souls is established."[1] Vidyānanda lays emphasis on two points. Firstly the perceptions of one and many are both experienced by us. We cannot select the one and reject the other. The condition of non-contradiction refers to a particular region, and hence it can yield only a partial truth. Secondly the absence of direct perception of other selves only negates such a possibility, and the conclusion that the others selves are non-existent is unwarranted. On the other hand the fact of self consciousness proves the existence of other selves, or it must lead to nihilism.

The Problem of the Plurality of Souls in the Liberated State

The Jaina upholds the view of plurality of souls both in its structural and functional aspects. The Sūtra says that the *Jīvas* are also substances, the plural use being meant to suggest the plurality of souls in their substantial aspect.[2] Akalaṅka observes that the plural use of the term *Jīva* is there to imply the manifoldness of souls.[3] Besides the substantial distinction Umāsvāti and Akalaṅka both distinguish among the liberated souls with respect to a number of factors. The substantial distinction among the souls in the liberated state must continue, for it is unintelligible how a distinct substance can lose its identity at some stage of its existence. The Jaina theory of substance admits only of the modal transformations through which a

1. Vidyānandin: *Tattvārthaśloka-vārtika*, 1.4.30-34
2. Umāsvāti: *Tattvārthasūtra*, 5.2 and 3
3. Akalaṅka: *Rājavārtika*, 5.3.4

substance persists. Substantial plurality of souls directly follows from the Jaina conception of the soul. Dr. Radhakrishnan is of opinion that the distinction among the liberated souls as propounded by the Jaina is not tenable. He observes: "Plurality of souls is a relative conception which really presents when we lay stress on sensation, feeling and bondage, as if they were really the true moments of the real. We were obliged to transcend the conception of an empirical centre and rise to a logical subject in the Jaina theory of knowledge.... In other words, to use Śaṅkara's famous expression, we have the doctrine of the plurality of *Jīvas* only so long as we treat the subject as an object."[1] A similar criticism is made by P.G. Kulkarni who observes: "If it is maintained that the soul remains quite pure and unaffected, there is no valid ground to maintain a plurality of such undifferentiated souls."[2] We have seen that the Jaina starts with the conception of the soul as a substance. The mundane and the liberated states are simply the modes of the soul's existence, they cannot be said to annihilate their substances themselves or reduce them to some other substances. The substance is the common possession of the varying modes, and so the souls as distinct substances must exist both in the mundane and the liberated states. The undifferentiated souls of the critic are the pure souls of the Jaina philosophy. The Jaina is very clear about the distinction among such souls. Such a distinction is possible on account of the *viśeṣas* (particulars), as held by the Naiyāyika. It is on this ground that the distinction among the liberated souls is upheld. In the liberated state, the *karma* adjuncts being absent, the souls approach each other very closely but they do not lose their *viśeṣas* thereby. The souls in liberation agree with each other in some characteristics, while they differ in others. By shaking off

1. Radhakrishnan: *Indian Philosophy*, vol. I, p. 337
2. *Journal of Philosophical Association*, Vol. III, Nos. 11-12, January, April, 1956, p. 66

their impurity they do not tend to be identical with each other, but both their special and general attributes become simply pure. Purity and individuality can coexist on account of the *viśeṣas.* Souls, for the Jaina, are distinct substances, and so they must remain distinct both in the mundane and liberated states.

Chapter 8

Jaina Eschatology

I

Statement of the Problem

We come across a profound use of the term *'karma'* in the oriental systems of philosophy. The doctrine of *karma,* in one or the other form, has unfailingly influenced Indian thought. It is considered to provide a sufficient explanation of the great riddle of misery, happiness and diversity in the world of living beings. Dr. Radhakrishnan observes: "The connection with the past at the human stage is denoted by the term *'karma'* in Hindu systems... Human growth is an ordered one, and its orderliness is indicated by saying that it is governed by the law of *karma.*"[1] The individuals differ among themselves in respect of their capacities, behaviour, material adjuncts and the consequent feelings of pain and happiness. The principle of *karma,* as the believers of the doctrine think, just reveals the secret of such variations and differences. The *karma* may, thus, be said to be the principle of limitation and obscuration of the powers of the soul. As nothing in the constitution of an entity can be detrimental to its own identity, the Jaina thinks that this obstructing factor, called the *karma,* must be alien to the soul's constitution. C.R. Jain says: "As our thought and deeds affect our character, and create or modify the tendencies of our soul, *karmas* must be recognized to be a force of some kind; for it would be ridiculous to maintain a thing could be affected

1. S. Radhakrishnan: *An Idealist View of Life,* p. 275

by that which had no substantiveness whatsoever."[1] Dr. Glasenapp has correctly observed that "*Karma* is not deed or work, nor invisible mystical force *(adṛṣṭa)* but a complexus of very fine matter, imperceptible to the senses, which enters into the soul and causes great changes in ti."[2] The uniqueness of the Jaina contribution to the doctrine of *Karma* lies in the fact he is able to conceive a substantial basis, though material, for the *karma* forces.

Karma as the Basis for Jaina Psychology

Acoording to the Jaina there is no psychology of the pure souls in the current sense of the term. Psychological problems arise only in case of the souls which are subject to *karmic* influence. The Jaina psychology is ultimately based on the joint-effect of the powers of the soul and the reactions due to the *karmic* energies. The doctrine of *karma* is, thus, the very foundation of the Jaina psychology. It is said: "One remarkable thing in this connection is that the Jaina thinkers have developed their psychological investigations on the foundation of the Doctrine of *Karma*. Since the whole of our life structure is based upon the working of *karma,* it is natural to seek the analysis and explanation of all our intellectual and motor activities through the assistance of *karma.* The Doctrine of *Karma* holds that every activity, whether it be physical or mental produces, besides its perceptible consequence, also an imperceptible effect which is known as *karma.* In other words, every action generates certain potential energies which on pasing a certain length of period change themselves into actual effects. This fact is not confined to the present life of a living being. The effect may also appear in life after death. Moreover, it is the force of *karmic* particles that destines the state after death."[3] Dr. Radhakrishnan makes a similar remark. He states: "Their

1. C.R. Jain: *Key of Knowledge,* p. 531
2. Glasenapp: *The Doctrine of Karma in Jaina Philosophy*, p. 3
3. M.L. Mehta: *Jaina Psychology* (Preface), p. XI

(of *karmas*) physical effects may be short-lived, but their moral effects (*saṁskāras*) are worked into the character of the self. Every single thought, word or deed enters into the living chain of causes which makes what we are.... *Karma* is not so much a principle of retribution as one of continuity"[1] The study of the conscious principle in its mundane exstence means its study in association with the *karma* forces.

The Conception of Karma in Different Systems of Thought
(i) The Nyāya-Vaiśeṣika and the Mīmāṁsā Connceptions

The Nyāya-Vaiśeṣika school of Indian philosophy enumerates *karma* as one of its categories. This *karma* is not at all concerned with the deteminations of the soul's conditions. In the present context *karma* generally means the principle which somehow determines the forms of existence of the soul. For this the Nyāya-Vaiśeṣika formulates the conception of the *adṛṣṭa* which has a direct bearing on and shapes the soul's structure and behaviour. Hence in the Nyāya-Vaiśeṣika system the parallel of the Jaina conception of *karma* is the *adṛṣṭa*. Thus the *karma* for him, may be taken to be the potency of the conscious self for future behaviour. The behaviour itself may also be called by the same name, as it would also generate a potency for future behaviour; but mainly the term is used to denote the potency generated by our past actions. The *adṛṣṭa* is something generated in our souls by our own actions. Our actions so affect our souls that they gain some capacity for further actions. So "it is maintained that our good actions produce a certain efficiency called merit (*puṇya*), and bad actions produce some deficiency called demerit (*pāpa*) in our souls and these persist long after our actions have ceased and disappeared. This stock of merit and demerit accruing from good and bad actions is called *Adṛṣṭa*."[2] "The qualities of dharma and adharma are jointly designated as *saṁskāras* or traces. These

1. S. Radhakrishnan: *An Idealist View of Life*, p. 275
2. Chatterjee and Datta: *An Introduction to Indian Philosophy*, p. 246

inhere in the soul and condition the creation of a new body in the next birth. *Adṛṣṭa* is responsible for the conjunction of soul with sense organs, mind and sense objects, and this conjunction is responsible for the experience of pleasure and pain."[1] Though for the Naiyāyika the soul is immutable and ubiquitous, yet on account of some non-eternal qualities it becomes subject to the effect of its own actions. This effect stored up in the soul is called the *adṛṣṭa,* and, where there is suitable occasion, it becomes a link between the soul and its empirical experiences. Like the *adṛṣṭa* of the Nyāya-Vaiśeṣika the Mīmāṁsaka also postulates a principle for generating a potency for various experiences in the soul and designates it as the *apūrva. Karma,* for him, means the enjoinment of religious duties which give rise to the *apūrva.* "It is held that the ritual performed here generates in the soul of the performer an unperceived potency (i.e. power for generating the fruit of the action) called *apūrva,* which remains in the soul and bears fruit when circumstances are favourable."[2] Like rituals all other actions must influence the soul by way of generating a capacity which goes to determine its future conditions. On its behavioural side such a *karma* may mean only the process of action as abstracted from the agencies whose action is meant; but on its structural side it must mean something positive like a distinct capacity generated in the substance behind actions.

(ii) The Sāṁkhya Conception

The Sāṁkhya holds ignorance as the sole cause of the soul's bondage. Ignorance is effective by way of *sāṁskāras* or impressions which are retained by the self for determining future behaviour. Though he assigns such limitation to *buddhi* or intellect only thereby safeguarding the *puruṣa's* immutability, yet his faith in the principle of bondage is equally firm. Expounding the Sāṁkhyan view of the self M.

1. Kaṇāda: *Vaiśeṣika-sūtra,* 5.2.25
2. Chatterjee and Datta: *An Introduction to Indian Philosophy*, p. 383

Hiriyanna observes: "The self in the empirical sense is not a detached entity like the *puruṣa,* but exhibits the result of innumerable forces that have acted upon it in the course of its beginningless history. It is consequently not passive and does not remain a mere spectator of whatever happens to be presented to it, but is active and meddles with the external object as it apprehends it."[1] For the Sāṁkhya there is a self, and the fact of its bondage is equally true. It results from an interaction between the self and the extenal world. Bondage really means the retention of the effect of this interaction in the form of traces or *sāṁskāras* generated in the self. The position of the Sāṁkhya, as regards the principle of *karma,* is almost the same as that of the Naiyāyika and the Mīmāṁsaka with the exception that the impressions, both actual and potential, are transferred to the region of intellect.

(iii) The Advaita Conception

The advaita philosophy propounds the truth of the principle of *māyā* to explain the worldly process which in the present context is chielfy concerned with the distortion of the powers of the self. This system of thought gets divided mainly into two groups as regards the status of the principle of *māyā.* On one hand Śaṅkara assigns totally a delusive status to it. *Māyā* is, in itself, a delusion and it gives rise to delusions which constitute the wordly process. On the other hand Rāmānuja and Aurobindo think that *māyā* is a real power of the *Brahma* and the wordly process is a real creation. "This power of self-limitation is necessarily inherent in the boundless all-existent. The infinite will not be infinite, if it could not assume a manifold finiteness; the absolute would not be absolute if it were denied in knowledge and power and will and manifestation being a boundless capacity of self determination."[2] Whatever may be the status of the principle of *māyā* in the two systems,

1. M. Hiriyanna: *The Essentals of Indian Philosophy*, p. 116
2. Aurobindo: *Life Divine*, p. 408

both require it to account for the worldly process. As Śaṅkara believes in the empirical reality of the world, his position marks a very close affinity with that of the Sāṅkhya who upholds the reality of the world but safeguards the immutability of the *puruṣa*. The position of Rāmānuja and Aurobindo is very much similar to that of the Mīmāṁsaka and the Nyāya Vaiśeṣika, as all of them agree in holding the limitations and distortions of the self to be real manifestations. Śaṅkara and Rāmānuja both hold *māyā* as the principle of bondage, the *Brahma* itself being insufficient to account for the process of bondage.

Purposive Psychology and the Yogācāra

The mental structure of the purposive psychology is also subject to modification by way of addition or diminution of complexes. The behaviour of the present moment is determined by the operative complexes in the mental structure, and it also generates a potency in the self for future behaviour. The character-complexes are tendencies and propensities gained by the mental structure in the course of its existence. Psychology explains the differences among the individual selves by means of differences in their mental structures existing in the form of constituent complexes. "The organised system of these tendencies, directed upon a variety of objects and towards the realization of various goals connected with these objects, constitute what we call character. Character is the system of directive conative tendencies. It may be relatively simple or complex; it may be harmoniously organised or lacking in harmony; it may be firmly or loosely knit; it may be directed in the main toward lower or toward higher goals."[1] This must mean that the mental structure possesses a capacity for being affected by the external stimuli and assimilates the effect in the form of complexes. This assimilation may be said to be the generation of a potency for future behaviour. The contents

1. Mc Duogall: *An Outline of Psychology*, p. 417

of our experience are not contained in the mental structure, but it gains, when it admits of the effect of a stimulus, in a capacity in the form of a tendency or a propensity to generate another experience. This very potency persists in the mental structure and becomes a cause of behaviour separated by an interval of time from the moment of generation of the potency. A similar position is held by the Yogācāra by replacing complexes by discrete cognitions. Psychology establishes the truth of the identity of the self by means of a process of integration of complexes, while the Yogācāra propounds the doctrine of the *vāsanās* to explain the same fact. The difference between the two conceptions lies in the fact that for psychology the process of integration yields something which transcends the diversity of complexes, while for the Yogācāra the principle of *vāsanā* does not lead to a unity objectively true. In spite of the aforesaid fact both believe in the modification of the complexes and the cognitions to effect the varying manifestations of the self.

Conclusion

This survey of the conception of *karma* or the principle of limitation of the self's powers in different systems of philosophy brings us to the following conclusions, Firstly, the self and its distortions are held to be valid at the levels of existence, where they are found to exist. In order to save the immutability of the soul the empirical level of existence is conceived; but at this level the self and its distortions both are considered to be true. The Nyāya-Vaiśeṣika does not introduce such a level, but postulates some non-eternal qualities in the soul to account for the self's distortion. The peculiarity of Śaṅkara's *advaita* lies in the fact that the empirical level is delusive as compared with the transcendental one. Secondly, the distortion of the self's powers is caused by something which is different from the self. Thus the secret of limitation, distortion and variation of the powers of the self is not alien to the self's constitution, it is inherent in the identity of the self. The limited and distorted self is only a form of the existence of the self. In being limited and distorted it has accepted the influence of the external world. It has undergone a transformation in its own powers on account of its association with the not-self. The capacity for distorted manifestation is the self's own quality which is tickled by the external factors. The Jaina also upholds the truth of the subjective side of the *karma* theory along with the other thinkers. He thinks that it is the soul itself which undergoes modifications which can be termed as the effects of the previous *karmas* and as the causes of the future ones. In other words the subjective *karma* is also interpreted in its two aspects, i.e., the causal and the consequential. Considered subjectively, for the Jaina, the *karmas* are a conscious manifestation of the soul; but he marks an advance over other thinkers by introducing the conception of materiality of *karmas.*

Materiality of Karmas

The general admission as regards the conception of *karma* is that they are the conscious impressions. On the subjective side the Jaina perfectly agrees with the view, but considered objectively he feels the necessity of something other than the soul which may stand for *karmas.* No substances can be obstructive to their own functions. there must be something alien to them to cause such an obstruction. The soul experiences limitation, obstruction and distortion of its powers, and the entity which causes them must not be the soul itself but something other than it. Prabhācandra establishes the materiality of *karmas* on the ground that the fall of the conscious soul must be due to something other than the soul itself.[1] Refuting the position of the *Yoga* it is said that the *karmas* cannot be the functions of the soul. If they are the qualities and the function of the

1. Prabhācandra: *Prameya-kamala-mārtanḍa*, p. 66

soul, they cannot be held responsible for the limitation of the soul.[1]

Nor can it be held that the *karmas* constitute an immaterial substance parallel to the soul. Akalaṅka objects to such a position, because "an immaterial entity cannot help or hinder the function of another immaterial entity. Just as space does not help or hinder the function of the other categories like the *dik* (direction), etc., in the same way an immaterial *karma* cannot help or hinder the function of the immaterial soul."[2] The underlying idea is that, if the *adṛṣṭa,* the *apūrva,* the *saṁskāra* or the *karma* is an immaterial principle, it cannot effect limitation and distortion of the soul's powers. Vidyānandin points out that "no *karmas* are seen to fructify directly or indirectly without the association of matter, so it cannot be held that the *karmas* are not material."[3] The former argument tries to deny immaterial nature of the *karma,* while the latter one affirms materiality of the *karmas.* Yośovijaya also argues that "Materiality of *karmas* is a correct notion because they effect other-determinedness (*pāratantrya*) of the soul. If it is held due to the soul's capacities, it cannot be effected at all. Necessarily that which is an attribute of something cannot effect its limitation or *pāratantrya.* Nor can we say that the *jīva* is not so limited.... The *karma* is material for the consciousness of pleasure, etc., takes place in its association. That in whose association pleasure etc. are felt is always seen to be material like food, etc. That which is not material is not seen to effect pleasure, etc., by its association like *ākāśa* or space."[4]

The Sāṅkhyan position involves a greater inconsistency on account of the absolute immutablity of the self. Das Gupta remarks that "If, again, by the varying states of pleasure and pain the nature of *puruṣa* cannot be affected, then in cannot be regarded as an enjoyer, and if could be

1. *Ibid.*, p. 66
2. Akalaṅka: *Rājavārtika*, 8.2.5
3. Yośovijaya: *Nyāyāloka*, p. 178
4. Yośovijaya: *Nyāyāloka*, p. 178

affected it would itself be changeable."[1] A similar inconsistency is involved in the conception of *māyā* and *Brahma* in Advaita Vedānta. "If one eternal consciousness is the one reality, there cannot be a distinction of false knowledge and right knowledge, bondage and emancipation. There being only one reality there is no right knowledge which need be attained."[2] C.R. Jaina observes: "Vedānta now takes refuge behind the nature of *māyā,* which it describes as inconceivable and for ever beyond the reach of the intellect. But it is really tantamount to throwing up the brief, for no one has a right to preach what is inconceivable to him. Now, if the Vedāntist maintains that he understands what he is talking about, *māyā* ceases to be incomprehensible, but if he says that he has not been able to comprehend it, then he is talking of things which he does not understand and has no right to be heard."[3] From the above discussion it may be concluded that the principle of limitation of the soul's powers cannot be unreal like *māyā,* nor can it leave the soul absolutely unaffected, nor can it be identical with the nature of the soul itself. Hence it must be alien to the constitution of the soul, but in some way able to effect the limitations of its powers. "*Karma,* thus, is a force which binds the soul to the consequences of its good or bad actions."[4] Being a force the *karma* must inhere in some substance, or as C.R. Jaina thinks "it would be ridiculous to maintain that a thing could be affected by that which has no substantiveness whatsoever."[5] Therefore the actions and desires to effect any change in us must transform themselves into a medium of homogenous nature with our physical constitution itself....Psychology shows that no desire, no feeling, no conation passes the threshold of our mind, without in some way, modifying the neural processes... the action-currents of human thought and will leave vestiges on its

1. Das Gupta: *Indian Idealism*, p. 141
2. *Ibid.*, p. 141
3. C.R. Jain: *Key of Knowledge*, p. 485
4. C.R. Jain: *Key of Knowledge,* p. 564
5. *Ibid.,* p. 531

experiential body which brings about a new arrangement in the atomic distribution of *karma-pudgala* composing the *karma-śarīra*."[1] It is for this reason that the Jaina conceives a very fine type of matter as the substratum of the *karma* forces. This matter constitutes what is called the *karma-śarīra*, the *linga-śarīra* or the aestral body in the various systems of thought. If these bodies are not material, they cannot be designated as bodies at all and we shall again come to the view of absolute subjectivity of the *karmas*. The *karma-śarīra* as a very fine material garment of the soul must be there to effect a linkage between the soul and the gross body.

Negativity of the Soul as the Root Cause of the Distortion of Its Powers

The position so far established brings us face to face with the problem why an immaterial soul is rendered susceptible to material influence at all. We want to find out the secret of the relation between the soul and the *karmas*, which makes the limitation and distortion of the former's powers by the latter possible. It is not only a problem for the Jaina, but all those that believe in the existence of the subtle body, the *linga-śarīva* or the aestral body have to face it. The Jaina presupposes such a susceptibility of mutual influence in the soul as well as in the *karma-pudgala*. Rājamalla says: "Both *jīva* and *pudgala* possess a power of negativity (*vibhāva śakti*) which effects a bondage of the two."[2] The real, on account of its natural powers, is possessed of natural as well as negative *(vaibhāvika)* activity. The negative manifestations of the soul do not originate from its association with *pudgala*, for the power which is non-existent in the *jīva* cannot be generated by anything else."[3] The underlying idea is that the negativity of the soul is also a positive element is its constitution like the other positive

1. Nahar and Ghosh: *An Epitome of Jainism*, p. 327
2. Rājamalla: *Pañcādhyāyī*, II, verse 45
3. *Ibid.*, verses 61 and 62

elements. "The manifestations of the negativity of the soul appear only when the soul is in union with the *karmas.* In the absence of the *karmas* the negative manifestations are suspended."[1] In the absence of all the *karmas* the power of negativity of the soul yields natural positive manifestations.[2] According to the Jaina the power of negativity does not stand on an equal footing with the soul's attributes like knowledge, etc. In other words negativity is not admitted of the soul at the level of attributes. If it were an attribute, the negative and the positive manifestations of the soul related to such attributes must be simultaneously perceived. Moreover negative and positive manifestations occur with respect to the same attribute. It means that in respect of an attribute two types of power can be affirmed. When the function of the soul with respect to an attribute is distorted by its conjunction with the *karmas,* we get the negative manifestations, but, when such a function is not obstructed the soul yields positive manifestations. Again it is said: "The various attributes of the soul possess a negative power as well. It becomes distorted *(vikṛta)* in the mundane existence of the soul on account of causes."[3] A distortion has been described as "the perversion of a natural power of a real."[4] The Jaina distinguishes between the implications of the two terms attribute and power. An attribute is an ever present constituent of a substance, and implies a plurality of powers. The variations in the potentiality of a substance are termed as the powers of the substance. When actualized these very powers give birth to the various modes. The negativity of the soul has been assigned the status of a power, and not that of an attribute. If negativity is held to be an attribute of the soul, the position will be doubly fallacious. Firstly, it must be admitted that one constituent attribute of a substance changes into another which

1. *Ibid.*, verse 86
2. *Ibid.*, verse 90
3. *Ibid.*, verse 946
4. *Ibid.*, verse 949

contradicts the dictum that "no attribute is transformed into another attribute."[1] Secondly, in the absence of the *karmas* the function of the attribute of negativity must be held to be suspended—which, according to the Jaina conception of substance, must result in the non-existence of the soul itself. Rāmānuja and Aurobindo also held *māyā* to be a power of self-limitation intrinsic to the constitution of *Brahma.* They also held that in the pure state this principle ceases to function. The Jaina conception of *vibbāva śakti* or negativity is in agreement with the view of the Viśiṣṭādvaita, and, by not assigning a status of an attribute to it. the Jaina very consistently unites the principles of self-limitation and self-manifestation in the soul.

The Relation Between the Soul and the Karmas

The *Jīva* and the material *karma,* thus, come in contact with each other on account of the negativity (*vibhāva śakti*) possessed by the two. The *Jīva* is said to possess the susceptibility of being affected by the *karmas* and the *karma,* in their turn, have the capacity of so modifying themselves that they become instruments in the process of psychic manifestations. Now the problem is whether this relation between the soul and the *karmas* should be designated as interactionism or parallelism.

We must bear in mind a basic conception of the Jaina philosophy which lies behind all such problems. The conception is that no substance can transform itself into another, the transformations are limited to the identity of the substance which may be interpreted in terms of its constitutive attributes. In other words in the proccss of transformation the modes do not transgress the limits laid by the attributes. Hence for the Jaina the question of transformation of the spiritual substance into the material one and vice versa does not at all arise. If interactionism means a mutual transformation of the energies of the soul

---

1. *Ibid.*, verse 1009

and matter, the Jaina does not propound such a theory. If parallelism means that the soul and matter yield two series of manifestations absolutely independent of each other, the Jaina position cannot be identified with it. According to the Jaina the power of distortion (*vibhāva-śakti*) possessed by the soul and matter both makes the two liable for mutual influence. This very power does not allow us to reduce the Jaina theory of mind-body relation to sheer parallelism. The Jaina rejects both parallelism and interactionism as absolute views, but unites the two to obtain a fuller view of the problem. He holds: "The *pudgala,* having obtained the conscious manifestations of the *Jīva* merely as an auxiliary cause, transforms itself into *karmas* by itself. The *karma-pudgalas* become simply auxiliary causes of the conscious manifestations of the soul undergoing transformations by itself."[1] "The material molecules, having the capacity of transforming themselves into *karmas* when they obtain the soul's manifestations, are transformed into *karmas;* they are not so transformed by the *Jīva*."[2] "Like the needle attracted by a magnet both the *Jīva* and the *karma-pudgala* possess the power of distortion which effects their mutual bondage."[3] The secret of such a relation lies in the Jaina theory of auxiliary causation, which is the only possible theory of causation so far as different substances are concerned. The underlying power of distortion in the *Jīva* and matter makes such a theory possible. Interactionism and parallelism embody simply the side views of the facts of relation between the souls and matter. By adopting the transcendental point of view the Jaina holds that the two series of the spiritual and the matarial manifestation run parallel and are not mutually determined. But from the empirical point of view the two series involve interaction. On account of the *vibhāva* power mind and matter both yield manifestations which are a little different from those which would have

---

1. Amṛtacandra: *Puruṣārtha-siddyipāya*, verses 12 and 13
2. Kundakunda: *pravacana-sāra*, II, verse77
3. Rājamalla: *Pañcādhyāyī*, II, verse 45

taken place, in the absence of such a power. The Jaina interactionism is completely free from mutual transformation of enegies of the soul and matter. The distorted transformations of both mind and matter follow from the individual substances themselves but after admitting the mutual auxiliary causation. It is from the *vyavahāra* or empirical view point that we may talk of the spiritualization of matter and the materialization of spirit. Both the soul and *karma-pudgala,* when in union, get energised in a particular way. Nemicandra holds: "From the empirical point of view the vitalities, the senses, respiration, etc., are the differentia of the *Jīva*; but from the real point of view consciousness alone is the differentia of the *Jīva.*"[1] "The deviations of the soul's manifestations when in association with the *karmas* are such as smell materiality, and those of matter are such as smell spirituality. Taking a fuller view of the facts the Jaina would unhesitatingly agree with Stout who holds: "My reason is, not that they are too loosely connected, but, on the contrary, that they are too intimately connected. The action of the mind is not action of the mind only, but action of mind and body in one."[2] In his commentary on the *Dravya-saṁgraha* Brahmadeva has very remarkably observed: "Here the pupil asks whether attachment and aversion, etc., are the products of the *Jīva* or of the *karma.* The answer is that they are the joint products of the two like the son born of the contact of the male and the female and the particular colour born of the mixture of lime and turmeric. Later on from the partially pure point of view they are said to be the products of *karmas.*In the same way from the impure realistic point of view they are said to be the products of the *Jīva*.... Then the question is from the pure realistic point of view whose products they should be held. The answer is that from the pure realistic point of view, like the son without the contact of the male and the female and like the particular colour without effecting a mixture of lime and turmeric they cannot

1. Nemicandra: *Dravyasaṅgraha,* verse 3
2. G.F. Stout: *Mind and Matter,* p. 92

be conceived to exist. How can we answer such a question?"[1] So while we are thinking about the soul, we very often forget the contributions made by *pudgala* in the form of *karmas,* the physical body and the environmental factors. If we interchange the positions of the soul and the *pudgala* in our discussion, we, under the same habit, are very likely to forget the contributions made by the soul and will take consciousness as a function of matter. The negation of the contributions of *pudgala* in the hands of the spiritualists and the negation of the contributions of the soul in the hands of the materialists are the absolute views. The negation of the substances of the soul and matter is not the only form of absolutism, but to transfer the qualities of one to the other or to deny their mutual contributions are equally harmful forms of absolutism. The right situation is quite different from these onesided views. The mundane soul, the substratum of the psychical functions and phenomena, is really a joint product of the soul and the *karma-pudgala.*

Beginningless Association of the Soul and the Karmas

We shall be winding up our exposition of the *karma* theory in general with a discussion of the temporal side of the soul's relation with the *karma.* We have already seen that the relation between mind and body is at all possible because of the inherent power of distortion *(vibhāva śakti)* which functions only when there is a union of the soul and the *karma-pudgala.* So we can imagine that in the life of a mundane soul there was never a moment when it was not in conjunction with the *karma-pudgala,* or the mundane existence of the soul would have been terminated then and there. "The bondage of the *jīva* and the *karma-pudgala* is beginningless and self-established. The question "How was it effected? Who effected it? and where was it effected? are impossible like the flower of the sky."[2] Just as the *jīva* and

1. Brahmadeva: *Dravyasaṁgraha-vṛtti,* p. 88
2. Rājamalla: *Pañcādhyāyī,* II, verse 54

the *pudgala* both have no beginning in time, in the same way the relation and the bondage of the two must be beginningless. This beginningless relation of the two is like that between the dross and the ore of gold, otherwise there will be the fallacy of mutual dependence."[1] If we suppose that this realiton had a beginning in time, then prior to it the soul must be supposed to exist in a pure state. Being in the pure state it must not have admitted of the effect of the *karma pudgala.* Hence its mundane existence could not have begun at all. Secondly, the mundane existence presupposes the soul's union with matter by which it is determined, and the soul's union with matter presupposes mundane existence by which it is determined. So there being no way out we must conclude that the union of the soul and the *karma pudgala* is beginningless. The fallacy of mutual dependence will arise only when this relation has a beginning in time.

II

Bondage of the Soul by the Karmas

We have seen that the soul falls a victim to *karmic* bondage on account of its inherent capacity for distortion. On this very ground we were able to establish the beginningless conjunction of the soul and the *karma-pudgala.* Hence the bondage of the soul by the *karma* is also beginningless. In mundane existence soul and matter live in association with each other. The soul's power for distortion is not sufficient to effect bondage, but without it no bondage would have been possible. Just as a brass needle is not attracted by a magnet, so also the soul would have stood unaffected by the *karma-pudgala,* had there been no power of distortion in it. It is on account of this power of distortion that soul is rendered susceptible to *karma* bondage. Neither the power of distortion nor the presence of the *karma-pudgala,* taken singly, is able to give rise to mundane

1. *Ibid.*, verses 35 and 36

existence; both of them stand in need of each other's contribution to effect the worldly life of the soul. Kundakunda conceives this bondage in its three aspects. "*Karma-pudgala* is bound with *karma-pudgala* on account of the qualities of smoothness and roughness of the *karma* molecules. The *jīva* is said to be bound on account of its impure manifestations like attachment etc. But the union of the soul and *karma-pudgala* is material-cum-spiritual, and it is the copresence of the two in the same space."[1] According to the Jaina this union of the soul and the *karma-pudgala* represents the structure of the wordly self. Modern psychology confines its vision only to one out of these three aspects, i.e., only to the soul's capacity for impure function. The *karma* psychology probes deep to get at the concomitane associate of the structure of the self in the form of the *karma-śarīra.* The Jaina, by allowing scope for all the three types of bondage, saves his position from the fallacy of one-sidedness.

The Cover of Karmas and Their Ghāti (Destructive) and Aghāti (Non-destructive) Types

This bondage of the soul by the *karmas* is generally understood to be a sort of covering; and a similar fact is suggested by the nomenclature used in case of the first two classes of *karmas* i.e., the *jñān-avaraṇīya* (knowledge-obscuring) and the *darśanā-vāraṇīya* (conation-obscuring). Just as the clouds cover the light of the sun, so also the *karmas* cover the faculties of the *jīva.*[2] Akalaṅka says: "The conscious *jīva* does not shine on account of *karmas* like a precious stone which has been defiled (*viddha*) by dirt."[3] It may suggest that behind the cover of *karmas* the soul remains unaffected by them; that is, the substence of the soul suffers no change on account of the *karmas.* This will mean that the soul under the

1. Kundakunda: *Pravacana-sāra,* II, verse 85
2. Devendra Sūri: *Karmagrantha* (Hindi), II, p. 12
3. Akalaṅka: *Nyāyaviniścaya,* III, verse 23

covering of *karmas* remains pure like the *puruṣa* of the Sāṁkhya. The Jaina position must be held to be different from it. The *karmas* do not effect merely a covering on the soul under which it may exist in its pure state. For the Jaina, under the influence of *karmas* the soul must also underge inpure manifestations. The *karmas* and the soul together yield a joint product which constitutes the personality of the mundane soul. It is said that "by the *karmas* the total destruction of knowledge or conation is not effected, because, then there will be the non-existence of the soul itself because of the non-existence of the attributes invariably tied with the soul."[1] Dr. Tatia also observes: "The remainder knowledge is variously covered by other sub-types of knowledge obscuring-*karma*, till a ray of light remains uncovered."[2] If *kevala-jñāna* or perfect knowledge is held to be an attribute of the soul, then the *kevala-jñānāvaraṇa karma,* being totally destructive will destroy the attribute of perfect knowledge completely and the soul will become unconscious like matter. From this it follows that the above mentioned *karma* should not be taken to destroy an attribute of the soul totally. Really speaking perfect knowledge is no attribute of the soul, because it is not always found with the soul. It is only a mode of the knowledge—attribute of the soul, and the appearance of this mode is obstructed by the *kevala-jñānāvaraṇa-karma.* It only affects the directness and simultaneity and wholeness of the knowledge-attribute, and these are nothing but the traits of the knowledge attribute. Different types of *karmas* have a bearing on different traits of an attribute, none of them can destroy the attribute totally. The confusion in this conection is also based on the lax use of the term attribute of *guṇa,* as has been already pointed out. Upon this very fact depends the distinction between the destructive (*ghāti*) and the non-destructive (*aghāti*) types of *karmas,* it is with reference to a particular mode of an attribute like the state of perfect knowledge that some

---

1. *Kaṣāyapāhuḍa*, p. 61
2. N.M. Tatia: Studies in Jainism, p. 240

karmas are called destructive, otherwise no *karma* is potent enough to destroy a constitutive attribute of the soul totally. Hence this distiction comes out to be a relative truth. All the *karmas* bring about a distortion of the faculties of the soul by obstructing their functions with respect to one or the other traits of the attribute. Mere distortion has also been taken to be destruction of the soul's faculties. The deluding *karma (mohanīya)* functions only by distorting the faculties of faith and conduct, and it is held to be a destructive type of *karma.* A distortion can never mean a total destruction of an attribute, it always embodies a deviation from the natural manifestation of an attribute. A limitation of any of the faculties of the soul may also be taken to be a distortion with respect to various traits of those faculties. Dr. Tatia has rightly observed: "It is in view of this fact that the karma covering pure and prefect knowledge is regarded as completely obscuring (*sarvaghātī*); while other sub-classes of knowledge obscuring *karma* are partially destructive *(deśaghātī).*"[1] The non-destructive *karmas* can never be held to effect no distortion of the attributes of the soul, then their clinging to the soul will be futile. They are *karmas*, and, hence, must agree with other *karmas* in respect of their general function. It is with respect to a particular state of the soul that some *karmas* are held to be non-destructive, they must also effect some sort of distortion of the soul's faculties. This brings us to the conclusion that the *karmas* affect the soul by distorting the latter's faculties. On analysis this distortion may be considered to be the result of the two types of forces emanating from the soul and the *karmas-pudgala.* The resultant of the spiritual and the *karmic* forces must not be absolutely spiritual or material, but must show symptoms of being a joint product of the two.

Classification of the Karma Forces

Now a classifiction of the *karma* forces may be attempted. In Jainism these forces have been divided into eight basic

1. N.M. Tatia: *Studies in Jainism,* p. 240

groups which are further divided into one hundred and forty-eight sub-classes called the secondary divisions or the *uttara-prakṛitīs.* In the present context the *karma* forces may be regrouped under the psychical, the physiological and the environmental classes. As a matter of fact no *karmas* can be said to allow the soul to exist unaffected by them. Of whatever type the *karmas* may be, it must have its bearing on the faculties of the soul. The manifestations of the soul resulting from its contact with the physique-making (*nāma*) *karma* have been counted among the operative type of the soul's manifestations.[1] Again the manifestations resulting from the power—obstructing (*antarāya*) *karma* have been enumerated among the subsidence-cum-destructive (kṣāyopaśamika) type of the soul's manifestations. The fact, that the physique-making and the power-obstructing *karmas* also cause a psychical change in the soul, suggests very clearly that no *karmas* can be held to be purely determining the psychical, bodily or environmental conditions of the *jīva.* Hence such a division can be upheld only with respect to the major effect of the *karmas* upon the soul. If the *karmas* have their bearing mainly on the soul, they may be said to belong to the psychical class. If the *karmas* have their bearing mainly on the physiology of the organism, they may be said to belong to the physiological class. If the *karmas* have their bearing mainly on the environment, they may be termed as the environmental type of *karmas.* "The *karma* which cause a distortion directly in the *jīva* is the *jīva-vipākī* (having fruition in the *jīva)* or the psychical type of *karma....* The *karmas* whose fruition is effected in the material body of the *jīva* is called the *pudgala-vipākī* (having fruition in the *pulgala*),"[2] Thus the *jñānāvaraṇīya* (knowledge obscuring), the *darśānāvaraṇīya* (conation-obscuring), the *vedanīya* (feeling determining) and the *mohanīya* (deluding *karma*) may be grouped under the psychical class. The *nāma* (phsique-determining) *karma* and

---

1. Umāsvāti: *Tattvārtha-sūtra*, 2.6
2. Vidyānanda: *Aṣṭasahasrī*, p. 266, (footnote)

the *āyuṣ* (age-determining) *karma* may be grouped under the physiological class. The *gotra* (status-determining) *karma* belongs to the environmental class. The *antarāya* (power-obscuring) *karma* has generally been described as obstructing the procurement of things, hence in can also be grouped in the last named class.

The Psychical Class of Karmas and the Self of the Jaina Psychology

The first enumerated class of *karmas,* i.e., the psychical ones is the basis of the *karma* psychology. C.R. Jain observes: "*karmas* (destiny) only act through the disposition, by altering and modifying the impulses."[1] There is a very intimate relation between the *karmas* and the psychical structure of the self. The accumulated stock of *karmas* just modifies the potentiality of the *jīva* by generating a capacity to give rise to different dispositions and complexes. In this way the *karmas* contribute towards the structure of the mind which endures and abides in time. When the *karmas* attain an operative stage, the soul's capacity for different dispositions and complexes gives rise to various psychological phenomena on their functional side. The *karma* psychology, thus, provides a concrete basis for both the structural and the functional facts. Besides it marks a deeper insight into the structure of the mundane self as a combination of the soul and the *karma-pudgala* which alone, according to Jaina philosophy, makes the existence of the psyche possible. Dr. Freud holds that the ultimate basis of his psychology is the sex-energy which he calls the libido. The Jaina thinks that the sex-energy is only a form of the soul's capacity when overpowered by the deluding *karma.* It is true that the psychical functions can be analysed into the component functions which colour each other. So, if Dr. Freud could see nothing but sex-energy in the structure of the self, he was not totally wrong. It was something like seeing the soul

1. C.R. Jain: *Jaina Psychology,* p. 63

as constituted of knowledge alone or bliss alone as Kundakunda did. The fallacy which Dr. Freud committed was that he took a partial truth to be the whole truth. The fault was felt by his successors, Alfred Adler and C.G. Jung. Adler replaced the sex-energy by a will-for-power, and widened the scope of the source of psychical functions. He holds that "the first problems of life are not sexual, but sex is a part of the life-problems. Mental disorders are not caused by the suppression of sexual desire but by being hampered by a style of life, a proper balance between the individual and the social drives."[1] "The sexual components cannot even be correctly estimated except in relation with the individual style of life."[2] This will-for-power or self-ascendency is seen by him as more fundamental than the sexual energy. Though Adler gives a wider meaning to the source of psychical function, yet he suffers from one-sidedness by holding the will-for-power as the only source of psychical functions. The Jaina takes Adler's self assertive impulse into consideration by enumerating pride as a sub-division of the deluding *karma,* when it is hampered by the power-obstructing *karma.* C.G. Jung felt the need of further widening the scope of the source of the psychical functions. He substituted will-to-live for the self assertive impulse, emphasizing thereby the fact that the ultimate source of psychical functions is the life energy only. In this respect he agrees with Schopenhaur and Bergson who propounded the conceptions of the will-to-live and the *elan vital.* Woodworth observes, "Jung used the term libido in an even broader sense than Freud, stripping it of its distinctively sexual character. He made it to include both Freud's libido and Adler's will-for-power, and in short the whole range of motives. He made it equivalent to Schopenhaur's will and Bergson's *elan vital."*[3] Mc Dougall isolates the characteristic of goal-sseking in the life energy and holds life energy itself

1. Cf. R.S. Woodworth: *Contemporary Schools of Psychology*, pp. 194-95
2. A. Adler: *Problems of Neurosis*, p. 93
3. R.S. Woodworth: *Contemporary Schools of Psychology*, p. 199

as the ultimate source of psychical phenomena. He says: "Instinct is not the whole of life. The mind is not only a bundle of separate instincts. For the solution of the central mystery of life and mind and will we must go behind instincts to find a life movement which is primitive and fundamental. The inadequacy of instincts as an explanation of the mental forces that maintain and shape all the life of the individuals and societies becomes manifest... in connection with the highest moral thought and conduct of man."[1] The ultimate source of all psychical functions must be held in the life energy itself, and not in the sexual energy or any other type of energy which is merely a differentiation of the basic energy. The Jaina very explicitly holds that the faculties and powers of the soul undergo various differentiations under the influence of different *karmas*, and that the life energy may be considered as one from the synthetic view-point and as many from the analytic view-point. The sub-classes enumerated under the psychical group of *karma* forces include much besides the various mental energies conceived so far. The Jaina has been able to give a more exhaustive and scientific classification of the self's power in relation with the *karma*-forces than one so far made by the philosophers and the psychologists.

The Physiological Class of Karmas

The growth of matter associated with life is different from that of lifeless matter. This marks a close relation between the organism and the principle of consciousness behind it. The organism is seen to be affected by the conciousness, which, in turn, is affected by the organic changes. The *karma śarīra* of the Jaina functions as a link between them. The physique-making *karma* is said to effect the condition (*gati*) of existence, i.e., the structure of the *jivas* material body and the transference to other conditions of existence. The secondary divisions of the *nāma* (pysique-

1. Mc Dougall: *Instinct and Personality*, p. 51

making) *karma* are connected with the organisation of the different parts of the body and its capacities. It should not be taken to mean that the physique-making-*karma* is wholly responsible for the production of the material body, and the matter of which the body is made has no importance. Just as different molecules of matter effect each other after the manner of auxiliary causation, in the same way the aforesaid *karma* has to make its own contribution towards the formation of the organism. This allows full scope for the functions of the *karma-pudgala* and the *pudgala* of the organism.

The Environmental Class of Karmas

The environmental class of *karmas* contributes towards the determination of the environment in which a particular soul happens to be placed. The *gotra* or the status-determining *karma* is concerned with the determination of the environment which helps or hinders the process of spiritual development. As this type of *karma* has no direct bearing on the psychical and the organic capacities of a living being, it is said to belong to the environmental class. The power-obstructive *karma* just effects a distortion and limitation of the power of the self. It is also held to determine the conjunction of the external objects required for the fulfilment of psychic functions like desire, etc. The latter aspect of this type of *karma* makes its enumeration among the environmental *karmas* possible. But the problem is how the environmental type of *karmas* which cling to the soul, are able to effect the behaviour of the things external to the soul and its organism. The answer may be sought in the concept of 'field' in psychology. Field psychology extends the scope of the psyche beyond the organism. Jacob Robert Kontor holds that "the real whole however, is not the organism but the organism in its efective environment."[1] Koffka says "that we should regard behaviour not composed

1. R.S. Woodworth: *Contemporary Schools of Psychology*, p. 239

of responses to stimuli but as governed by a field, the organismic field of interacting forces, a field that is self-organized into definite though changing patterns."[1] Conscious experience is often influenced by the rest of the field as unconscious or vaguely conscious desires. "For Levin, the field means the life space containing the person and his psychological environmemt."[2] According to the Jaina the germs of such an extension of the self in the 'field' are rooted in the structure of the self in the form of the environmental *karmas.* The presence of these *karmas* with the soul makes the latter capable of extending its effect outside the organism. Inside the field some objects may be supposed to have a positive valence, while others have a negative valence. The environmental class of *karmas* of the Jaina philosophy must generate such a field through which they may contribute to the course of things. Action-currents may be supposed to emanate, on account of the presence of the environmental *karmas*, from the self to effect changes in the external world. These *karmas* work so secretly that they allow an intelligible explanation of the physical events in terms of physics and chemistry. Above all as the Jaina is not a believer of absolute opposition, for him the cosmos is a harmoniously organized system of elements. There is an aspect of the world which makes us hold that every element coordinates its function with those of others so as to make the entire cosmos a coherent system. Then it is not very surprising that the self and its environment are found to function in coordination with each other.

Coordination among Different Types of Karmas

Again a question may be raised as regards the coordination among different types of *karmic* energies. The *karmic* energies have been grouped under eight types, according to the traditional exposition of the *karma* theory,

---

1. *Ibid.,* p. 137
2. *Ibid.,* p. 153

and under three types in the present dissertation. We want to know whether there is any principle of coordination working among the different sub-classes of the *karmas*. The Jaina holds that generally the *karmas* work in coordination with each other, and this co-ordination takes place not only among the three types of *karmas* taken singly but also as taken in relation with each other. If once the age-determining *karma* for the next life is bound, no other *karma* of the same class can be bound in the same life. Various *karmas* may be bound at different times, but *karmas* having contradictory fruition cannot fructify simulataneously. Among the psychcal *karmas* when the fruition of one *karma* requires the fruition of another, then the fruition of the two must take place simultaneously. For the appearance of sensuous knowledge the conation-obscuring and the knowledge-obscuring *karmas* must both be in a state of destruction-subsidence simultaneously. Not only this should be allowed but as the process of perception is dependent upon the connected physiology, the physiological class of *karmas* must attain an operative stage at the same time. In the same way the environmental type of *karmas* must yield an agreeing function with the other *karmas*. If the power-obstructing *karma* so functions as to obstruct the soul's function in some way, it is most likely that the environment is also in agreement with the general situation. As the working processes concerning the different types of *karmas* also depend upon factors other than the *karmas* themselves, such factors must be allowed due freedom. This would mean an exception to and a deviation from the general theory of coordination of *karmic* energies. If there is a blind man, he may be lacking in psychological capacity for occular perception or his physiology for such perception may be distorted. It is quite possible that he may be lacking in both the respects, but we do not see reason enough why the aforesaid disagreement among the functions of the various *karmas* should not exist. The author of the Viśeṣāyaśyaka-bhāṣya holds that "from the view-point of psychological attainment all the *jīvas* are five sensed."[1] It means that fruition of psychical *karmas* can exist without the fruition of the corresponding physiological *karmas*. It also implies that the psychical *karmas* may remain bound with the soul without the physiological *karmas*. The writer of the 'Dhavalā' commentary on the 'Saṭkhaṇḍāgama' is of opinion that for the appearance of a physiological sense, it is necessary that the conditions for the appearance of the psychical sense must be fulfilled."[2] Though the physiological sense presupposes the psychological sense, yet there is no strict correspondence, when a reverse situation is meant. It is said in the '*Bhagvatī-śūtra*' that "one who has the knowledge-obscuring *karma* may have or may not have the deluding *karma;* but one who has the deluding *karma* must have the knowledge obscuring *karma*....One who has the feeling *karma* may have or may not have the deluding *karma,* but one who has the deluding *karma* must have the feeling *karma.*"[3] It is also mentioned that the physical capacities resulting from ithe subsidence or the destruction-subsidence of *karmas* pass away unrealized in the absence of proper physiology and environment. In the hellish condition of existence the pleasure-feeling *karma* fructifies as the pain-feeling *karma* on account of the lack of proper environment. In the state of meditation and study of scriptures undesirable *karmas* come to maturity but they fall fruitless because of the lack of proper environment. It can be easily believed that the presence of proper physiology and environment is not utilised in the absence of the necessary psychological attainment. So we come to the conclusion that there is no perfect correspondence among the different types of *karmas*, but at the same time the mutual correspondence is not totally absent so as to reduce the system to a mere chaos. If there is no absolute coordination among different types of *karmas*, we do not also see a total absence of coordination among them. But

1. Jinabhadra: *Viśeṣāvaśyaka-bhāṣya,* verse 2999
2. *Ṣaṭkhaṇḍāgama*: 'shudraka-bandha', part II, vol. 7, p. 65
3. *Bhagavatī-sūtra*, p. 708-09

the mundane existence of the soul is not possible without such coordination among the *karma* forces. So we see that there is coordination among the various *karmas* if it is essential to the consequent process.

The Life-History of Karmas or the States of Karmas

The history of a *karma* begins from the very moment it is bound with the soul. If a *karma* is considered in its subjective aspect, this history will be found almost the same as the life-history of an instinct or a disposition. The union of a *karma* with the soul marks the first state in the life-history of a *karma*. This state is known as the *bandha* (state of bondage). No *karma* is able to effect the faculties of the soul immediately after the state of *bandha*. It requires a period to become mature. This period is technically known as the *ābādhā* or the period of maturity. Nemicandra says: "The period for which the material molecules, that have come to the soul in the form of *karmas* do not gain the capacity of effecting the soul, is called the *ābādhā*."[1] This period is necessary in case of every *karma* because a new *karma* is to be assimilated in the existing structure of the self. Unless it is so assimilated it cannot be said to be a part in the soul's structure, though it is bound with it. Just as an instinct must become ripened before it actually influences the behaviour, so also the *karma* stands in need of getting mature before it can bring about its fruition. The Jaina philosophy gives three main states of *karmas*. First of all a *karma* is bound with the soul, then there must be the period of preparation of realization, and then will follow the state of operation. The first is the state of *bandha* (bondage), as we have already mentioned; and the other two are known as the *sattā* (endurance) and *udaya* (operation), We come across a similar division of *karmas* into *āgāmī*, *prārabdha* and *sañcita* in some of the systems of Indian Philosophy. The *prārabdha karmas* mean those that are operating and the *sañcita karmas*

1. Nemicandra: *Gommaṭasāra* (*Karmakāṇḍa*), verse 4

are those that lie accumulated with the soul. These divisions correspond to the operative and enduring states of the *karmas* in Jaina philosophy. As regards the *āgāmī karma* Sriniwas Iyengar observes: "Every present act, every present thought, every present desire becomes stored in his subtle body as *āgāmin* (augmentative)."[1] So the *āgāmī karmas* may be taken to correspond to the *bandha* state. The elements in the mental structure are also distinguished in the same way. Every complex or disposition has a moment of assimilation; and before it begins to function it remains there as an element in the unconscious. It then rises to the operative state and after effecting its function it passes away. The *karma* phenomenology of the Jaina also mentions that after the operative state of *karmas* they become detached from the soul. Kundakunda observes: "Just as a fruit, when ripe, falls from the tree and cannot remain attached to it; in the same way the *karmas* do not attain the state of operation, when they are once shed off."[2] This fact may again be compared with the psychological conception of the death of an instinct. Mc Dougall says: "In some few cases it appears that an instinct, if it is not excited are brought into play soon after the date at which it normally matures, fades away or at least becomes incapable of being excited."[3] In the same way not only an instinct but every element in the mental structure must come to an end. The *karmas* also have a definite duration after which they fall off from the soul.

Besides the above three a few more states of the *karmas* may also be distinguished. Nemicandra mentions ten states of the *karmas* out of which three have already been discussed. The accumulated *karmas* may be affected in respect of their duration, fruition and transformation. In respect of duration or fruition or both if an increase is effected the *karmas* are said to be in the state of *utkarṣaṇa* (increased realization); and a state of decrease is similarly termed as *apakarṣaṇa*

1. Sri Niwas: *Outlines of Indian Philosophy,* p. 62
2. Kundakunda: *Samayaprābhṛta,* verse 192
3. Mc Dougall: *An Outline of Psychology,* p. 111

(decreased realization). When a *karma* is transformed into another type of *karma,* the state is called saṁkramaṇa or transformation. Regarding such a trasformation of mental elements Mc Dougall thinks: "Two (or more) instincts may be simultaneously excited. If their tendencies are not incompatible, behaviour is then a blend of the two actions characteristic of the two instincts, each being modified by the other. If their tendencies are opposed, we may witness a struggle, with alteration of the movements of opposite kinds, until one gains the upper hand."[1] There is not much of doubt about such a change of mental elements in respect of their duration, function and transformation. Dr. Tatia says: "Tranformation is the process whereby the soul transforms the nature, the duration, the intensity and the numerical strength of one kind of *karmic* matter into those of another which it is binding at the time by means of manifestation of a particular kind of energy. Transformation is mainly the process of change of one kind of *karmic* energy into another, the change of duration and fruition in the same kind of *karmic* energy being included in the *utkarṣaṇa* and the *apakarṣaṇa* states."[2] The *karmas* that are in the state of *apakarṣaṇa* must get mature earlier than they are due. This sort of realization of *karmas* constitutes another state called *udīraṇa* or immature realization. Endurance or *sattā* is the state in which a *karma* exists in a potential form without producing its effect like an instinct whose moment of maturity has not yet come. This state must be distinguished from the state of subsidence of *karmas*. Devanandi defines subsidence: "As the non-uprising of the *karmas* in the soul on account of its own power."[3] This state requires an effort on the part of the soul to suppress the effect of the *karmas*; while the state of endurance is not based upon such a application of the power of the soul. The *karmas* that are incapable of immature realization and transformation are

1. *Ibid.*, p. 113
2. N.M. Tatia: *Studies in Jainism,* p. 252
3. Devanandin: *Sarvārthasiddhī,* p. 82

said to be in the state of *nidhatti;* while those that admit of no change but follow their own course are said to be in a state termed as the *nikācita.*[1] All the ten states do not occur necessarily in the life of a *karma.* Some states become possible only by negating others. The essential states through which a *karma* must pass are the bondage, the endurance and the realization after which it must get detached from the soul.

III

The Five Types of Conscious Manifestations

The union of the *jīva* with the *karmas* in their various states gives rise to the theory of the five types of conscious manifestations of the *jīva. Karmas* in their different states of existence give birth to various forms of thought and activity. These manifestations are the *aupaśamika* (subsidential), the *kṣāyika* (destructive), the *kṣāyopaśamika* (destructive-subsidential), the *audayika* (operative) and the *pāraṇāmika* (natural) ones.[2] The ten states of the *karmas* give rise to only three types of conscious manifestations, the destructive being determined by the absence of the *karmas* and the natual one, by the *jīva* itself.

The Aupaśamika (Subsidential) and Kṣāyika (Destructive) Manifestations

The state of endurance (*sattā*) of the *karmas* does not affect the soul at all, because herein the *karmas* do not attain maturity. As we have seen that the states of endurance and subsidence are not the same, the effect of the subsidential state is there in the soul. Actually speaking the power of the soul prevents the *karmas* from becoming operative; and it will have meaning only when the *karmas* are supposed to be

---

1. Nemicandra: *Gommaṭasāra (Karmakāṇḍa),* verse 440
2. Umāsvāti: *Tattvārthasūtra,* 2.1

almost mature.[1] When the *karma* forces get subsided, they are, then, as good as non-existent, "The purity of the subsidential and destructive types of soul's manifestations is the same; but there is only this much of difference that in the former the destructive *karmas* exist, while in the latter no such *karmas* are there."[2] This also explains the nature of the destructive manifestations. "The manifestation which appears on the total destruction of the obstructive *karmas* in the destructive one; and it is pure and natural.[3] So the subsidential and destructive types of manifestation are quite similar on the functional side, but their structural sides are different because of the presence of *karmas* in case of the subsidential manifestations. Now the nomenclature adopted shows that in the determination of the aforesaid two types of manifestations the subsidence and the destruction of the *karmas* play the main role. But, when the *karma*-energies are not functioning, we must hold that the soul's powers are manifesting in an unobstructed way, and, so the manifestations are pure and natural. But as the soul's powers evince the negation of the corresponding *karmas* and as they had been so far affected by them, the spiritual manifestations of this type have been named after their negative traits.

The Kṣāyopaśamika (Destructive-Subsidential) Manifestations

The natural and pure powers of the soul being the positive elements, the consequent manifestations must be supposed to be determined by them. Subsidence or destruction of *karmas* is not directly responsible for such determination. The third type of the soul's manifestations has been described "as one which arises on the non-realization (*anudaya*) of the totally destructive *karmas* and

1. Cf. Devanandin: *Sarvārthasiddhi,* p. 82
2. Umāsvāti: *Sabhāṣya Tattvārthāhigama-sūtra,* p. 76
3. Rājamalla: *Pañcādhyāyī,* II, verse 965

the realization (*udaya*) of the, partially destructive *karmas*"[1] Nemicandra says: "Where the *karmas* are obstructing the soul's faculties and still where the faculties are manifesting partially, it is the destructive-subsidential manifestation."[2] Akalaṅka contends that the mixed manifestation has a dual nature like the partially obstructed intoxicating power of an inferior type of rice (*kodon*).[3] We must remember that no *karmas* are able to destroy the attributes of the soul totally, hence in the present context destruction must be taken with reference to some modes of an ever present attribute of the soul. The subsidential-destructive type of manifestations require the non-operation of the totally destructive *karmas*, so as to avoid complete disappearance of the soul's faculties, and the operation of the partially destructive *karmas* so as to effect a distortion and limitation of the soul's powers. The positive and the negative conditions that determine the mixed type of manifestations are thus clearly mentioned. Akalaṅka again observes: "In the absence of the operation of the totally destructive *karmas* and in the presence of their subsidence the destructive-susbsidential type of manifestations appear on account of the operation of the partially destructive *karmas*."[4] The positive and negative conditions that determine the mixed type of manifestations are thus clearly mentioned. Again it is said: "when the totally destructive *karmas* are operative, the faculties of the soul do not manifest at all. Therefore the disappearance of their operation is taken to be their destruction. The presence of such totally destructive *karmas* is said to be their subsidence because their potency is not actualized. In such a non-appearance of the operation of totally destructive *karmas* the operation of the partially destructive *karmas* gives rise to the destructive-subsidential manifestations on account of the absence of total destruction."[5] The effect of

1. *Ibid.*, verse 966
2. Nemicandra: *Gommaṭasāra* (*Karmakāṇḍa*), verse 814
3. Akalaṅka: *Rājavārtika*, p. 100
4. *Ibid.*, 2.5.3
5. *Ibid.*, p. 106

the destructive *karmas* is, thus, avoided by way of their endurance and subsidence, and not by way of destruction after which the pure function of the soul's attributes must follow. The non-operative and subsidential states of the totally destructive *karmas* prepare the ground upon which the partially destructive *karmas* work and generate the destructive-subsidential manifestations. The non-operation or the subsidence of *karmas* is as good as their non-existence, and it must have brought about the pure manifestations but for the operation of partially destructive *karmas*. Hence this type of manifestations would mean the distortion and limitation of the soul's powers by the partially destructive *karmas*. It is a little strange to note that neither destruction nor subsideence (the terms used in the nomenclature) suggest the other aspect of the mixed manifestations, i.e., their determination by the partially destructive *karmas*. We know that sensuous knowledge, which is enumerated as a mixed manifestation, presupposes the operation of the perfect knowledge-obscuring *karma* which is totally destructive. So it follows that the mixed manifestations appear only when the total and partial obscurations have been taken in respect of different faculties. Akalaṅka takes a durable mode of an attribute as an attribute (*guṇa*), and thus propounds the truth of total disappearance of an attribute.

The Audayika (Operative) Manifestations

Then we come to the operative type of the soul's manifestation. It is defined as the manifestation determined by the operation of the *karmas*."[1] "The fruition of the *karmas* when helped by the auxiliary causes is the operation."[2] This type of manifestations is solely determined by the operation of *karmas*, and it does not presuppose the existence of non-operation of any type of *karmas* like the mixed manifestations.

1. Rājamalla: *Pañcādhyāyī*, II, verse 967
2. Devanandin: *Sarvārthasiddhi*, p. 82

Now the question is whether the pure or the impure faculties of the soul are affected by the operative *karmas*. If there are pure faculties of the destructive type, they cannot be obscured by any *karmas*. If there are pure faculties of the subsidential type, they can be obscured by the operation of those very *karmas* only which will arise later on. From this it follows that the operative manifestations are nothing but manifestations doubly affected by the *karmas*. Sensuous knowledge is a mixed type of manifestation. It presupposes the covering of the *kevalajñānāvaraṇa* without which it cannot be effective. The *kavalajñānāvaraṇa* is not totally destructive to the attribute of knowledge but is so only with respect to some traits of knowledge. Even the wrong type of sensuous knowledge, i.e., the *kumati* has been enumerated among the mixed manifestations, while one more manifestation, i.e., *ajñāna* (non-cognition) depending upon the knowledge attribute has been conceived and designated as the operative manifestation.[1] As regards the identity of the manifestation of non-cognition it is said: "Among the three types of knowledge (i.e., *mati, śruta* and *avadhi)* the non-cognition is destructive-subsidential, it is never operative. The non-cognition which is conceived to be operative is void, because, the body is unconscious."[2] Akalaṅka takes non-cognition in the sense of the worng type of cognition and calls it a destructive subsidential manifestation."[3] Again non-cognition as an operative manifestation has been identified with the absence of knowledge.[4] But as the total absence of knowledge in not possible in any of the living beings, non-cognition must be taken only in a relavtive sense. Non-cognition cannot be a mode of the knowledge attribute. It can only be a trait of the actualized power for cognition. Every living being possesses a positive power for cognition. This very power evinces non-cognition in the form of its own limitation. So we find nothing like an independent mode which could

1. Umāsvāti: *Tattvārtha-sūtra,* 2.6
2. Rājamala, *Pañcādhyāyī,* verses 1018-19
3. Cf. Akalaṅka: *Rājavārtika,* 2.6.5
4. *Ibid.,* p. 109

be called a non-cognition. It is the actually manifesting knowledge which has been doubly named. In can be called destructive-subsidential with respect to the positive implication of the mode. It can also be called operatve with respect to its negative implication. Just as there are no *karmas* which can be called absolutely destructive, so also absolutism with reference to destructive-subsidential and operative types of manifestations cannot be maintained. The manifestations which in their major aspects are determined by the operation of *karmas* have been designated as opertive, their minor aspects being dependent upon the subsidence or the endurance or the operation of *karmas.*

The Pāriṇāmika (Natural) Manifestations

Now we take up the discussion of the natural manifestations of the soul. There are some faculties of the soul that do not yield to the *karmic* forces. These faculties are responsible for the generation of natural manifestations. "The manifestations depending upon the soul alone are natural."[1] They are independent of the operation, destruction, subsidence and the destruction-subsidence of the *karmas.*"[2] So the natural manifestations will be the same both in the mundane and liberated states of the soul's existence. Some faculties of the soul may not be subject to the influence of the particular type of *karma,* but they will not lead to the natural manifestations. Actually speaking only those faculties can yield natural manifestations, which are no subject of *karmic* influence. Brahmadeva distinguished between the pure and impure types of natural manifestations.[3] The question is when the natural manifestations are not determined by the *karmas* in any of their states of existence what other factor should be conceived to destroy their purity. Brahmadeva supports his

1. Devanandin: *Sarvārthasiddhi,* p. 82
2. Akalaṅka: *Rājavārtika,* 2. 712
3. Brahmadeva: *Dravya-saṅgraha-vṛtti,* p. 16

view on the ground of the subdivision of natural manifestations as given by Umāsvāti. Actually speaking these manifestations are the implications of the modes resulting from different attributes of the soul. The modes themselves are not identified with them. The subdivisions of the natural manifestations suggest that they represent the generality of a number of the soul's manifestations. Vidyānanda contends: "The ability of being emancipated by right faith, knowledge and conduct is the manifestation of *bhavytva* (liberability). The opposite of it is the manifestation of *Abhavyatva* (non-liberability). These are to be held natural, because they are ever present being independent of the operation of *karmas,* etc. They are caused by the beginningless manifestation of the soul."[1] This clearly shows that the natural manifestations depend upon various attributes and modes which form a beginningless series. The modes of an individual soul so exist that they all fall within a sphere, and the natural manifestations embody the generality of such spheres. As the existence of these modes may be contaminated by the *karmas*, their generality may also be seen as contaminated by them. This allows scope for the impure natural manifestations, as held by Brahmadeva. Such impure natural manifestations do not require the help of any further *karmas* for their appearances. So they are said to be natural. It is in this respect that all the three manifestations as enumerated by Umāsvāti may be held to be natural.

To be brief the soul's manifestations may be grouped only into two classes, i.e., the operative and the non-operative ones. When the operative manifestations presuppose the existence of destruction-subsidence of some *karmas*, they become the destructive-subsidential manifestations; and when they are not so based, they are said to be simply operative ones. The non-operative manifestations may presuppose destruction or subsidence of *karmas* thus giving rise to the destructive or subsidential types of manifestations.

---

1. Vidyānandin: *Tattvārtha-ślokavātika*, p. 316

If these non-operative manifestations are not so based, they are said to be natural manifestations. This two fold or five fold division of the conscious manifestations of the *jiva* is the very foundation of the Jaina or the *karma* psychology which aims at going deeper into the very nature of the self and the causes of the variations of its powers. We cannot agree with the view of modern psychology which makes a great use of the powers of the psyche but does not believe in a substratum for such powers. B.L. Atreya correctly odserves: "In the zeal to acquire the status of an exact science psychology has really lost its soul and has been wasting much of its time in aping the lower sciences of Mathematics, Physics and Chemistry, which are built on a Method which fails in the field of psychology, unless supplemented by another which is pecularly its own"[1] C.R. Jain also makes a similar remark. He says "The Jaina or Higher psychology as it might be termed, is not connected with that elementary branch of the subject which exhausts itself in the measurement of sensations, the effect of emotions on the outer physical body and the like, but which studiously avoids to ascertain whether the soul be a reality or myth. Its province in the higher department of thought which seeks to understand the nature of the thing whose presence is the source of life and light in the body and also of action and the inhibition of action, and of the diversified impulsions and promptings of the mind."[2]

IV

The Problem of Karma-Determinism, Indeterminism and Freedom

If the relation between the soul and the *karmas* is to be designated as an interactionism, it is an interactionism in which neither the substance nor the attributes of the one are

1. B.L. Atreya: *An Introduction to Para Psychology*, p. 1
2. C.R. Jain: *Jaina Psychology* (Preface)

transformed into those of the other. The same is the limitation when the *karmas* are said to determine the physiology and the environment connected with a *jīva*. The *karmas* become simply an occasion or a *nimitta kāraṇa* in the determination of the psychic, physiological and environmental variations. Under this limitations *karma*-determinism can mean simply an agreement between the potency of the *karmas* and the consequent variations in the above mentioned three spheres. Our problem is to discern whether this type of *karma*-determinism can be consistently maintatined.

Samantabhadra objects to absolute *karma*-determinism as "If things are accomplished solely by the fate (or *karmas*), then it cannot be maintained that fate can also be determined by effort (*puruṣārtha*). If fate is determined by another fate then emancipation becomes impossible and effort, fruitless."[1] There is a basic inconsistency in holding the absolute *karma*-determinism, it will allow no scope for effort. We have already seen that there is no perfect co-ordination between the operation of *karmas* and the environment. The fact of the atrophy of *karmas* is an obstruction in the way of absolute *karma*-determinism. Every *karma* requires a suitable ground for its realization; and failing to get such a ground it sheds off fruitless. This atrophy is threefold according to the three classes of *karmas*. It is possible that the psychological accomplishment is there, but the physiological and the environmental factors are suffering in some way. In such a situation the psychical *karmas* will not realize their end fully, *karmas* both in their operative and destructive-subsidential states suffer in the above manner. All this leads to the conclusion that *karma* determinism in its absolute form is not a tenable theory.

We cannot go to the other extreme of absolute indeterminism and hold that the will can be perfectly independent of the *karmic* influence. The absolutism of indeterminism directly leads to the futility of the *karma* doctrine. If *karmas* have no bearing on the behaviour of

---

1. **Samantabhadra:** *Āptamīmāṁsā*, verse 88

living beings, they are as good as non-existent. In the absence of the *karmic* influence, the individual differences become inexplicable. Samantabhadra again observes: If things are accomplished by effort only, effort cannot be held to be determined by *karmas* or fate. If fate is also determined solely by effort, then effort will become fruitlful in case of all living beings"[1] No living being is absolutely free to choose and act. Such a limitation is felt by every individual and it speaks to the truth of *karmic* influence.

The concept of freedom or indeterminism may be taken to yield two meanings. Firstly it may stand for creating a situation which balances the effect of the *karmas. Karmas* alone cannot yield something which is detrimental to their own working. Hence this effort must be due to the soul itself. It is on account of the soul's own powers that it is able to maintain itself against the *karmas.* The freedom of the soul may be held to lie in this maintenence. Secondly freedon finds its full meaning only in the *kṣāyika* (destructive) type of conscious manifestations. Such manifestation are determined by the soul itself and hence they may be termed as free. It is self-determinism and is perfectly consistent with freedom. "Determinism in the sense of self-determination is not inconsistent with freedom," as H. Rashdall held.[1] Absolute freedom, as distinct from self-determinism, is a meaningless conception.

The Jaina View of Determinism and Indeterminism

Thus the conceptions of freedom and determinism cannot be thought of in isolation from each other. They mutually imply each other. It is said that "liberty and necessity both co-operate harmoniously in the production of every human thought. Every human life and conduct therefore is but a reconciliation between liberty and necessity.[2] Mundane personalities are the joint effects of the soul's powers and

1. Rashdall: *Theory of Good and Evil*, II, p. 309
2. Nahar and Ghosh: *An Epitome of Jainism*, p. 384

the *karma*-forces. From the synthetic point of view the two types of forces yield a single resultant in the form of mundane personalities. From the analytical point of view the two components of the mundane personalities can be distinguished. Greater magnitude of one or the other signifies freedom or determinism. Actually speaking the personality of an individual is beyond both determinism and freedom. It does not negate them but transcends them. It is why neither determinism nor freedom is able to give its full description. On the application of the Jaina *nayavāda* the same entity can be seen as determined or free, because it smells out determinism and indeterminism at the same time. Jayasena in the commentry of the *Pravacanasāra* describes the soul from the deterministic (*niyati*) and indeterministic (*aniyati*) view-points.[1] Hence according to the Jaina determinism and indeterminism are partial truths valid only when appropriate reference-systems are defined. The *karmas* work in such a way that they allow freedom for the members involved in the process; and freedom is so effected that it does not oppose *karma*-determinism. In conclusion it may be added that "Necessitarianism quarrels with libertarianism and libertarianism is not prepared to agree with necessitarianism, but the doctrine of *karma* quarrels with none, since it agrees with both to an intelligible extent."[2]

The Jaina on Moral Accountability

The Jaina *karma*-determinism presents no moral difficutly. The problem of moral accountability is well solved only when there is *karma*-determinism of the above type. In absolute determinism moral accountability becomes unjustified. In absolute indeterminism the appearance of the action itself becomes impossible. Moral accountability requires both determinism and freedom. "...there is nothing

1. Cf: *Pravacanasāra* (Com. by Jayasen), p. 371
2. M.L. Mehta: *Jaina Psychology*, p. 8

incompatible with morality in this necessary determinism inseparable with human nature, a deteminism which is the condition of freedom with responsibility."[1] Not only freedom presupposes determinism, but the reverse is also true. It is true because determinism and freedom are very intimately put together in the personality of a living being. In terms of Jaina philosophy moral accountability may be interpreted as a liability for bondage. But this bondage does not take place totally according to the operation of *karmas*. The fact how an individual receives the fruition of *karmas*, plays an important part in the determination of bondage. The external behaviour being the same, milder types of bondage are due to the less passionate reception of the fruition of the *karmas*. Kundakunda says: "One who entertains attachment binds *karmas*. The soul free from attachment does not bind *karmas*. This is the preaching of the Jina."[2] Such is in brief the Jaina theory of bondage of the soul by the *Karmas*.

1. A.B Lathe: *An Introduction to Jainism*, p. 101
2. Kundakunda: *Samayaprābhṛta*, verse 160

Chapter 9

The Jaina Theory of Liberation and the Non-absolute

The Basic Implications of the Theory of Liberation

The mundane existence of the self and the variations of its powers suggest that there may be a state of the self's existence where it is free from the mundane limitations and distortions. It means that then the liberated soul will have no obstruction to the manifestations of its powers. In Jaina philosophy the doctrice of *karma* provides the principle of the soul's fall from its pure state. The disappearance of the *karmic* influence from the soul will lead to its pure and self-determined functions. The seven principles of Jaina philosophy give us the various stages on the path to liberation. Thus the theory of liberation presupposes the existence of the soul and its bondage by the *karmas*; liberation, then, is the freedom of the soul from the bondage of the *karmas*. The possibility of this freedom is another implication of the theory of liberation. Along with the existence of the soul the truth of its bondage and the possibility of freedom from *karma* may be taken to be the basic conceptions upon which the rise of the soul from its mundane existence to the liberated state depends.

The Nyāyā and the Mīmāsṁā Conceptions of Mokṣa

In almost all the systems the conception of mokṣa is very closely connected with the conceptions of the soul and its bondage. To begin with, for the Nyāya the soul is a substance in which the attributes of knowledge, feeling, desire, etc., inhere on account of the category of *samayāya*.

Even consciousness is an accidental attribute of the soul. In liberation the soul becomes free not only from suffering and pain but also from knowledge and consciousness. They are found in the soul on account of its asscociation with the body. Hence in liberation the soul exists as a pure substance. It is also held that the fall of the soul is due to false knowledge—a knowledge that does not distinguish between the soul on one hand and the body and other objects on the other.[1] Knowledge alone is potent to remove ignorance and to free the soul from the worldly fetters. It is strange that the existence of this knowledge is also negated in liberation. M. Hiriyanna observes: "As a consequence it (the soul) will be devoid of thought, feeling and will, and mokṣa thus becomes a condition of perfect gloom from which there will be no re-awakening. Such a state has rightly been condemned by the opponents of the doctrine as a remedy worse than the disease which it prosposes to cure."[2] It must be supposed that in liberation the soul gains a power which enables it not to admit of the effect of the category of *samavāya.* Such a soul is said to be the pure substance. The Mīmāṁsā conception of liberation or mokṣa marks an advance over the Nyāya conception which it otherwise mostly resembles. According to the Mīmāṁsā the soul has no consciousness in liberation, because its connection with the body and the senses are then totally cut off; but still it retains a potentiality for consciousness. About the Mīmāṁsā conception of mokṣa it is said that "it is a state where the soul remains in its own intrinsic nature, beyond pleasure and pain. The soul in its intrinsic state can be defined only as substance having existence and a potentiality for consciousness though no actual consciousness."[3] But for this potentiality for consciousness the Naiyāyika and the Mīmāṁsaka hold almost similar views.

---

1. cf. Chatterjee and Datta: *An Introduction to Indian Philosophy*, p. 239
2. M. Hiriyana: *Essentials of Indian Philosophy*. p. 103
3. Chatterjee anc. Datta: *An Introduction to Indian Philosophy*, p. 390

The Buddhīstic Conceptīon of Mokṣa

Coming to the Buddhistic conception of mokṣa it cannot be consistently taken to be an absolute non-existence, as the use of the term *nirvāṇa* may imply. If Buddhism holds such a view, then its position will go far behind that of the Naiyāyika; and, in this respect, it may be likened to that of the Cārvāka for whom liberation is totally an empty concept. In Buddhism liberation is sought to put an end to one's own miseries and to enable oneself to do the same for others, as Lord Buddha did. However cessation of worldly miseries and sufferings is not the only content of the Buddhistic liberation but peace results there in the liberated state. Hence it has a positive content which may be held to exist in accordance with the general law of momentariness. According to T.R.V. Murti "Buddha has taught the doctrine of momentariness not as an ultimate proposition but a step leading to relativity (śūnyatā)."[1] Buddha's silence on this point should not be taken to mean that liberation is an utter void (śūnya), wherein he found nothing to comprehend; but it must mean that there is something which cannot be comprehended in terms of ordinary experience. "The silence of Buddha is a classical illustration of the truth that final truths cannot be expressed in words: to take Buddha to be a nihilist is to mistake his philosophical stature."[2] Thus the Buddhistic mokṣa is rich with contents which language fails to describe. This simply leads to the inexpressibility of the state of liberation. This state which escapes all expression, is what T.R.V. Murti means by śūnyatā or relativity. Such a state is beyond expression, but is held to be comprehensible by direct experience.

The Sāṁkhyan and the Advaitist Conceptions of Mokṣa

The Sāṁkhya reserves an immutable position for the *puruṣa* in his philosophy. Still he agrees with others in

1. T.R.V. Murti: *The Central Philosophy of Buddhism,* p. 122
2. Naga Raja Rao: *The Schools of Vedānta,* p. 31

holding that liberation means a total cessation of pain and suffering. According to him pain and pleasure belong to *buddhi* or intellect and the mind, the *puruṣa* is totally beyond their reach. Actually speaking in the Sāṁkhya system we cannot talk of the liberation of the *puruṣa;* still bondage is held to be a real fact, it is in no way a delusion. The Sāṁkhya conceives another entity, born of *prakṛti,* which is made subject to bondage. Buddhi or mind comes very near the *puruṣa* and it so behaves that it is taken to be conscious. So it is really the bondage of *prakṛti;* and hence it is the *prakṛti* that is to be liberated. Unless the *puruṣa* in some way suffers from the bondage, liberation can have no meaning. The gain of consciousness on the part of *prakṛti* will not solve the problem but raise the *prakṛti* to the status of the *puruṣa.* Still the Sāṁkhya may be given credit for maintaining consciousness as an essential attribute of the soul and its bondage as an existential fact. On the other hand the Advaitin starts with the monism of *Brahma.* The entire universe is *Brahma. Brahma* is the only reality of the universe. At the same time it is immutable. To explain the visible manifoldness and differences of the world the principle of *māyā* is formulated. It causes the existence of both the individual *jīva* and its bondage. But the principle of *māyā* is not granted any reality parallel to the *Brahma. Māyā* and its effects are true only at the empirical level, while the empirical level has no validity as compared with the transcendental level. Thus the Advaitism agrees with the Sāṁkhya in holding the immutability of *Brahma* or *Puruṣa;* but its bondage in his hand is reduced to a mere delusion. It does not stand parallel to the Sāṁkhyan bondage which is an existential fact. Though Śaṁkara assigns empirical reality to bondage, yet the conception does not gain in tenability on account of the non-est principle of *māyā* in the root. If the *Sāṁkhya* is said to have no bondage of the *puruṣa,* the Advaitin also holds a position which is not very much different from it. The former attributes the phenomenon of bondage to the *prakṛti,* the latter reduces it to a delusion. In Advaitism bondage is a delusion born of another delusion.

Actually speaking there is nothing to be deluded, because the only reality of Advaita Vedānta, i.e., the *Brahma*, being immutable, cannot itself be deluded. The delusive appearance must be actually comprehended by some one though it may be caused by the preceiving mind itself. Unless there is someone to be deluded, the talk of delusion cannot be meaningful. Again delusion is not the nature of *Brahma*, hence *Brahma* itself cannot be the cause of delusion. *Māyā* must come out to be a distinct antithesis of *Brahma*, if any reality is granted to the individual soul and its bondage. To make ethics real bondage and the mundane existence of the *jīva* must be taken to be true. Samantabhadra remarks that in the absolutism of Advaita there is no possibility of science and nescience, and bondage and liberation.[1] Actually speaking both for the Sāṁkhya and the Advaitin there is no liberation, because for the former the individual self was never fallen while for the latter there is no individual self at all.

The Jaina Conception of Mokṣa

The Jaina conception of Mokṣa is based on the Jaina theory of the soul and its bondage by *karmas*. The soul and the *karmas* both are existential categories of Jaina philosophy. Hence liberation must be an actual event in the life-history of the soul. No member in the Jaina theory of the soul's bondage and liberation is reduced to featurelessness or a delusion. The soul, its bondage and its liberation are all existential facts. At the same time inspite of depriving the soul of its attributes the Jaina grants an undisturbed pure manifestation of the faculties of the soul in the state of liberation. *Karmas* obscured and distorted these faculties, hence freedonm from *karmas* would mean their liquidation from the soul. Umāsvāti describes mokṣa as the total expulsion of the *karmas* from the soul.[2] Śubhacandra says:

---

1. Samantabhadra: *Āptamīmāṁsā*, verse 25
2. Umāsvāti: *Tattvārthasūtra*, 10.2

"The differentia of the mokṣa is the breach of the association of all the *karmas* with the soul."[1] Limitations of the soul cannot take place by themselves, they are affected by the operation of *karmas*. So, if the *karmas* are shed off somehow, the soul must attain its natural form of existence. Nemicandra distinguishes between the subjective and the objective types of *mokṣa*. He says: "The soul's manifestation which is the cause of destruction of all the *karmas* is the subjective *mokṣa*, the objective *mokṣa* means the expulsion of the *karma-pudgala* from the soul."[2] This distinction emphasizes both the psychological and the physical aspects of the process of liberation. Like the bondage by the physical *karmas* and the resulting psychology of the *Jīva* the process of liberation is made concrete by the introduction of the distinction between the subjective and the objective types of liberation.

The Jaina on the Possibility of Liberation

Though the association of *karmas* with the soul is beginningless, yet it comes to an end. The Jaina thinkers have advanced some arguments to show the possibility of liberation. Umāsvāti states that "the *mokṣa* is possible on account of the absence of causes of bondage and the expulsion of the accumulated *karmas*, from the soul."[3] The mundane existence of the soul is maintained and prolonged by the influx of *karmas* and the fruition of the *karmas* already bound with the soul. Hence liberation must result from the negation of the aforesaid two conditions. In other words, if the influx of the *karmas* can be exhausted, the liberation of the soul must follow as a necessary consequence. This seems to be the basic argument advanced in support of the possiibility of liberation.

Vidyānanda gives further arguments to support the

1. Śubhacandra: *Jñānārṇava*, p. 82
2. Nemicandra: *Dravyasaṅgraha*, verse 37
3. Umāsvāti: *Tattvārthasūtra*. 10.2

aforesaid two conditions. In support of the cessation of bondage in some *jīva* he states: "The absence of bondage is proved by the presence of right faith, etc., which are the opposites of the causes of bondage."[1] Supporting the possibility of the expulsion of *karmas* from soul he observes: "In some soul the *karmas* are totally shed off, because their existence is terminated by their fruition. The termination of *karmas* by their fruition is proved by the fact their fruition is not found to be eternal."[2] As regards the first argument the absence of bondage is proved by the presence of such causes as oppose the process of bondage. In this respect the validity of the presence of the necessary causes still requires a proof. How can we show that the conditions like the right faith, etc., are attainable? On the contray in Jaina pholosophy we find a mention of such souls that can never attain these conditions.[3] Hence in this respect the argument seems to provide insufficient ground. Coming to the second argument of Vidyānanda it is held that the existence of all the *karmas* is terminated by their fruition. But this fruition itself becomes a cause of further bondage, and thus the chain of bondage continues. The fruition of *karmas* is not a necessary condition for that expulsion (*nirjarā*) of *karmas* which we require for liberation. Moreover it is said that for liberation the '*akāma*'[4] type of *nirjarā* or expulsion of *karmas* is required and it is effected by means of penances and meditation. Expulsion of *karmas* in general, which is a common attainment of all the souls, is not a sufficient

---

1. Vidyānandin: *Āptaparīkṣā*, p. 2
2. *Ibid.*, p. 2.
3. Nemicandra: *Gommaṭasāra (Jīvakāṇḍa)*, verse 557
4. The Jaina coneives the principle of *nirjarā* or the expulsion of *karmas* as having two varieties. The *karmas* when mature bear their fruits and fall from the soul. This is the first or the *sakāma* type of *nirjarā*. It is not sufficient for the attainment of liberation. so the devotee has to make special efforts to effect another type of *nirjarā,* the *akāma-nirjarā* which brings about a speedy expulsion of a larger amount of *karmas*. This type of *nirjarā* is very essential for the final emancipation of the soul.

condition for liberaton. Hence to hold that the mere termination of the existence of the *karmas* by their fruition is a sufficient proof for the total expulsion of *karmas* from the soul is wrong.

One more argument is advanced by Samantabhadra in support of the possibility of liberation. He says. "The destruction of the obscurations and the obscuring *karmas* must be complete on account of its causes, because there are rising degrees of such a destruction."[1] Again, just as the rising degrees of destruction of *karmas* are noticeable, so also the rising degrees of their effect are also noticed. Hence on the ground of the above argument it also follows that at some moment of time the effects of *karmas* must be complete so as to destroy the faculties of the soul totally. At this point the argument may seem to lose its force. But it may be supplemented by the fact that what is connected with a substance as an attribute cannot be totally destroyed. Knowledge, etc., are connected with the soul in the aforesaid manner, and so the *karmas* cannot destroyed them totally. On the other hand *karmas* are substantially distinct from the soul, and, therefore, they can be severed from the soul. Samantabhadra's argument gains in force when it is conssidered along with the Jaina theory of attributes.

It may also be said that the beginninglessness of the *karma*-association is a obstacle in the way of liberation. When this association as extended in the past has never been broken, it may continue eternally in future in the same way. The oft quoted example of the ore and the dross does not necessarily imply the beginninglessness of their association. So the argument based on this example stands only as a weak analogy which does not yield the necessary support we expected from it. The idea behind the example may be taken to suggest that the beginninglessnes of the *karma*-association has nothing to do with the end of this association. It is brought about by some causes, while its end, by others different from the former ones. So wherever

1. Samantabhadra: *Āptamīmāṁsā*, verse 4

the proper causes are available the *karma*-association must come to an end irrespective of the fact that it had no beginning in the past. Das Gupta says: "Though it is beginningless yet it can be removed by knowledge, for to have a beginning or not to have it does not in any way determine whether the thing is subject to dissolution or not, for the dissolution of a thing depends upon the presence of the thing which can cause it; and it is a fact that when knowledge comes illusion is destroyed, it does not matter whether the cause which produced the illusion was beginningless or not."[1] It appears that this aspect of *karma*-philosophy did not much attract the attention of the Jaina thinkers themselves. Like others they also did not doubt the possibility of liberation, because it is the great hope for which the entire system of philosophy is constructed. It may be said that behind all these arguments lies the fact of the substantial distinction between the soul and the *karmas*, and it is responsible for the possiblity of liberation. It does not make liberation as essential event in the life of every soul; but where the proper causes are present liberation must follow.

Negativity of The Soul and Liberation

We must remember that according to the Jaina the bondage of the soul is fundamentally due to its negativity (*vibhāva-śakti*). This negativity functions only when the soul in under the influence of the *karma*-forces. The Jaina does not see any fault in this mutual dependence between negativity and *karma*-bondage, because the series of bondage extends infinitely in the past. As step by step the layers of *karmas* are being thinned, the negativity of the soul also loses its potency. Thus, when there is a total expulsion of *karmas*, the soul's negativity must also suspend its function. We cannot suppose that in the liberated state negativity is deprived of its function, because in Jaina philosophy it

1. Das Gupta: *A History of Indian Philosophy*, vol. I, p. 453

cannot be granted the status of a attribute. The attributes of the soul are such as admit of negative function in the presence of *karmas*; and these *karmas* being eliminated the attributes must function self-determinedly. Rājamalla remarks: "In the absence of *karmas* the power of negativity changes into a natural power."[1] In the absence of negativity the soul loses all attraction for *karmas*, and there is no further bondage. *Karmas* are the only enemies of the soul which cause a distortion of its nature. By destroying these enemies the soul becomes self-determined and self-contained (*svastha*). The etymological meaning of sanskrit term '*svastha*' finds its just application to this state of spiritual realization, while its hygienic meaning is only derivative. This state is the full realization of what Nemicandra mentions as the state wherein the soul may be said to be absorbed or lost in itself.[2] It, then, continues through the manifestations of its own pure attributes.

Manifestation of the Soul's Power in Liberation

As the *karmas* were regrouped into three classes the freedom of the soul is also effected in three ways. What were called the psychical faculties of the soul are now free from all limitations. So no psychical phenomena, as the modern psychology understands, can appear in a pure soul. In other words there is no sensuous or perceptual knowledge and the feelings of anger, pride, deceit, greed, pain and pleasure in the pure soul. Pure knowledge and pure feeling are no subjects for psychology, hence the pure soul refuses to abide by its laws. In this sense alone we can hold that there is no psychology of the pure souls. On the destruction of the physiological classs of *karmas* there is no determination of the body. Thus the physiological limitations, which worked as instruments to psychical functions, come to an end. Now the soul's power of cognition and affection can

---

1. Rājamalla: *Pañcādhyāyī*, II, verse 90
2. Nemicandara: *Dravyasaṅgraha*, verse, 56

effect a pure function independent of the body. Similarly the environmental *karmas*, which, were responsible for help and hinderance lose their potency. The soul is then able to continue with its infinite powers.

According to the traditional theory of *karma*-classification eight qualities are said to emerge in the *siddhas* or the liberated ones on the destruction of eight *karmas*. They are perfect knowledge, perfect conation (*darśana*), complete loss of obstruction (*avyābādhatva*), right faith, extreme subtlity (*paramasaukṣmaya*), interpenetration (*avagāhana*), complete loss of mass (*agurulaghutva*) and infinite power (*anantavīrya*).[1] The traditional viewpoint enumerates the qualities of the liberated ones in a detailed way. All the qualities point to the unobstructed manifestations of the soul's attributes. Rājamalla enumerates conduct, conation, bliss, knowledge, power, right faith, subtlity, interpenetration, complete loss of obstruction (*avyābādha*) and complete loss of mass (*agurulaghutva*) as the qualities of the pure *jīva*."[2] The latter list agrees with former with the exception of the qualities of bliss and conduct which should also be supposed to be distinct faculties of the soul. The qualities of subtlity, interpenetration, and complete loss of mass refer to the elimination of such characteristics as are held to be associated with the soul on account of the body. Actually speaking they cannot be attributed to the soul, being the qualities of matter. The enumeration of the quality of conduct refers to that state of the soul where no tinge of passions (*kaṣāyas*) is found in it. The passionate states of the soul were the impure manifestations of the soul, and so they must presuppose an attribute behind them. Thus by the quality of conduct we may mean passionlessness or the peaceful steadiness of the soul which was distorted by the conduct deluding *karma*, a sub-class of the deluding *karma*. On the same ground the enumeration of bliss is also justified. Bliss is one of the four infinite attributes of the emancipated

1. Amṛtacandra: *Tattvārthasāra*, verses 37, 38, 39 and 40
2. Rājamalla: *Pañcādhyāyī*, II, verses 942, 943

souls, and so it cannot be removed from the list of the pure qualities of the siddhas. Moreover it has been shown and established that bliss is also an attribute of the soul. When the *karmas* are exhausted, this attribute must be left there to undergo a process of pure manifestations. This very faculty must be identified with the infinite bliss of the *kevalis* or the perfect ones.

Extension of the Liberated Souls

The Jaina theory of substance makes extension an essential aspect of every substance, so the soul must have an extension even in liberation. This extension is a mode of expression of the soul's capacity of having *predeśas (pradeśavatva).* The soul has many such *pradeśas* and occupies a definite position in space, though offering no resistence to other substances. We should not think that the soul has extension only so far as it is in association with the body. Extension is an existential implicate of its own existence. Its association with the body or, to go still deeper, its association with the *karmas* is responsible for contraction and expansion. Akalañka says: "On account of the body-making *karma,* like the light of a lamp, the soul is said to possess contraction and expansion."[1] This capacity results from the negativity of the soul. In the absence of the *karmas* it loses all its potency, and the soul is left with a fixed extension. As regards this extension of the soul in liberation the Jaina is of opinion that it has the same dimension as the last body the soul possessed.[2] We can deduce this conclusion from the premises the Jaina has established. Up to the attainment of the last body the *karmas* remain there to determine contraction and expansion of the soul. They work up to the moment just preceding the soul's liberation. Then the soul is left free from *karmas.* So the extension left with it is the same as that of the last body. With the disappearance of the

1. Akalaṅka: *Rājavārtika*, 10.4.14
2. Nemicandra: *Dravyasaṅgraha*, verse 14

karmas the soul's capacity for contraction and expansion also vanishes. Hence for a liberated soul there is only one changeless extension, i.e., the extension of the last body.

Eternality of the Liberated State

In pursuance of a similar line of reasoning it may be shown that a liberated soul can never return to mundane existence. Liberation is said to be possible on the attainment of those conditions which oppose the causes of mundane existence; and these conditions are self-determined. Once such obstructions are removed we find no reason why they should at all reappear. The Jaina also thinks that the transmigration of the soul was due to the presence of *karmas*. If were *karmas* that dragged the soul from one life to another. In the total absence of the *karmas* this transmigration should also come to an end. It means that once liberation is attained the soul must continue in its pure state for ever.

Dynamism in Liberation

The attainment of the perfect state by a soul is very likely to suggest that there is no dynamism in liberation. On the contrary the theory of substance holds that, if dynamism is suspended, the substance will lose its existence. In the process of gradual release from the *karmas* the soul was really developing its faculties, and it may be said to be evolving. When it was able to destroy the *karmas* totally, it must have attained the summit of self-evolution. Then there being no higher heights to be attained and a fall being impossible, the soul may be supposed to lose its dynamic nature. But the Jaina position is different from it. It is true that there is no higher state the soul may aspire to attain, but it is no proof of the suspension of its dynamism. The Jaina thinks that in liberation the change is not towards the higher but towards the similar. The modes that successively appear in liberation are so like each other that their comprehension is beyond ordinary knowledge. In nature there is simply dynamism, the idea of evolution is attached to it by us in accordance with a purpose in view. Dynamism does not care whether there is evolution or not. It can go on with very slight variations in which the distinctive part is reduced to a minimum. It is known in Jaina philosophy as the *sadṛśā pariṇamana* (change by similarity). Rājamalla mentions similar and dissimilar variations under the conception of *tadatadbhāva*, the former are found in the liberated ones while the latter belong to the mundane *jīvas*.[1]

II

Kundakunda's Treatment of the Pure Soul

Kundakunda describes the soul from the pure view-point (*śuddha naya*) by which he means a description made by keeping the pure state of the soul in mind. In his 'Samayasāra' he repeatedly draws a distinction between the soul's description made from the realistic (*niścaya*) and the empirical (*vyavahāra*) points of view. He says: "The non-distinguished one soul is most desirable in the universe. When there is the story of its bondage, it becomes untrue."[2] "The knower is said to be having conduct, conation and knowledge from the *vyavahāra* point of view. From the pure point of view there is neither knowledge. nor conduct nor conation, but it is the pure knower."[3] The soul is a unity and its division into various faculties can be made only from the empirical view-point. Further it is said: "He is the knower who knows that the soul is not the doer of the *karmas* and of the quasi-*karmas*, i.e., the body and the environment."[4] Again "from the *niścaya* or the realistic point of view the soul is the doer of itself and enjoys itself."[5] These couplets

1. Rājamalla: *Pañcādhyāyī, I,* verse 326
2. Kundakunda: *Samayaprābhṛta*, verse 3
3. *Ibid.*, verse 7
4. *Ibid.*, verse 80
5. *Ibid.*, verse 89

aim at cuting off all the relations between the soul and the *karmas* and the body. The soul is supposed to have no connection with what is other then itself and is confined to its own identity. Again it is emphasized that "the soul neither does nor enjoys the *karmas* of various types. It simply knows the fruition of *karmas*, meritorious and demeritorious."[1] When asked what the soul's identity is, Kundakunda replies that it is one unity indistinguishable even into its various faculties, and is perfectly confined to itself. In the above statements Kundakunda sees the soul as perfectly independent and goes to the extent of denying the auxiliary causation by which we are able to explain the mystery of the mind-body relation. Just as the conception of *māya* in Advaīta Vedānta has been interpreted as a device to arouse the spirit of renunciation among the followers, in the same way it may be said that Kundakunda has also thought of a method in the form of the pure view-point to arouse an ethical awakening without which a devotee is not fit to advance on the path of the soul's development. This interpretation of the view point of Kundakunda savours inconsistency, "when one reads that "the *vyavahāra* view-point is false and the pure view point is true. A right believer invariably resorts to the true reality."[2] Rājamalla is also of opinion that the *vyavahāra* is false and gives us false preaching.[3] This brings us to a consideration of the validity which is implied by the pure point of view.

Validity of the Niścaya Naya

It is strange to note that the *niścaya naya* or the realistic view-point does not appear in the metaphysical discussions. There the main *nayas* are the *dravyārthika* (substantial) and the *pryayārthika* (modal) ones. Umāsvāti enumerates seven *nayas* which have been described as the sub-divisions of the

1. *Ibid.*, verse 348
2. *Ibid.*, verse 13.
3. Rājamalla: *Pañcādhyāyī*, I, verse 628

two basic *nayas.*[1] It is Kundakunda who mentions the *niścaya* and the *vyavahāra nayas* and the tradition is followed by Nemicandra. The absence of this tradition in metaphysics shows that Kundakunda's *nayas* are formulated from the ethical point of view. We must be aware of the fact that the *vyavahāra* of Kundakunda is not the same as that of Umāsvāti. Vidyānanda holds the *vyavahāra naya* to be a variety of the *dravyarthika naya*"[2] while the popular belief identifies the *niścaya* with the *dravyārthika* and the *vyavahāra* with the *paryayārthika nayas.* The *niścaya naya* has been again divided into pure and impure ones as we clearly see in Nemicandra. Brahmadeva thinks that with reference to the pure view-point the impure *niścaya-naya* is also a *vyavahara-naya.*[3] The former sees the soul as free and pure, while the latter takes its mundane existence into consideration but independently of the material *karmas.* So the *nayas* of Kundakunda are concerned with the various states (modes) of the soul as abstructions from an existing reality. Hence in metaphysics they must fall under the *paryāyārthika-naya.* But on the other hand ethics must study things with reference to the ideal of the pure soul, which raised the importance of the *niścaya-naya* considerably. In spite of this fact the *niścaya* is only a *naya*, a view point, and it cannot yield the whole truth. The association of *karmas* with the soul is only a *nimitta,* an auxiliary cause, for the soul's manifestations. Anger, sensuous knowledge, etc., are the soul's own manifestations, or the soul must be held to be static as the Sāṁkhya does. The impure view-point considers such distorted manifestations of the soul, but it carries almost no import in the ethical realm. It is why Kundakunda recommends an advance over the *vyavahāra* and the impure view-points. These view-points must be held to be false with respect to the pure view-point, because every partial

1. Umāsvāti: *Tattvārthasūtra*, 1,33.
2. Vidyānandin: *Tattvārthaślokavārtika*, 1.33.3
3. Brahmadeva: *Dravyasaṅgraha-vṛtti*, p. 89

truth must become false if a wrong reference-system is attributed to it. Kundakunda's universe of discourse is confined to the pure soul and so the truths depending upon the impure and the *vyavahāra* view-points must come out to be false. But this validity of the pure view-point and the falsity of the impure and the *vyavahāra* view-points are only relatively true, i.e., they must be accommodating to each other. Moreover no *naya* proceeds on something positive to determine the emergence of the *vyavahāra* and the *aśuddhaniścaya nayas.* Rājamalla says that they proceed on account of the negativity of the soul.[1] A *naya* is never without the support of something real in the existent, or there will be no regulative principle for the formulation of *nayas.* So we come to the conclusion that what Kundakunda thinks ethically false cannot be so metaphysically.

Kundakunda gives a description of the soul from the view-point of pure *niścaya-naya* and thinks it to be valid. When a question is raised as to the thesis of the *niścya-naya,* Rājamalla states that not this (*neti*) is its thesis and for this reason its is also a *naya.*"[2] The subject-matter for the *niścaya-naya* is the negation of the *vyavahāra,* and it is the highest reality.[3] From the view-point of *niścaya-naya* "there is neither substance, nor attribute, nor both of them, nor their totality. There is only the non-dualism of sat which may be taken to be an attribute of a substance."[4] The description of the soul may be effected from different view-points. No proposition can give us its full description. Whatever is predicated of the soul affirmatively just excludes the other possibilities. Hence a better description must consist of negative statements. Being a negative statement it cannot touch the reality of the soul derectly, but it is more suited as it guards us from taking any one characteristic for the whole of the

1. Rājamalla: *Pañcādhyāyī*, I, verse 531
2. *Ibid*., verse 601
3. *Ibid*., verse 598
4. *Ibid*., verse 635

soul. But at the same time there is a danger that the soul may be taken to be a void. It is for this reason that we cannot eliminate the positive statements in the soul, they have their own importance. So we shall have to maintain that the antithesis of '*neti*' in the form '*tadeveti*' (that it is) is also descriptive of the soul. When the two theses are combined together, as is the aim of the *anekānta* philosophy, we shall get still a fuller description of the soul. The aforesaid theses represent the ordinary way of our thinking. Reality cannot be exhausted by these partial truths, but at the same time the partial descriptions of the soul must be held true in their proper universes of discourse. When the *niścaya-naya* simply negates the *vyavahāra,* it will have nothing positive as its content. As absolute negation has no meaning and it is always the affirmation of something implied by it implicitly, the *niścaya naya* must be pointing to something positive, it cannot be a mere negation. At the same time it is simply a *naya* bound with some thesis. Our conclusion then, is that the *niścaya naya* must not be purely negative. From this *niścaya* point of view Kundakunda (in his Samayasāra) and Nemicandra (in his Dravyasaṁgraha) make a number of statements which convey a positive information. Thus we cannot agree with what Rājamalla holds that the *niścaya naya* is negative and inexpressible. The truths yielded by the *niścaya naya* may be held to be valuable, because ethically they are most useful. Kundakunda repeatedly establishes the pure cognitive nature of the soul from the pure point of view. We know that knowledge is one of the attributes of the soul, and the identity of the soul is not exhausted by it. So the soul as only a pure knower is an isolation from a totality. This isolation may be important again from the ethical viewpoint, but the absence of attachment and aversion in the soul are presupposed by it. Thus the *niścaya naya* yields an information which falls short of complete and true description of the soul.

Kundakunda's Theory of Samayasāra or the Essence of the Soul

The grandeur of Kundakunda's philosophy of the soul, does not lie in viewing the soul as pure but in the search of a truth beyond all the *nayas.* "The soul is bound with the *karmas* or not bound with them are the theses (pakṣas) of *nayas.* What is beyond these theses is the essence of the soul."[1] the commentator Amṛtacandra Sūri states: "Those, who leave attachment of all the theses and are safe within their identity *(svarūpa),* enjoy the nectar with a peaceful mind being free from the network of the mental vicissitudes *(vikalpas).*[2] One and many, permanent and transitory, expressible and inexpressible, bound and unbound are all the theses of the *nayas;* reality, *paramārtha* or the *vastu* transcends all these theses. Again what the above lines aim to establish is that no thesis is able to give a true picture of reality and that for every thesis there is an antithesis. If reality is described as one *(eka),* the thesis of many (*aneka*) emerges to disturb our judgment and vice versa. But one and many are both predicable of reality in their proper reference systems. One and many both belong to the same reality. Hence reality is held to transcend these theses, if it is to be comprehended in its fullness. Vidyānandin also states that reality or the *vastu* is something beyond one and many and is different from them.[3] Rājamalla himself has admitted that the grandeur of the experience of self is different from the thesis of the *niścaya naya.*[4] The ideal of Jaina metaphysics is neither the truth of the *niścaya naya* nor that of any other viewpoint, but it is a transcendence of all these view-points and it is held to be indescribable. Again the Jaina does not like to hold the indescribability of the soul to be absolute. If so, it will be impossible to predicate

1. Kundakunda: *Samayaprābhṛta*, verse 152
2. Amṛtacandra: *Samayasāra-kalaśa*, verse 70
3. Vidyānandin: *Aṣṭasahasrī*, p. 290
4. Rājamalla: *Pañcādhyāyī*, II. verse 646

even indescribability to the soul, Moreover the analytical view-point effects an analysis of the same reality, and this analysis is not false if we mean it from the analytical view-point. Hence the *parmārtha* cannot be said to be absolutely indescribable. Samantabhadra says: "It is the nature of a proposition that it moves by negating the contents of other propositions."[1] It is true that we cannot effect a complete description of the soul; but by that we cannot mean that the partial descriptions are absolutely false. They are false, no doubt, with respect to the complete comprehension of reality; but their falsity consists only of onesidedness. Such a nature of reality can be summed up only by the non-absolute, because it defies all the absolute views. The *parmārtha* is not the absolute, but it is the non-absolute. It is the non-absolute in which one and many, unity and difference, position and negation and permance and impermanence are peacefully united.

Absolute in Advaita Vedānta

Kundakunda's conception of the essence of the pure soul brings us to a consideration of the theories of the absolute or the ultimate reality of the universe as propounded by various thinkers. The absolute in Advaita Vedanta is ultimately identified with the universal of existence. In our experience we come across many mutually distinct objects, and the commonest element in them is existence. Advaita Vedānta upholds the absolutism of this element by negating all the distinctions with which it is found intermingled. This universal of existence or *sat* constitutes the body of the advaitin's absolute. This is the way we can effect an approach to the absolute. The existence of the absolute or *Brahma* is actually proved by a consideration of the lower. We cannot make a start from the higher, because the higher is beyond our comprehension. When the particular and the universal are seen together,

1. Samantabhadra: *Āptamīmāṁsā*, verse 3

how can we select the one and call the other false and non-existent? By rising to the higher categories we are never negating the lower. The globe is certainly a higher category than the north and the south poles. When we advance from the poles to the globe, we never mean a globe without poles. On the contrary the globe takes the poles into its womb without exhausting their existence. It is why when we come down to the lower again the poles are seen to emerge again. In the same way we can reach the ultimate universal of existence, but by that we cannot negate the reality of the particulars. The particular and the universal together constitute the reality. It is only an abstract way of thinking that we talk of the universal alone or the particular alone. Neither of them can exist without the other.

Again the absolute is held to be one hence without distinctions. Distinctions belong to the lower levels of existence. Even existence (*sat*), consciousness (*cit*) and bliss (*ānanda*) are said to exist in it only from the lower view-point. Distinctions arise out of particularity, so if particularity is attributed to the absolute, distinctions must belong to it. If there is nothing in the absolute to determine the perception of distinctions like the perception of the existence-universal, then we do not understand why the percepton of distinction should at all appear. There must be a principle to regulate our perceptions of distinctions. Advaita Vedānta assigns this function to *māya,* but again the difficulty is that *māyā* is itself a category of the lower level. If Advaita Vedānta wants to give a meaningful explanation of the world, its *māya* must be somehow connected with the absolute and must stand parallel to the absolute. Contrasting Saṅkara's position with that of Nāgārjuna it is maintained that the phenomenal world, for Śaṁkara, is not absolutely unreal like the horn of a hare."[1] There must be some community between the phenomenal and the absolute worlds, and we can talk of this community only when the reality of the two worlds is first admitted. "The very contrast between the

---

1. A.C. Mukerjee: *Nature of Self*, p. 303

real and the unreal would be impracticable without their common basis in the category of being."[1] This implies that the two worlds and their common basis must be simultaneously true. Perhaps for some similar reasons Rāmānuja and Aurobindo both think of *māyā* to be a real power of *Brahma*. It seems that all the differences and distinctions in the absolute have been summed up under the term *māyā*, and then *māyā* is held responsible for their existence and perceptions. The very fact that the empirical world is not a chaos gives a hint that it is not based on something absolutely unreal. There must be something in the Absolute itself which accounts for distinctions. Consciousness, existence and bliss are not random ascriptions of the absolute, it is the absolute itself which gives us these three views along with its all inclusiveness. The absolute is one in such a way that it takes the manifold into its womb.

A satisfactory description of the absolute, it is said, is effected by the term *neti*, i.e., not this. It is true that whatever we predicate of the absolute does not give us a full picture of the absolute; but it cannot be held absolutely false. The truth that is seen in such predications is due to the absolute itself. Existence, consciousness and bliss do not give an absolutely false description of the absolute. A.C. Mukerjee thinks that *satyam-sivam-sundaram* (true, good and beautiful) is the fittest description of the absolute.[2] He further holds: "It is true that the absolute is indescribable; but in spite of this it may be indirectly described by using the highest categories of thought when the latter are not taken in their individual meaning."[3] The same fact is further confirmed in the following words. "We cannot be said to advance a single step in the way of establishing the truth of the absolute by raising it entirely above all categories. Śaṁkara's absolute is not such a transcendent principle, though it is

1. *Ibid.*, p. 268
2. *Ibid.*, p. 265
3. *Ibid.*, p. 267

not definable in the ordinary way."[1] However limited the descriptions of the absolute may be, they cannot be absolutely false. The absolute is not absolutely beyond descriptions. The truth of the partial descriptions of the absolute is again due to something positive in the absolute itself, otherwise anything could have been predicated of it. The absolute is so constructed that no proposition is able to give its full picture. Moreover, if the absolute is only existence-universal (*sattā sāmānya)* and nothing else, then there remains nothing but the existence-universal which can be described. Hence the existence-universal must be taken to be complete description of the absolute which, thus, becomes perfectly describable. The conclusion from the above discussion is that the absolute is neither absolutely describable nor absolutely indescribable. To draw a distinction between the transcendental and empirical levels of existence just brings the two levels on the same footing under a common genus. The truths of the transcendental level become false on the empirical level and vice versa. This reduces the transcendentalism of Advaita Vedānta only to a partial truth.

Thus we see that what Advaita Vedānta thinks to be the one, immutable and inexpressible absolute comes out to be a vision of the Jaina's non-absolute viewed from the pure pount of view. Kundakunda's exposition of the soul from the pure point of view mostly agrees with the description of the absolute in Advaita Vedānta. Reality transcends both the trenscendental and the empirical levels of existence. Trancessendentalism and empiricism both give us only the partial views of reality. What is beyond these partial views is the true reality, as Kundakunda held. This reality is one and many, permanent and changing and expressible and inexpressible at the same time. The *parmārtha* or the non-absolute of the Jaina can yield all these views consistently.

1. *Ibid.*, p. 304

The Śūnya or the Bhūtatathātā of Buddhistic Philosophy

Buddha's silence on the problem of the nature of reality has been generally taken to imply two things. Firstly, Buddha kept silent, because there are no contents in reality which may be described. It means that the indescribability of reality is due to a total absence of features in it. Secondly, Buddha kept silent because the nature of reality is not at all touched by words. The first view leads to featurelessness of reality, while the second negates its describability. The common conclusion from both the implications is that reality is absolutely indescribable. As regards the first view Samantabhadra says: "If the indescribable means something devoid of all features, then it is non-reality."[1] This position reduces itself to the theory of pure being which we have seen to be untenable. As a matter of fact even being cannot be attributed to such a principle, because it is also a feature. T.R.V. Murti states that for the Mādhyamika the partial comprehensions about reality are absolutely false, because they are ascriptions of features non-existent in reality.[2] This again means a total negation of features in reality. So the descriptions of reality which we generally make may be held to be true only from the empirical viewpoint (*saṁvṛti*). At the same time this *saṁvṛti* is absolutely false because it ascribes to reality something which is totally non-existent in it. Hence our descriptions of reality are not at all faithful to it. If the *śūnya* is interpreted as a complete void, the problem of the falsity of *samvṛti* also falls to the ground. So the *śūnya* has been taken to mean the indeterminate—which implies that reality is something positive but is no subject of comprehension based on reason. It is said that "the Mādhyamika dialectic tries to remove the conflict inherent in Reason by rejecting both the opposites taken singly or in combination. The Mādhyamika is convinced that the conjunctive or disjunctive synthesis of the opposites is but another view.... The function of the

---

1. Samantabhadra: *Āptamīmāṁsā*, verse 48
2. T.R.V. Murti: *The central Philosophy of Buddhism*, p. 240

Mādhyamika dialectic, on the logical level, is purely negative, analytic."[1] Above all the *dṛṣṭis* there is *prajñā* (intuitional insight) which is the abandonment of all *dṛṣṭis.*[2] What is grasped by the intuitional insight is purely a negation implying nothing positive. The position is again reduced to sheer nihilism. Hence what *prajñā* comprehends must be something positive which always escapes the grip of our ordinary knowledge. Affirmation in the form of permanence or momentariness must not be taken to be absolutely false but as a step leading to *śūnya.* In the same way negative prepositions perform the same function from the other end. None of the affirmative or the negative prepositions are totally false, but being analytical in nature they fail to give the complete nature of the *śunya.* They are false, as the Jaina declares only with respect to the whole reality—which means only a partial falsity. If they are partially false, they must be partially true. With this interpretation the negative function of the Mādhyamika dialectic can be said to have some value as leading towards the *sūnya.* The *śūnya* as indeterminate can only mean that it is beyond both the negative and affirmative prepositions, it can never mean an empty concept. Das Gupta has very correctly remarked: "This *bhūtatathātā* is neither that which is existence; nor that which is non-existence, nor that which is at once existence and non-existence, nor that which is not at once existence and non-existence; it is neither that which is plurality, nor that which is at once unity and plurality, nor that which is not at once unity and plurality. It is a negative concept in the sense that it is beyond all that is conditional and yet it is a positive concept in the sense that it holds all within it. It cannot be comprehended by any kind of particularization or distinction. It is only by transcending the range of our intellectual categories of the comprehension of the limited range of finite phenomena that we can get a glimpse of it. It cannot be comprehended by the

1. *Ibid.*, p. 128
2. *Ibid.*, p. 123

particularizing consciousness of all beings, and we may thus call it negation, *śūnyatā,* in this sense."[1] We cannot suppose that affirmation and negation are pure ascriptions totally false, for, then, they cannot lead to the truth of reality. The *bhūtatathātā* or the *śūnya* must be such as includes all the opposing *dṛṣṭis* and is still above them. For the Buddha it is above the four *koṭis* (forms of predication) and for the Jaina it is above the seven *bhaṅgas* (form of predication). This again brings us to the same position where Kundakunda's philosophy culminates. The *śūnya* or the *bhūtatathātā* must be the same principle as the non-absolute of the Jaina.

Hegelian Absolute

According to Collingwood Hegel's reality is neither a delusion nor a mere appearance which may be said to exist with respect to the perceiving minds, but it is something which exists independently of them.[2] Though it is of the nature of thought yet its transformation are such as savour materiality. For Hegel, what we call matter is only a form of intelligence—a petrified intelligence.[3] The movement of Hegelian dialectic is such as gives rise to contradiction. "The finite, as implicitly other than what it is, is forced to surrender its own immediate or natural being, and to turn suddenly into its opposite." For every thesis there is the antithesis, but the process does not end at this contradiction. Then there comes the synthesis wherein the contradiction is supposed to disappear. Hegel proceeds from the lower to the higher, and thus, when he reaches the highest (if it is at all attainable) the contradiction totally disappears. This is the absolute of Hegel. W. James observes: "Hegel considers that the immediate, finite data of experience are 'untrue' because they are not their own others. They are negated by

1. Das Gupta: *A History of Indian Philosophy.* Vol I, p. 130
2. Cf: R.G. Collingwood: *The Idea of Nature,* p. 124
3. W. James: *A Pluralistic Universe*, p. 85

what is external to them. The absolute is true because it and only it has no external environment, and has attained being its own other."[1] Though contradiction is the very soul of Hegelian dialectic, yet it appears to lose its import in the Hegelian absolute. Mc Taggart says: "Hegel regards the Absolute as a unity. He regards it, not as an external or mechanical unity, not even as an organic unity, but as the deepest unity possible one in which the parts have no meaning but their unity, while that unity again, has no meaning but its differentiations."[2] K.C. Bhattacharya is also of opinion that "the Hegelian subordinate distinction to unity while the *Nyāya* assigns priority to distinction."[3] Herein we see a great resemblance between Hegelian and Śaṅkarite conceptions of the absolute. Both are obtained by rising to the higher and higher systems or universals, and in ultimacy contradiction and opposition vanish totally. The former holds the differences to be real, while for the latter they are delusions. But when the thesis and the antithesis are mutually different and opposed without implying any unity, the unity of the absolute cannot be obtained from them. P.T. Raju has correctly remarked: "How the contradiction is solved? If the terms that contradict are left as such, then they do not cease to conflict. If they are not left as such then the terms themselves cease to be."[4] Actually speaking by simply rising to the higher systems contradiction cannot be got rid of. Dr. Haldar has also pointed out that "Hegel goes from the lower to the higher without solving the contradictions of the former, and wants to include them under the latter."[5] As already mentioned T.R.V. Murti draws a distinction between the Hegelian and the Jaina dialects by calling the former as conjunctive and the latter as disjunctive. By this he means that "Hegel takes the synthesis as a

1. *Ibid.*, p. 108
2. Mc Taggart: *Studies in Hegelian Cosmology*, p. 58.
3. *Studies in Philosophy*, Krishnacandra Bhattacharya. (Edited by Gopinath Bhattacharya), p. 333
4. P.T. Raju: *Thought and Reality*, p. 81
5. *Ibid.*, p. 78

newer, richer, more comprehensive, and therefore higher idea providing the basic for differences."[1] Hegel's absolute, thus, is a unity which is, at the same time, a basis for differences, It is on account of the latter aspect of the absolute that Hegel is said to go to the higher without solving the contradiction of the lower. For Advaita Vedānta differences being mere delusions the problem of solving the contradiction does not arise. When we rise to higher systems; it does not mean that the contradiction of the lower ones is wiped out. The globe does not negate the existence of the poles, we cannot think that there are no poles on the globe. On the contrary there is no globe without the poles, poles are peacefully united in the globe. The globe implies the existence of the poles along with its own identity. In the same way Hegel must not think that his absolute can be unity only, it must imply difference as well. Difference and unity are harmoniously put together in the absolute which has its own identity beyond both unity and difference. This again brings us to the same position as Kundakunda holds about his *paramārtha* which transcends all the theses.

If Hegel's dialectic is universal, his absolute can never be attained. It must ever remain in the process of rising higher and higher. Thus the ultimate unity of the absolute is only a figment of imagination. If the unity of the absolute is attainable, the dialectical process must be suspended. So if the dynamism of reality is saved, the unity of the absolute is lost; and if the unity of the absolute is saved, the dynamism or reality is lost. On the other hand the Jaina holds that the perfect state of the soul is attainable and is still subject to dynamism. The principle of dynamism works on account of the capacities both for unity and difference in the Jaina *paramārtha* which is identified neither with unity nor with difference. If the absolute is supposed to attain absolute unity it can never be dynamic. The Jaina *paramārtha* or the non-absolute includes both unity and difference, and is on that very ground, dynamic.

---

1. T.R.V. Murti. *The Central Philosophy of Buddhism,* p. 301

Bradleian Absolute

In Bradley we see that the necessity of reconciling oppositions is not so great as in Hegel. He holds: "No appearance is lost in the absolute. Each one is indispensable and contributes to the whole. Take away from the absolute any one of its elements and it is at once reduced to nothing. None of the fundamental aspects of the world can be resolved into others, and none is useless and insignificant."[1] It is further maintained that "the Absolute is not other than its appearances. At the same time it is not to be identified with any particular appearance or with any combination of them. It is not mere intellect, nor mere will, nor mere feeling. It is the unity of which these are but partial aspects and in which all things are brought together and transmuted though not equally."[2] Hegel wanted to solve the contradiction in the absolute, while for Bradley differences become essential constituents of the absolute. Bradley must presuppose that the absolute so exists that differences are shown by it. At the same time it is held to be a unity which must not oppose differences even in the ultimate state. When unity and difference both exist in the absolute, we can simply attach equal importance to both of them, and the absolute must not be identified with either of them. It cleartly means that it must be beyond unity and difference, but should despise neither of them. What other identiy can we attribute to such an absolute except that which Kundakunda has assigned to his *paramārtha?* In Śaṅkara the differences were delusive, in Hegel they were absent in the ultimate reality but in Bradley they become throughout real. It does not help us even a little in the present situation, to say that "the appearances in the absolute do not remain the same as they are for us, but acquire a new meaning and value."[3] Whatever may be the form of appearances in the

---

1. H.L. Haldar: *Neo Hegelianism*, p. 242
2. *Ibid.*, p. 243.
3. *Ibid.*, p. 256

absolute, they must imply difference. Bradley has certainly granted greatest importance to differences among the idealist thinkers, he marks an advance over Hegel in this respect. It may be taken to be an important step towards the non-absolute.

Bradley's conception of the absolute combines unity and difference, permanence and change harmoniously, but he is said to give no explanation as regards the togetherness or permanence and change. When change and permanence or unity or difference are supposed to be copresent, the problem is how their simultaneous function is possible. The same was the problem for the Jaina, when unity and difference were taken to be attributes of the same substance. It seems that Bradley also admitted the identity of unity and difference at the level of attributes. Then neither unity nor difference can perform its function being hostile attributes of the same substance. The Jaina solves the difficulty by probing deep into the region of traits where the opposing elements lose their contradiction and become necessary and mutually complementary forms of existence of a real. Unity and difference are affirmed of a real not in the same context, because, then they will be contradictory. The Jaina saves his position from contradiction by introducing contexts or reference systems.

Bradley may be taken to condemn this position of the Jaina when he holds, 'Our usual procedure is to evade the difficulty by shutting our eyes now to the aspect of unity, now to the aspect of diversity as suits our purpose. This is a make-shift practically convenient but theoretically the problem remains unsolved."[1] Bradley himself calls the relational way of thought "a make-shift, a device, a mere practical compromise, most necessary, but in the end most indefensible."[2] But the question is whether unity and diversity really belong to reality or they are mere ascriptions affected by the perceiving mind. Bradley must resort to the first

1. *Ibid.*, p. 220
2. **Bradley:** *Appearance and Reality*, p. 33

alternative. Then knowledge of reality as unity or as diversity must not be designated as a make-shift. The only defect in such a knowledge is that it is unable to comprehend reality as a whole. Reality admits of analysis, and the partial truths which result from an analytical consideration of reality must not be held to be absolutely false. If proper reference-systems are given, the partial truths do not lack validity. This is certainly a relational way of thought which gives only partial views of reality. What is called an appearance is the truth obtained by following the machinery of terms and relations. When these appearances are supposed to be present in the absolute, it is wrong to say that the relational truths are totally false. Bradley clearly admits that "fully to realize the existence of the Absolute is for finite beings impossible, but a limited idea of the Absolute seems fully attainable by the finite intellect."[1] It should be remembered that the relational and non-relational are the two implicates of a real. The relational and the non-relational inhere in the same real as change and permanence and unity and diversity do. By negating the relational side of reality we do not get the true nature of reality but only another side of it. The non-relational which Bradley considers to the nature of his absolute is simply a partial view of reality. Reality or the absolute must be beyond both the relational and the non-relational. It cannot be identified with either of them. The relational way of thought is due to the various characters present in reality, it is not merely a subjective construction of the percepient's mind. Bradley cannot consistently rest in the non-relational, he must go beyond not only the relational but also the non-relational. His absolute must come out to be what Kundakunda means by his *paramārtha* or what is generally known as the non-absolute in Jaina philosophy.

1. Quoted by D.M. Datta in his *Chief Currents of Contemporary Philosophy*, p. 48

Concluding Remarks

These various conceptions of the absolute may be so graded as to give us an idea of the passage from the absolute to the non-absolute. The general impression which we get about the various conception of the absolute is that it is ultimately a unity. Diversity finds a place in the systems only as belonging to the lower levels. Śaṁkara has given us absolute unity, non-distinction and oneness; diversity, distinction and manifoldness are reduced to the status of a delusion. Śaṅkara grants no status to the empirical world as against the absolute. In the Mādhyamika, as interpreted by T.R.V. Murti, the absolute is a positivity but it always evades expressibility. It is not a unity, it is also not a diversity. Our expressions are limited to unity or diverity or both or neither. The absolute always evades all these expressions. Hence the Mādhyamika marks an approach to reality beyond all the *dṛṣṭis* or views, which is certainly creditable. For this reason we may think that in the Mādhyamika school the conception of the *śūnya* or the *bhūtatathātā* as inexpressible is more consistent than that of the absolute in Śaṅkara's Vedānta. Another distinction between the views of the aforesaid two schools is that for the Mādhyamika unity and difference are supposed not to belong to reality at all, while Śaṅkara affirms unity of the absolute to the negation of all diversity. In Hegel unity is obtained through diversity, diversity is held to be organic to unity. It appears that, though diversity finds a very important place in Hegel, yet an attempt is made to maintain the supremacy of unity. Hegel deviates, in a way, from the positions of Śaṅkara and the Mādhyamika by recognizing greater importance of negation, though in the absolute all diversity is overcome by unity. Hegel's position may be taken to mark a drift from unity to diversity. But it is in Bradley that this drift becomes very explicit, as he recognizes the presence of diversity in the absolute. For him diversity is not only a truth of the lower level, but it is equally true of the absolute. Unity and diversity are copresent in Bradleian absolute. This marks a further advance of the drift from unity to diversity. Bradley, like other idealist thinkers, fails to detach himself from the idea of unity as the sole constituent of reality. Somehow these thinkers must recognize the ultimacy and supremacy of unity in the absolute. Waiving aside this overwhelming aspect of the conception of the absolute we may take these various conceptions about the absolute as steps on the passage from unity to diversity. The position of the Mādhyamika yields two interpretations. If it is considered from the view-point of the reality of *dṛṣṭis* it comes next to Śaṅkara. If this transcendence over unity and diversity is taken into account, he comes after Bradley. The Mādhyamika is chiefly credited for his insight beyond unity and diversity both. The Jaina may be taken to represent the last step on this passage. Unity and diversity are granted an equal status and are grounded in the very nature of reality which transcends both of them. The recognition of these characters in the region of traits of *dharmas,* as the Jaina calls them, and not at the level of attributes, saves the Jaina position from being inconsistent. Really speaking the nature of reality is best explained by the *paramārtha* of Kundakunda or, to be more general, by the non-absolute of the Jaina.

Kundakunda in his 'Samayaprābhṛta', from where we get his theory of the *paramārtha,* is mainly concerned with an exposition of the soul's nature. This work contains very little of the exposition of matter. This part of the Jaina philosophy becomes the main theme in his other works like the *Pañcāstikāya* and the *Pravacanasāra*. So Kundakunda must not be taken to uphold the substantial reality of the soul alone. He cannot be classed with the idealists. He follows the general dualistic trend of the Jaina philosophy. Hence his *paramārtha* may be taken to represent the nature of the soul. The non-absolute is a general term to include the reality of the material and the spiritual which are held substantially different in Jaina philosophy. This non-absolute is said to be the fundamental reality of the Jaina system, and is held to be beyond all theses, *dṛṣṭis* or *pakṣas.*

Bibliography

(Vikrama Era = V.E., Vīra Nirvāṇa Era = V.N.E., Śaka Era = S.E.)

A Critical History of Greek Philosophy (1953)	W.T. Stace
A Critique of Logical Positivism	C.E.M. Joad
A Critique of the Organ of Knowledge (Bhārtīya Jaina Pariṣat, Calcutta 1946),	Tatia and Mookerjee
A Groundwork of Educational Psychology	J.S. Ross
A History of Indian Philosophy, Vol. II (1952)	J.N. Sinha
A History of Philosophy (Indian edition) 1949	F. Thilly.
A Hundred Years of Psychology (Gerald Duckwort & Co. Ltd., London, 1951)	J.C. Flugel
Ālāpapaddhati (Translated by Dīpacandra, V.N.E. 2459)	Devasena
Analysis of Mind (George Allen & Unwin, London, 1951)	B. Russell
Anekāntajayapatākā	Haribhadra
An Epitome of Jainism (Calcutta, 1917)	Nahar & Ghosh
An Essay on Metaphysics (1950)	R.G. Collingwood

An Idealist View of Life (George Allen & Unwin Ltd., London, 1947)	S. Radhakrishnan
An Introduction to Indian Philosophy (University of Calcutta, 1944)	Chatterjee & Datta
An Introduction to Parapsychology	B.L. Atreya
An Outline of Abnormal Psychology (12th Edition)	Mc Dougall
An Outline of Psychology (6th edition)	Mc Dougall
Āptamīmāṁsā (Jaina Saṁskṛti Sodhana Mandala, Kashi)	Samantabhadra
Āptaparīkṣā (Kashi, 1913)	Vidyānanda
A Pluralistic Universe	W. James
Aṣṭasahasrī (Nirṇaya Sāgara Press, Bombay, 1915)	Vidyānanda
Āvaśyakaniryukti	Bhadrabāhu
Berkeley's Immaterialism (1950)	A.A. Luce
Beyond Realism and Idealism (George & Unwin Ltd., London 1949)	Wilbur
Bhagavatī-sūtra	
Bhāratīya Darśana (1957)	Umesh Misra
Bhāratīya Darśana Paricaya	Harimohan Jha
Brahmasūtra (2nd edition, 1948)	Swāmī Vīreshwa-rānanda
Bṛhat-svayambhū-stotra	Samantabhadra
Buddhist Philosophy of Universal Flux	S. Mookerjee
Contemporary Schools of Psychology (1952)	R.S. Woodsworth
Contributions to Analytic Psychology (Translated by H.G. and Carry F. Baynes, 1943)	C.G. Jung

Cosmology Old and New	G.R. Jain
Creative Evolution (Translated by Arthur Mitscell, 1944)	Henri Bergson
Critical Realism (Macmillan & Co. Ltd., London; 1938)	G. Dawes Hicks
Critique of Difference (1936)	S.S. Suryanarayana Shastri
Dhavalā (Jīvasthāna, Satprarūpaṇā, Commentary on Ṣaṭkhaṇḍāgama)	Vīrasena
Dictionary of Philosophy and Psychology vol. I (1928)	Baldwin
Divine Life vol II	Aurobindo
Dravya-saṅgraha	Nemicandra
Dravya-saṅgraha-vṛtti (Central Jaina Publishing House, Arrah)	Brahmadeva
Energies of Men (1948)	Mc Dougall
Essays on Truth and Reality (Clarendon Press, London, 1944)	F.H. Bradley
Essentials of Indian Philosophy (2nd edition, 1951)	M. Hiriyanna
Fundamental Questions of Indian Metaphysics and Logic (1956)	S.K. Maitra
Gommaṭasāra (Karmakāṇḍa) (Paramaśruta Prabhāvaka Jaina Mandala Bombay, 1928)	Nemicandra
Gommaṭasāra (Jīvakāṇḍa)	Nemicandra
Guide to Modern Thought	C.E.M. Joad
Guide to Philosophy (1953)	C.E.M. Joad
Hegelianism and Personality (1893)	Andrews Seth
Historical Introduction to Modern Psychology (1949)	Murphy Gardener

History of Philosophy, vols. I, II, III and IV — S.N. Das Gupta

History of Philosophy, vol. I (1957) — Umesh Misra

History of Philosophy—Eastern and Western — Ministry of Education, Govt. of India

Idealism: A Critical Survey (Methew & Co. London) — A.C. Ewing

Idealistic Thought in India (1953) — P.T. Raju

Indian Idealism (Cambridge University Press, 1933) — S.N. Dass Gupta

Indian Philosophy vol. I (1929) — S. Radhakrishnan

Indian Philosophy vol. II (1931) — S. Radhakrishnan

Indian Philosophy vol. II (1952) — Max Müller

Indian Psychology, Perception (1934) — J.N. Sinha

Indian Realism (1938) — J.N. Sinha

Instinct and Personality — Mc Dougall

Introduction to Modern Philosophy — C.E.M. Joad

Introduction to Philosophy (1935) — G.T.W. Patrick

Jaina-darśana — Mahendra Kumar

Jaina-darśana (1956) — Nyāyavijaya

Jainism — Herbert Warren

Jaina Psychology (1934) — C.R. Jain

Jaina Psychology (1955) — M.L. Mehta

Jaina tarka-bhāṣā (Singhi Jaina Series No. 8, 1938) — Yaśovijaya

Jñāna-bindu-prakāśa (Singhi Jaina Series No. 16) — Yaśovijaya

Jñānārṇava (Raicandra Jaina Śāstramālā, Bombay, 1927)	Śubhacandra
Karmagrantha II (Ātmānanda Jaina Prakāśaka Maṇḍala, Agra)	Devendra Sūri
Kasāyapāhuḍa (with Jayadhavalā) Part I (Bhāratīya Digambara Jaina Sangha, Mathura, 1944)	Guṇadhara
Key of Knowledge (3rd edition, 1928)	C.R. Jaina
Knowledge and Perception (Oxford Clrandon Press, 1950)	H.A. Pichard
Logic of Hegel (1892)	William Wallace
Lokaprakāśa	Vinayavijaya
Mind and Matter (Cambridge University Press, 1931)	G.F. Stout
Modern Materialism	Mc Dougall
Nature of Consciousness	S.K. Saxena
Nature of Reality	R.G. Collingwood
Nature of Self (Indian Press Ltd., Allahabad 1938)	A.C. Mukerjee
Nandisūtra (Commentary by Haribhadra)	
Nayas—Way of Approach and Observation	N.M. Tatia
Naya-vivaraṇa	
Neo Hegelianism (1927)	H.L. Haldar
Niścaya-dvātriṁśikā	Sidhasena
Niyamasāra	Kundakunda
Nyāyāloka (Jaina Grantha Prakāśaka Sabhā, Ahmedabad)	Yaśovijaya
Nyāya-kumuda-candrodaya vol. I and II. (edited by Pt. Mahendra Kumar, 1941)	Prabhācandra

Nyāyaviniścaya, vol. II	Akalañka
Our Knowledge of the External World (George Allen & Unwin Ltd., London)	B. Russell
Outlines of Indian Philosophy (Banaras) (1909)	Sriniwas Ayangar
Outlines of Indian Philosophy (1951)	M. Hiriyanna
Outlines of Jaina Philosophy (1954)	M.L. Mehta
Pañcāstikāya (Commentary by Prof. A. Chakravarti, Central Jaina Publishing House, Arrah, 1920)	Kundakunda
Perception	H.H. Price
Phenomenalogy of Mind (1949)	Hegel
Philosophy, An Introduction (1953)	Archie J. Bahm
Pramāṇamīmāṁsā (Singhi Jaina Series, 1939)	Hemacandra
Pramāṇanaya-tattvāloka (Edited by Himānśuvijaya)	Vādideva
Prameya-kamala-mārtaṇḍa (Nirṇaya Sāgara Press, Bombay)	Prabhācandra
Pravacanasāra (with Tattva-dīpikā and Tātparya vṛttis, V.N.E. 1969)	Kundakunda
Problems of Neurosis	A. Adler
Problems of Philosophy	B. Russell
Process and Reality (Cambridge University Press, 1929)	A.N. Whitehead
Puruṣārtha-siddhyupāya (V.E. 2471)	Amṛtacandra
Pūrvī aur Paścimī darśana	Devarāj
Rājavārtika. Parts I (1952) and II (1957) (Edited by Pt. Mahendra Kumar)	Akalaṅka

Ratnakaraṇḍa-śrāvakācāra	Samantabhadra
Religion and Science of Life	Mc Dougall
Riddle of Life	Mc Dougall
Sabhāṣya Tattvārthādhigama-sūtra (Parama-śruta Prabhāvaka Maṇḍala, Bombay (1932)	Umāsvāti
Samayaprābhṛta (with Tātparya-vṛtti and Ātmakhyāti commentaries, Kashi, 1914)	Kundakunda
Samayasāra Kalaśa	Amṛtacandra
Samayasāra (commentary by Prof. A. Chakravarti, Bhāratīya Jñānapītha, Kashi)	Kundakunda
Sapta-bhaṅgī-taraṅgiṇī—(Parama śruta Prabhāvaka Mandal, Bombay, V.N.E. 2431)	Vimaladāsa
Sarvadarśana-saṁgraha	Mādhavācārya
Sarvadarśana-samuccaya	Haribhadra
Sarvārthasiddhi (Solapur, S.E. 1839)	Devanandi
Śāstravārtā-samuccaya. (Commentary by Yośovijaya)	Haribhadra
Ṣaṭkhanḍāgama (Khudaka-bandha)	
Schools of Vedānta (Bhāratiya Vidya Bhavana, Bombay, 1943)	Naga Raja Rao
Science and Unseen World	Eddington
Science versus Idealism (1955)	Corinforth
Six Existentialist Thinkers (1953)	H.J. Blackham
Structure and Growth of Mind	Mitchell
Studies in Hegelian Cosmology	Mc Taggart

Studies in Jainism (Jaina Cultural Society, Banaras, 1951)	N.M. Tatia
Studies in Philosophy (edited by Gopinath Bhattacharya, 1956)	Krishna Chandra Bhattacharya
Studies in Post Śaṅkarite Dialectic (University of Calcutta, 1936)	Asutosha Bhattacharya
Sūtrakṛtāṅga (commentary by Śīlāṅka, Āgamodaya Samiti Mahesānā)	
Svarūpa-sambodhana (Laghiyas-trayādi-saṅgraha, V.E. 1972)	Akalaṅka
Syādvādamañjarī (edited by Dr. Jagdish Chandra, 1935)	Malliṣeṇa
Syādvāda-siddhi	Vādībhasiṁha
Tattvārtha-śloka-vārtika(Tattvartha-cintāmaṇi commentary by Pt. Manikya candra, Kunthusāgar Grantha Mālā Solapur) Vols. I,II,III and IV	Vidyānanda
Tattvārthasāra	Amṛtacandra
Tattvārtha-śloka-vārtika (Nirṇaya Sāgara Press, Bombay, 1918)	Vidyānanda
Tattvārtha-sūtra	Umāsvāti
Tattvārtha-vṛtti (Bhāratiya Jñānapītha, Kāshī)	Śrutasāgar Sūri
The Central Philosophy of Buddhism (1955)	T.R.V. Murti
The Chief Currents of Contemporary Philosophy	D.E. Datta
The Doctrine of Karma in Jaina Philosophy	Glessnapp
The Ego and Ed (95th edition, 1949)	S. Freud

The Fundamental Questions of Philosophy (Routledge & Kegan Paul & Ltd., London)	A.C. Ewing
The Idea of Nature (Clarendon Press. Oxford, 1945)	R.G. Collingwood
The Jaina Philosophy of Non-Absolutism (Bhāratiya Jaina Pariṣat, Calcutta, 19440.	S. Mookerjee
The Life Divine Vol. I. (Arya Publishing House, Calcutta)	Aurobindo
The Meeting of East and West (1946)	F.S.C. Northrop
The Nature of Thought Vol. II (1941)	B. Blanshard
The Nature of Truth (2nd edition, 1939)	Harnold H. Joachim
The Nyāya Theory of Knowledge (University of Calcutta, 1939)	S.C. Chatterjee
The Philosophical Works of David Hume, Vol. I. (Combridge; Allen and Farnham Printers)	
The Philosophy of Kant	Watson
The Principles of Philosophy (1948)	H.M. Bhattacarya
The Reign of Relativity (1921)	Viscount Haldane
The Self and Nature (1971)	D. Witt H. Parkar
The Vedānta Philosophy	Sridhar Majamudar
Thinking and Experience (Hutcheson's University Library, London, 1953)	H.H. Price
Theory of Good and Evil (2nd edition, 1948)	V. Rashdall
The theory of Knowledge and Existence (1932)	W.T. Stace

Theory of Relativity	Albert Einstien
The Right and the Good (Clarendon Press, London, 1930)	W.D. Ross
Thought and the Brain (1950)	Henri Pieron
Thought And Reality (George Allen & Unwin Ltd., London, 1937)	P.T. Raju
Vaiśeṣika darśana	Ganganath Jha
Viśeṣāvaśyaka-bhāṣya	Jinabhadra
Viśvadharma darśana, (Vihār Rāṣtrabhāsa Pariṣat, 1953)	Bihari Lal
Woking of Mind.	C.E.M. Joad

Journals

Ātmadharma	Bhādrapada V.N.E. 2482
Agra University Jounral of Research Letters	
Dārśanika	Jan. 1957
Jaina Siddhānta Bhāṣkara,	December, 1934, June 1936 December, 1952
Journal of Philosophical Association	Jan. & April, 1956
Journal of the University of Bihar	Vol. III. No. 1. Nov. 1957
	Vol. IV. No. 1. Nov. 1958
Mind	Vol. 45, 1936
Philosophical Quarterly.	July 1937 April 1940

April 1941

Jan. 1955

April 1955

Philosophy Vol. 13, 1938

Oct., 1940

Proceedings of the Indian National Congress, 1950

The Indian Philosophical Congress, 1944

Ranade ka Darśana. Darśana Pariṣat, Allahabad University, 1958

णाणं

पयासयं

वीर नि॰ 2470

ईसन् 1944

भारतीय ज्ञानपीठ